THE BOOK OF
REVELATIONS

THE BOOK
OF REVELATIONS

Selections from the Holy Qur^cān
with interpretations by Muhammad Asad,
Yusuf Ali, and others

Selected and prepared by
Kabir Helminski

THE BOOK FOUNDATION
BRISTOL, ENGLAND AND WATSONVILLE, CALIFORNIA

THE BOOK FOUNDATION
www.thebook.org

Special thanks to Talal and Nadia Zahid for their support.
Publication Design & Cover Art by Threshold Productions and Ahmed Moustafa.

Closely based on Muhammad Asad's *The Message of the Qurᶜān*,
including translations by Kabir Helminski,
and from *The Light of Dawn* by Camille Helminski
Research and Editing by Subhana Ansari

First Book Foundation edition published 2005.

British Library Cataloguing in Publication Data
A catalogue record of this book is available from the British Library

Library of Congress Cataloging-in-Publication Data
The Book of Revelations: Selections from the Holy Qurʾān
with interpretations by Muhammad Asad, Yusuf Ali, and others
Selected and prepared by Kabir Helminski.
Bristol, England & Watsonville, California: The Book Foundation, 2005.

ISBN 1-904510-12-4
BP 130.4 H
1. Islam. 2. Qur'an 3. Quranic Interpretation
I. Kabir Helminski II. The Book Foundation

Table of Contents

Introduction

This is a sourcebook of Quranic selections and accompanying interpretations. These selections were made, above all, to highlight the fundamental spiritual principles contained in the Qur'an. If you are new to the Qur'an, we hope that this book will provide a balanced view of the Heart of the Qur'an. If you are already a student of the Qur'an, we hope that these selections will perhaps awaken a new appreciation for the universal spiritual wisdom of the Book.

The interpretations are not meant to be the final word, but rather a point of entry to the universe of meaning offered to us by Revelation. The reader will encounter a variety of viewpoints and understandings and will be encouraged to deepen his or her understanding by reflecting upon the material offered here. In some cases the interpretations offer background information that establish a context for the ayāh. In other cases one might be opened to a direct soul encounter with the words themselves.

The translations we offer remain close to the widely respected translations of Muhammad Asad, and, to a lesser extent, Yusuf Ali. Where substantive changes have been made from the accepted translations of Ali and Asad, they are in the direction of even greater faithfulness to the root meanings of the words, rather than toward freer interpretation. In other words, we have tried to take as few liberties with the text as possible. We have also made minor changes in the direction of a more contemporary idiom, yet one that is dignified and sacred without being ponderous or archaic.

The selections are followed by one or more interpretations, with the name of the interpreter in parentheses at the end of the selection. The bibliography at the back gives more details about each author and the publications.

Any selection from the Qur'an will inevitably be somewhat subjective and, perhaps, arbitrary. Nevertheless, it is also true that certain passages have become often-quoted favorites. We apologize if some of your favorites may seem to be missing. We have done our best to include selections that touch upon the major spiritual themes of the Qur'an. May people profit from these pages and may Allah be pleased with our efforts.

~Kabir Helminski

The Selections

The Opening:
Seven Often-Repeated Verses

In the Name of God, the Infinitely Compassionate, Most Merciful.
All praise is God's,
the Sustainer of all worlds,
the Infinitely Compassionate and Most Merciful,
Sovereign of the Day of Reckoning.
You alone do we worship
and You alone do we ask for help.
Guide us on the straight path;
the path of those who have received Your favor,
not the path of those who have earned Your wrath,
nor of those who have gone astray.

[*Sūrah al-Fātiḥah* 1:1-7, complete]

This *sūrah* is also called *Fātiḥat al-Kitāb* ("The Opening of the Divine Writ"), *Umm al-Kitāb* ("The Essence of the Divine Writ"), *Sūrat al-Ḥamd* ("The *Sūrah* of Praise"), *Asās al-Qurʾān* ("The Foundation of the Qurʾān), and is known by several other names as well. It is mentioned elsewhere in the Qurʾān as *As-Sabʿ al-Mathānī* ("The Seven Oft-Repeated [Verses]") because it is repeated several times in the course of each of the five daily prayers. According to Bukhārī, the designation *Umm al-Kitāb* was given to it by the Prophet himself, and this in view of the fact that it contains, in a condensed form, all the fundamental principles laid down in the Qurʾān: the principle of God's oneness and uniqueness, of His being the originator

3

and fosterer of the universe, the fount of all life-giving grace, the One to whom man is ultimately responsible, the only power that can really guide and help; the call to righteous *action* in the life of this world (*guide us the straight way*); the principle of life after death and of the organic consequences of man's actions and behavior (expressed in the term *Day of Judgment*); the principle of guidance through God's message-bearers (evident in the reference to *those upon whom God has bestowed His blessings*) and, flowing from it, the principle of the continuity of all true religions (implied in the allusion to people who have lived—and erred—in the past); and, finally, the need for voluntary self-surrender to the will of the Supreme Being and, thus, for worshipping Him alone. It is for this reason that this *sūrah* has been formulated as a prayer, to be constantly repeated and reflected upon by the believer.

"The Opening" was one of the earliest revelations bestowed upon the Prophet. Some authorities (for instance, ʿAlī ibn Abī Ṭālib) were even of the opinion that it was the very first revelation; but this view is contradicted by authentic Traditions quoted by both Bukhārī and Muslim, which unmistakably show that the first five verses of *Sūrah* 96 (*Sūrah al-ʿAlaq*, "The Germ Cell") constituted the beginning of revelation. It is probable, however, that whereas the earlier revelation consisted of only a few verses each, "The Opening" was the first *sūrah* revealed to the Prophet in its entirety at one time: and this would explain the view held by ʿAlī. (Asad, p. 1)

Guidance for the God-Conscious

Alif. Lām. Mīm.[1]

This Divine Writ—let there be no doubt about it—
is meant to be a guidance for all the God-conscious,
who believe in the existence
of that which is beyond the reach of human perception,
and are constant in prayer,
and spend on others out of what We provide for them as sustenance;
and who believe in that which has been bestowed
from on high upon you, O Prophet,
as well as in that which was bestowed before your time:
for it is they who in their innermost are certain of the life to come!
It is they who follow the guidance which comes from their Sustainer;
and it is they, they who shall attain to a happy state!

[*Sūrah al-Baqarah* 2:1-5]

The second *sūrah* starts with a declaration of the purpose underlying the revelation of the Qurʾān as a whole: namely, man's guidance in all his spiritual and worldly affairs.

A guidance for all the God-conscious: the conventional translation of

---

[1] The mystical letters: Preceding about a quarter of the Qurʾānic *sūrahs* are combinations of letters sometimes referred to as "openings" (*fawātiḥ*). They are always pronounced individually. Though various theories as to their meaning exist, their true meaning rests in the Mysterion. As Abū Bakr, close companion of the Prophet and the first of the Caliphs to guide his community after his passing, said, "In every Divine Book there is mystery—and the mystery of the Qurʾān is indicated in the openings of some of the *sūrahs*."

5

muttaqī as "God-fearing" does not adequately render the *positive* content of this expression, namely the awareness of His all-presence and the desire to mold one's existence in the light of this awareness. The interpretation adopted by some translators, *one who guards himself against evil* or *one who is careful of his duty,* does not give more than one particular aspect of the concept of "God-consciousness."

Beyond the reach of human perception: al-ghayb (commonly, and errone-ously, translated as "the Unseen") is used in the Qurʾān to denote all those sectors or phases of reality which lie beyond the range of human (sense) perception and cannot, therefore, be proved or disproved by sci-entific observation or even adequately comprised within the accepted categories of speculative thought. These include, for instance, the exis-tence of God and of a definite purpose underlying the universe, life after death, the real nature of time, the existence of spiritual forces and their inter-action, and so forth. Only a person who is convinced that the ulti-mate reality comprises far more than our *observable* environment can attain to belief in God and, thus, to a belief that life has meaning and purpose. By pointing out that it is *a guidance for those who believe in the existence of that which is beyond human perception,* the Qurʾān says, in effect, that it will—of necessity—remain a closed book to all whose minds cannot ac-cept this fundamental premise.

And spend on others out of what We provide for them as sustenance: provi-sion of sustenance applies to all that may be of benefit to man, whether it be concrete (like food, property, offspring, etc.), or abstract (like knowl-edge, piety, etc.) The "spending on others" is mentioned here in one breath with God-consciousness and prayer because it is precisely in such selfless acts that true piety comes to its full fruition. It should be borne in mind that the verb *anfaqa* (literally, "he spent") is always used in the Qurʾān to denote spending freely on, or as a gift to, others, whatever the motive may be.

That which was bestowed before your time: this is a reference to one of the fundamental doctrines of the Qurʾān, the doctrine of the historical continuity of divine revelation. Life—so the Qur'ān teaches us—is not a series of unconnected jumps but a continuous, organic process: and this law applies also to the life of the mind, of which man's religious experience (in its cumulative sense) is a part. Thus, the religion of the Qur'ān can be properly understood only against the background of the great monotheistic faiths which preceded it, and which, according to Muslim belief, culminate and achieve their final formulation in the faith of Islam. (Asad, pp. 3-4)

Their Hearts and Hearing Are Sealed

Behold, as for those who are bent on denying the truth—
it is all one to them whether you warn them or do not warn them:
they will not believe.
God has sealed their hearts and their hearing,
and over their eyes is a veil;
and awesome suffering awaits them.

[*Sūrah al-Baqarah* 2:6-7]

In contrast with the frequently occurring term *al-kāfirūn* ("those who deny the truth"), the use of the past tense in *alladhīna kafarū* indicates conscious intent, and is therefore appropriately rendered as *those who are bent on denying the truth*. This interpretation is supported by many commentators, especially Zamakhsharī (who, in his commentary on the verse, uses the expression *those who have deliberately resolved upon their* kufr). Elsewhere in the Qurʾān such people are spoken of as having *Hearts with which they fail to grasp the truth, and eyes with which they fail to see, and ears with which they fail to hear* [7:179]. [For an explanation of the terms *kufr* ("denial of the truth") and *kāfir* ("one who denies the truth").

Over their eyes is a veil: this is a reference to the natural law instituted by God, whereby a person who persistently adheres to false beliefs and refuses to listen to the voice of truth gradually loses the *ability* to perceive the truth, "so that finally, as it were, a seal is set upon his heart" (Rāghib). Since it is God Who has instituted all laws of nature—which, in their aggregate, are called *sunnat Allāh* ("the way of God")—this "sealing" is attributed to Him: but it is obviously a consequence of man's free choice

8

and not an act of "predestination." Similarly, the suffering which, in the life to come, is in store for those who during their life in this world have willfully remained deaf and blind to the truth, is a natural consequence of their free choice—just as happiness in the life to come is the natural consequence of man's endeavor to attain to righteousness and inner illumination. It is in this sense that the Qur'anic references to God's "reward" and "punishment" must be understood. (Asad, pp. 4-5)

The Bond with God

In this way[2] does He cause many a one to go astray,
just as He guides many a one aright:
but none does He cause thereby to go astray except the iniquitous,
who break their bond with God
after it has been established [in their nature],
and cut asunder what God has bidden to be joined,
and spread corruption on earth:
these shall be the losers.

[*Sūrah al-Baqarah* 2:26-27]

The *bond with God* (conventionally translated as *God's covenant*) apparently refers here to man's moral obligation to use his inborn gifts—intellectual as well as physical—in the way intended for them by God. The "establishment" of this bond arises from the faculty of reason which, if properly used, must lead man to a realization of his own weakness and dependence on a causative power and, thus, to a gradual cognition of God's will with reference to his own behavior. This interpretation of the *bond with God* seems to be indicated by the fact that there is no mention of any specific "covenant" in either the preceding or the subsequent verses of the passage under consideration. The deliberate omission of any explanatory reference in this connection suggests that the expression *bond with God* stands for

---

[2] The preceding *āyāts* say: *Behold, God does not disdain to propound a parable of a gnat, or something even less than that. Now, as for those who have attained to faith, they know it is the truth from their Sustainer—whereas those who are bent on denying the truth say, "What could God mean by this parable?"*

10

something that is rooted in the human situation as such, and can, there-fore, be perceived instinctively as well as through conscious experience: namely, that innate relationship with God which makes Him: *closer to man than his jugular vein* [50:16]. For an explanation of the subsequent refer-ence to *what God has bidden to be joined,* see 13:21. (Asad, pp. 7-8)

God's Representative on Earth

He it is Who created for you all that is upon the earth; then He turned toward the
heaven and made seven firmaments,
and He has perfect knowledge of all things.
And behold! Your Sustainer said to the angels:
"I am about to establish upon earth a representative, a khalīfah."
They said: "Will You place on it
one who will spread corruption thereon and shed blood—
whereas it is we who proclaim Your limitless glory
and praise You and hallow Your name?"
God answered: "Truly, I know that which you do not know."
And He imparted to Adam the names of all things;
then He brought them within the ken of the angels and said:
"Declare to Me the names of these,
if what you say is true."
They replied: "Limitless are You in Your glory!
No knowledge have we save that which
You have imparted to us.
Truly, You alone are all-knowing, truly wise."
Said He: "O Adam, convey to them the names of these."
And as soon as Adam had conveyed to them their names,
God said: "Did I not say to you, 'Truly, I alone know
the hidden reality of the heavens and the earth,
and know all that you bring into the open
and all that you would conceal?'"

[*Sūrah al-Baqarah* 2:29-33]

The term *khalīfah*—translated here as "representative"—has also the meaning of "one who shall inherit." It is derived from the verb *khalafa*, "he succeeded [another]." The accent is on God's having caused man to inherit the earth by endowing him with specific faculties and abilities. Its use elsewhere in the Qur'ān implies the grant to humanity of the ability to discern between right and wrong, truth and falsehood.

And He imparted to Adam the names of all things: literally, *all the names.* The term *ism* ("name") implies, according to all philologists, an expression "conveying the knowledge [of a thing] . . . applied to denote a substance or an accident or an attribute, for the purpose of distinction": in philosophical terminology, a "concept." From this it may legitimately be inferred that the "knowledge of all the names" denotes here man's faculty of logical definition and, thus, of conceptual thinking. That by "Adam" the whole human race is meant here becomes obvious from the preceding reference, by the angels, to *such as will spread corruption on earth and will shed blood,* as well as from 7:11. (Asad, pp. 8-9)

Adam is man, and man is the secret of God's Self-knowledge, "the secret of the heavens and the earth." Whatever is to be found in the heavens and the earth, the names of all things which are also the Names of God, are all to be found in man. By the matter of our physical bodies we are mineral. By our unconscious physiological processes we are vegetable. By our ability to move and sexually reproduce and respond to the world around us we are animal. By our ability to reason and choose, we are human. By our ability to conceive of invisible, celestial realities, we are angelic. And by our ability—necessarily limited—to conceive of the reality and nature of God, we participate—indirectly, and as it were by analogy—in God's Divinity, though we do so not by our own exertions, but by His free gift.

Have you ever noticed how characters like those which belong to

13

entire animal species, in the case of man seem to belong to single individuals? We all know people we would describe as peacocks, or lions, or snakes, or foxes, or gazelles. In our separate individuality we may be "dominated" by specific Names of God, something which is fairly easy to see in the case of the great leader, the great craftsman, the great athlete, the great physician, the great poet. But in our intrinsic humanity, we are all of these things. Everything in God is reflected, in one way or another, in the human state. And because this is true, by God's generosity, man can potentially know the seeds or prototypes of things; his art, his science, his philosophy, and his spiritual realization are clear proofs of this. The angels in this verse are the intrinsic prototypes or Names of all created things, all things in the heavens and the earth; and since all things are signs of God, these Names are both the names of created beings, and the Names of God which form and animate those beings. The angels are symbols or representatives of these Names, but they don't *know* these Names; only Adam, only humanity, can tell the angels their own names.

It is this knowledge which gives man his central and sovereign position in the created order—a power which, when appropriated by the ego, makes man capable of destroying the earth. According to verse 29 of this *sūrah, He it is Who created for you all that is upon the earth.* We know that without earth there would be no man; but the deeper truth is: without man there would be no earth. (Upton)

What is Needed for Salvation

Those who have attained to faith,
and those who follow the Jewish Scriptures
and the Christians and the Sabians,
and who believe in God and the last day and who do good works
shall have their reward with their Sustainer;
on them shall be no fear nor shall they grieve.

[*Sūrah al-Baqarah* 2:62]

There seems to be a human tendency in almost every religion to claim some exclusive salvation for its adherents. Clearly, many Jews and Christians have made this claim. Many Muslims, including well-known commentators on the Qur'ān, have also expressed this belief despite the fact that there are numerous places in the Qur'ān that make spiritual attainment independent of professed beliefs or ethnic origin, and dependent on mindfulness of God (*taqwā*) and moral action (*ṣalihāt*).

Muḥammad Asad writes about *All who believe in God and the last day and who do good works shall have their reward with their Sustainer: on them shall be no fear nor shall they grieve:* "The above passage—which recurs in the Qur'ān several times—lays down a fundamental doctrine of Islam. With a breadth of vision unparalleled in any other religious faith, the idea of 'salvation' is here made conditional upon three elements only: belief in God, belief in the Day of Judgment, and righteous action in life. The statement of this doctrine at this juncture—that is in the midst of an appeal to the Children of Israel—is warranted by the false Jewish belief that their descent from Abraham entitles them to be regarded as 'God's chosen peo-

15

ple.'" (Asad, p. 14)

Yusuf Ali writes in a similar vein: "*On them shall be no fear nor shall they grieve.* Compare 2:38, where the same phrase occurs. And it recurs again and again afterwards. In *Sūrah al-Baqarah* (the second *sūrah*) it occurs in verses 38, 62, 112, 262, 274, and 277. The point of the verse is that Islam does not teach an exclusive doctrine, and is not meant exclusively for one people. The Jews claimed this for themselves, and the Christians in their own origin were a sect of the Jews. Even the modern organized Christian churches, though they have been, consciously or unconsciously, influenced by the time-spirit, including the historical fact of Islam, yet cling to the idea of vicarious atonement, which means that all who do not believe in it or who lived previously to the death of Christ are at a disadvantage spiritually before the Throne of God. The attitude of Islam is entirely different. Islam existed before the preaching of Muḥammad on this earth; the Qur'ān expressly calls Abraham a Muslim (3:67). Its teaching (submission to God's will) has been and will be the teaching of religion for all time and for all peoples." (A. Yusuf Ali, pp. 33-34)

According to Mahmoud Ayoub: "Commentators have differed concerning the intent of this verse and the reason for its revelation. The verse is one of many general statements in the Qur'ān in which faith is raised above any religious or ethnic identity. Commentators have, however, sought to limit its universal application in several ways. Four main approaches may be distinguished. The first was to declare the verse abrogated and therefore inapplicable. The second was to limit the application of the verse by assigning the reason for its revelation to a specific group of people. The third approach has been to limit the verse to a strictly legalistic interpretation, and the fourth has been to accept the universality of the verse until the coming of Islam, but thereafter to limit its applicability only to those who hold the faith of Islam." (Ayoub, p. 110)

The weakness of the argument for abrogation is that while God may abrogate a legal ruling, it would seem absurd for God to abrogate a spiritual principle, which would amount to redefining the nature of what is essentially good.

Some commentators, including Tabarsi, have maintained, for instance, that the above verse is abrogated by: *If anyone desires a religion other than Islam (submission to God), it will never be accepted from him* [3:85]. When one examines the context of this verse, we see that it is preceded by this very broad statement: *Do they seek for other than the religion of God, while all creatures in the heavens and upon the earth have willingly or unwillingly submitted* (i.e., become *muslim*)? [3:83].

Clearly "islam" in this context is a universal and natural state of submission, not a religion as such. This is followed by the *āyāts: Say: "We believe in God, and in what has been revealed to us and what was revealed to Abraham, Ismā῾īl, Isaac, Jacob, and the tribes, and in the books given to Moses, Jesus, and the Prophets from their Lord: we make no distinction between one and another among them, and to God we submit."* [3:84].

To limit the verse to the time before the coming of the Prophet Muḥammad Σ is based on a certain story related by As-Suddī. In this story, Salman Farsi, a close companion, was asking the Prophet whether some of his pious friends who had died before meeting the Prophet were in heaven or hell. The Prophet is said to have replied, "They are people of the Fire," which disturbed Salman very much. Later this verse was revealed, supposedly correcting Muḥammad's misperception.

If we accept this story, we must accept that the Prophet spoke something that was patently false regarding an essential spiritual matter and that he then needed to be corrected by God. Obviously this raises serious problems since the Prophet said, "If I advise you on worldly matters and you know better, then I may be wrong, but if I advise you on spiritual matters, you must believe me."

Furthermore, according to this interpretation, Muḥammad is reported to have said that this refers only to those who died before the advent of his prophethood. Why then did God not clearly refer to the past in some way, such as: "Those before the coming of the Qur᾽ān and the Prophet Muḥammad"?

17

This verse is a clear lesson in a very fundamental principle of Qurʾanic interpretation: Take God at His word. Look at the primary and obvious meaning of the text. Do not allow the text to be contradicted or obscured by commentaries, or even by purported *ḥadīth* that may contradict those truths and principles that are repeatedly found in the whole of the Qurʾān. The Qurʾān is guaranteed reliable. No *ḥadīth* is absolutely guaranteed in the same way.

The *ḥadīth* collections were assembled about three centuries after the life of Muḥammad. About a million supposed *ḥadīth* were reduced by sincere scholars down to some tens of thousands, using the best methodology they could develop at the time. Scholarship of recent centuries, however, has raised questions about the reliability of even the sound *ḥadīth* collections. While a substantial portion of the *ḥadīth* literature undoubtedly represents the spirit, and the exact words of Muḥammad, nevertheless there must be admitted the possibility of inaccurate or fabricated *ḥadīth* finding their way into the *ḥadīth* collections.

A safe and secure principle might then be to give our attention to those *ḥadīth* that are beautiful and inspiring and that do not contradict or modify what is explicitly said in the Qurʾān, and to take the Qurʾān at its word. (Helminski)

Essential Submission

Truly, one who submits his whole being[3] to God,
and is in a state of virtue,
shall have their reward with their Sustainer;
these need have no fear, neither shall they grieve.

[*Sūrah al-Baqarah* 2:112]

This verse follows the argument between Christians and Jews, each of whom claims that the other will not enter Paradise. Here we have the definitive answer to anyone who claims that nominal adherence to a belief system will bring salvation. As always, the Qurʾān refocuses us on what is essential: the surrender of one's whole self to God and the beautiful state of consciousness (*iḥsān*) that results.

Iḥsān is a word that is difficult to translate. It is the third element of the canonical definition of Islam (*islām, īmān, iḥsān*) and was described by the Prophet Muḥammad in this way: "Worship (or serve) God as if you saw Him, but even if you don't see him, know that you are seen." *Iḥsān*, which is related to the root meaning of "beauty" (*ḥasan*), implies doing something in the most excellent and beautiful way. The Prophet once remarked upon seeing a certain grave, which had been hastily shoveled, that a Muslim should do everything well, and requested that the gravesite be properly finished.

So, for those who surrender and become a *muḥsin*, a person of excellence, they shall have no fear *(khawf)* or grief. Surrender then leads to the overcoming of fear, including the fear of God. What we should have in-

---

[3] Whole being: *literally,* face.

stead of fear of God is *taqwā*, the vigilant awareness of God's presence and the guarding of ourselves from our own neglectfulness (*ghaflah*).

Just a few verses later, the word *face* appears again. This time we are reminded that we can see God's face everywhere.

It is essential to understand the relationship between surrendering our whole being to God, on the one hand, and being free of fear and grief, on the other. (Helminski)

Freedom of Religion

Hence, who could be more unjust than those
who bar the remembrance of God's name
from any of His houses of worship (masājid)
and strive for their ruin,
although they have no right to enter them save in fear?
For them, in this world, there is nothing but disgrace;
and for them, in the life to come, awesome suffering.

[*Sūrah al-Baqarah* 2:114]

It is one of the fundamental principles of Islam that every religion which has belief in God as its focal point must be accorded full respect, however much one may disagree with its particular tenets. Thus, the Muslims are under an obligation to honor and protect any house of worship dedicated to God, whether it be a mosque or a church or a synagogue (see 22:40), and any attempt to prevent the followers of another faith from worshipping God according to their own lights is condemned by the Qur'ān as a sacrilege. A striking illustration of this principle is forthcoming from the Prophet's treatment of the deputation from Christian Najrān in the year 10 A.H. They were given free access to the Prophet's mosque, and with his full consent celebrated their religious rites there, although their adoration of Jesus as "the son of God" and of Mary as "the mother of God" were fundamentally at variance with Islamic beliefs. (Asad, p. 24)

Wherever You Turn . . .

To God belong the East and the West.
Wherever you turn, there is the face of God.
Indeed, God is infinite, all-knowing.

[*Sūrah al-Baqarah* 2:115]

Here *the East and the West* also mean the sunrise and the sunset, so we are given a beautiful picture of both the directions of East and West, as well as these moments in time when we witness the splendid display of nature.

We can be reminded of God's presence by the sunrise and sunset, and we can be reminded that *wherever we turn our gaze, there we can see God's "Face."* The face of a human being is that by which we can most easily recognize that person, so here we are also being told that God's most recognizable feature can be seen anywhere, anytime, if we are in the right state of openness.

Furthermore in many places in the Qur'ān we are told to witness. (*In this, behold, there is indeed a reminder for everyone whose heart is wide-awake—that is, who listens and witnesses* [50:37] and *O believers, be steadfast before God, witnesses for justice* [5:8]) To witness means to see for ourselves with all the faculties that are given to us. In the same way that we say: "I witness that there is no god but God," we can witness God's recognizable signature wherever we look. This is an astounding proposition, yet we would not be asked to witness in this way if it were not possible for us. God is infinite and all-knowing. God's perception and intelligence permeate everything. The signs of it are the lawfulness that science uncovers, the beauty and order of nature, as well as the meaning that relates one thing to another, as well as the sense of significance in all of this that the human heart experiences. God is not a distant abstraction, not merely

22

some utterly transcendent "truth," but something that is also here and now before our very eyes and hearts. (Helminski)

The Reciprocity of Remembrance

So remember Me, and I remember you.

[*Sūrah al-Baqarah* 2:152]

.

The Qur'ān calls upon us to remember God. But how are we to do this? To remember something is to call it to mind, to cause it to take place in our minds. But there is no room in our little human minds for the vastness of God. Only the human spiritual Heart has room for Him, and the Heart exists on a deeper level than the work of deliberate, constant, and conscious Remembrance we are commanded by the Qur'ān to carry out.

In verse 151 of this *sūrah,* it is made clear that the thing which gives us the power to remember God is the *Messenger . . .who recites to you Our revelations.* So God first remembered us, in our helpless need, and then commanded us to remember Him, thus making Remembrance synonymous with gratitude. But if, after His merciful act of remembering us, we fail to remember Him, He may not remember us again.

By His own act, He implants the Remembrance of Him in our Hearts. In the first case, the Remembrance is a response to revelation; in the second, the Remembrance itself *is* the revelation; this refers, on one level, to an "infused Remembrance," a Remembrance of God implanted in our Hearts by the direct action of God; to the unveiling of Divine realities; to the direct knowledge of God.

Remembrance of a distant object takes work; remembrance of an "object" so overwhelmingly present that It can have no rival is a foregone conclusion. As God says in a *ḥadīth qudsī* (transmitted by Tirmidhī), "What is difficult for some is easy for those for whom Allāh has made it easy." The work of remembering God can never bring us to Him—yet if we fail to remember Him, what can we expect? We remember Him, and fall infinitely short of His Reality. He remembers us, and reaches us in a heartbeat, or even sooner.

It is We Who have sent down to you the Remembrance.
[*Sūrah al-Ḥijr* 15:9]

He was, in fact, already here. His Remembrance of us *is* our Remembrance of Him within us. In a certain sense, we *are* that Remembrance. (Upton)

Signs for the Intelligent

Truly, in the creation of the heavens and of the earth,
and the succession of night and day:
and in the ships that speed through the sea with what is useful to man:
and in the waters which God sends down from the sky,
giving life thereby to the earth after it had been lifeless,
and causing all manner of living creatures to multiply thereon:
and in the change of the winds,
and the clouds that run their appointed courses between sky and earth:
these are messages indeed for people who use their intelligence.

[*Sūrah al-Baqarah* 2:164]

This passage is one of the many in which the Qurʾān appeals to *those who use their intelligence* (*yaᶜqilūn*) to observe and reflect upon the wonders of nature, including the evidence of man's own ingenuity (*the ships that speed through the sea*), as so many indications of a conscious, creative Power pervading the universe. Everywhere there are signs that call us to wake up and notice how miraculous this life is. People with intelligence can have their hearts filled with awe and thus be led to what is essentially a religious consciousness. Faith and intelligence can serve each other. (Helminski)

Virtue

Virtue is not that you turn your faces to the East or West,
but virtue is to be faithful to God, the Last Day,
and the angels, and the Book, and the Messengers;
to spend of your substance out of love for Him,
for your kin, for orphans, for the needy, for the traveler,
for those who ask and for the ransom of slaves;
to be steadfast in prayer, to offer regular charity,
to fulfill the contracts you have made,
to be firm and patient in pain and adversity,
and throughout all periods of panic.
Such are the sincere and God-conscious.

[*Sūrah al-Baqarah* 2:177]

As if to emphasize again a warning against deadening formalism, we are given a beautiful description of the righteous and God-fearing man. He should obey salutary regulations, but he should fix his gaze on the love of God and the love of his fellow-men. We are given four heads: (1) our faith should be true and sincere, (2) we must be prepared to show it in deeds of charity to our fellow-men; (3) we must be good citizens, supporting local organization; and (4) our own individual soul must be firm and unshaken in all circumstances. They are interconnected and yet can be viewed separately.

To be faithful to God: faith is not merely a matter of words. We must realize the presence and goodness of God. When we do so, the scales fall from our eyes; all the falsities and fleeting nature of the Present cease to

27

enslave us, for we see the Last Day as if it were today. We also see God's working in His world and in us; His Powers (angels), His Messengers, and His Message are no longer remote from us, but come within our experience.

To spend of your substance out of love for Him. Practical deeds of charity are of value when they proceed from love, and from no other motive. In this respect, also, our duties take various forms, which are shown in reasonable gradation: our kith and kin; orphans (including any persons who are without support or help); people who are in real need but who never ask (it is our duty to find them out and they come before those who ask); the stranger, who is entitled to laws of hospitality; the people who ask and are entitled to ask, i.e., not merely lazy beggars but those who seek our assistance in some form or another (it is our duty to respond to them); and the slaves (we must do all we can to give or buy their freedom). Slavery has many insidious forms, and all are included.

To be steadfast in prayer, to offer regular charity, to fulfill the contracts you have made. Charity and piety in individual cases do not complete our duties. In prayer and charity we must also look to our organized efforts; where there is a Muslim State, these are made through the State, in facilities for public prayer, and public assistance, and for the maintenance of contracts and fair dealing in all matters.

Then come the Muslim virtues of firmness and patience. They are to "preserve the dignity of man with soul erect" (Burns). Three sets of circumstances are especially mentioned for the exercise of this virtue: (1) bodily pain or suffering, (2) adversities or injuries of all kinds, deserved and undeserved, and (3) periods of public panic, such as war, violence, pestilence, etc. (A. Yusuf Ali, pp. 69-70)

Fasting

O you who have attained to faith!
Fasting is ordained for you as it was ordained for those before you,
So that you might remain conscious of God:
During a certain number of days,
but whoever of you is ill or on a journey,
Shall instead fast a number of other days,
And it is incumbent on those who can afford it
to make the sacrifice of feeding a needy person.
And whoever does more good than he or she is bound to do
thereby does good to himself or herself;
for to fast is to do good to yourselves—if you only knew it.

[*Sūrah al-Baqarah* 2:183-184]

Fasting has been a nearly universal practice in the spiritual history of humanity. Islam continues this by prescribing it for one lunar month for all believers.

"Fasting is the bread of the Prophets, the sweet morsel of the saints," wrote a Muslim saint of the twentieth century, Hasan Shushud. Fasting is meditation of the body, and meditation is fasting of the mind. Fasting helps the body to purify itself of the toxins that accumulate through the impurities of food and incomplete digestion.

Fasting, as long as it is not excessive, is based on a positive relationship to the body, for it eases the burdens the body must carry. Indulgence—whether in food, intoxicants, or pleasures—is a form of cruelty toward the body because of the price the body must pay for our so-called pleasures.

Purification leaves the body, especially the nervous system, in a more responsive state. Hunger reduces the need for sleep and increases wakefulness. Eating our fill hardens the heart, while hunger opens the heart and increases detachment. In hunger some of the veils between us and what is real are removed; remembrance becomes a way of life. Fasting has been a catalyst for awakening in all sacred traditions. Rumi says: "If the brain and belly are burning clean with fasting, every moment a new song comes out of the fire." (*Open Secret,* translated by John Moyne and Coleman Barks, p. 42.)

With gratitude for being embodied we will listen to what the body has to tell us and use it well. As always, gratitude will restore the proper perspective and remind us that the body is a means for awakening the soul.

Yusuf Ali writes: "The Muslim fast is not meant for self-torture. Although it is stricter than other fasts, it also provides alleviations for special circumstances. If it were merely a temporary abstention from food and drink, it would be salutary to many people, who habitually eat and drink to excess. The instincts for food, drink, and sex are strong in the animal nature, and temporary restraint from all these enables the attention to be directed to higher things. This is necessary through prayer, contemplation, and acts of charity, not of the showy kind, but by seeking out those really in need. Certain standards are prescribed, but much higher standards are recommended." (A. Yusuf Ali, p. 72)

In the final lines we are given two principles. The first is to do more than the bare minimum of goodness, to stretch ourselves and thus to do good to ourselves, as in supererogatory fasting. To live with the attitude that I am going to do just enough to get by is not the way of life suggested by the Qur'ān. We are the recipients of our own generous and good deeds. Benefiting others benefits ourselves. The fundamental principle is to live generously, to do even more good than we are obligated to do.

The second idea in these *āyāts* is that fasting is doing good to ourselves. It may not be immediately obvious in our ordinary state of consciousness, when we are preoccupied with satisfying our desires and hungers, but there is a benefit in intentionally abstaining from certain lawful and necessary things, for a limited, prescribed period of time, and with a spiritual intention. This helps us to develop a healthy sense of sacrifice. It develops our will and ultimately our freedom of choice, thus making us even more human. (Helminski)

Divine Relationship

And if My servants ask you about Me—witness, I am near;
I respond to the call of the one who calls,
whenever he calls Me:
let them, then, respond to Me, and have faith in Me,
so that they may follow the right way.

[*Sūrah al-Baqarah* 2:186]

If My servants ask you. . . . Not everyone lives at the same level of faith or knowledge of the Truth. Some people may confide in others, seeking some evidence or reason to have faith, because often the struggles and disappointments of life may shake people's faith in the beneficent order of life.

We are told to "witness." To witness means being in that state where we know that God is real, as if we saw Him in front of us at this very moment. *Wherever you turn is the Face of God* [2:115]. When we are in that state, that *hal*, we can truly be of service to others, sharing with them by our own conviction and kindness, that God is near and always responds to the one who calls, whenever He is called.

When much of the world seems blind to the Truth of God's nearness and Mercy, the faithful, the *muᶜminūn*, are the ones who must carry this responsibility as the living witnesses of God's generosity and responsiveness, until people can know this for themselves. (Helminski)

Defensive Warfare

And fight in God's cause against those who wage war against you,
but do not commit aggression—for, truly, God does not love aggressors.
And slay them wherever you may come upon them,
and drive them away from wherever they drove you away—
for oppression is even worse than killing.

[*Sūrah al-Baqarah* 2:190-191]

These verses lay down unequivocally that only self-defense (in the widest sense of the word) makes war permissible for Muslims. Most commentators agree that the expression *lā taʿtadū* signifies, in this context, *do not commit aggression;* while by *al-muʿtadīn* "those who commit aggression" (*aggressors*) are meant. The defensive character of a fight *in God's cause*—that is, in the cause of the ethical principles ordained by God—is moreover self-evident in the reference to *those who wage war against you,* and has been still further clarified in 22:39: *permission [to fight] is given to those against whom war is being wrongfully waged.* According to all available Traditions, that constitutes the earliest (and therefore fundamental) Qurʾanic reference to the question of *jihād* or holy war. . . . That this early, fundamental principle of self-defense as the only possible justification of war has been maintained throughout the Qurʾan is evident from 60:8 and 4:90-91, both of which belong to a later period than 22:39.

As for those who do not fight against you
on account of [your] faith,
and neither drive you forth from your homelands,

33

God does not forbid you to show them kindness
and to behave towards them with full equity,
for truly, God loves those who act equitably.

[*Sūrah al-Mumtaḥanah* 60:8]

Thus, if they let you be, and do not make war on you,
and offer you peace, God does not allow you to harm them.
You will find others who would like to be safe from you
as well as safe from their own folk, but who,
whenever they are faced anew with temptation to evil,
plunge into it headlong.
Hence, if they do not let you be, and do not offer you peace,
and do not stay their hands,
seize them and slay them whenever you come upon them:
for it is against these that We
have clearly empowered you [to make war].

[*Sūrah an-Nisāʿ* 4:90-91]

The injunction *slay them wherever you may come upon them* is valid only within the context of hostilities already in progress (Rāzī) on the under-standing that *those who wage war against you* are the aggressors or oppressors (a war of liberation being a war *in God's cause*). The translation in this context of *fitnah* as oppression is justified by the application of this term to any affliction that may cause man to go astray and to lose his faith in spiritual values. (Asad, p. 41)

Preserve the Regularity of Prayer

Preserve and be continuously mindful of the prayers,
and of praying in the most excellent way;
and stand before God in devoted surrender.

[*Sūrah al-Baqarah* 2:238]

This verse reminds us to preserve and protect the regularity and rhythm of the ritual prayers, which set up a sacred pattern in our lives and help us to continue on in a state of remembrance at all times. Some translators have taken the second part of the *āyāh* to mean, *especially the middle prayer,* while others take it to mean *the most excellent prayer.* Muḥammad ʿAbduh suggests that *praying in the most excellent way* may mean "the noblest kind of prayer—that is, a prayer from the fullness of the heart, with the whole mind turned towards God, inspired by awe of Him, and reflecting upon His word" (*Manār* II, 438, as quoted by Asad, p. 53). Finally, we are enjoined to maintain a state of awe and devoted surrender as we pray. (Helminski)

The Throne Verse

God—there is no deity but Hū,[4]
the Ever-Living, the Self-Subsisting Source of all Being.
No slumber can seize Him nor sleep.
All things in heaven and on earth belong to Hū.
Who could intercede in His Presence
without His permission?
He knows what appears in front of and behind His creatures.
Nor can they encompass any knowledge of Him
except what He wills.
His throne extends over the heavens and the earth,
and He feels no fatigue in guarding and preserving them,
for He is the Highest and Most Exalted.

[*Sūrah al-Baqarah* 2:255]

This is the *Āyāt-ul-Kursī*, the "Verse of the Throne." Who can translate its glorious meaning or reproduce the rhythm of its well-chosen and comprehensive words? Even in the original Arabic the meaning seems to be greater than can be expressed in words.

The attributes of God are so different from anything we know in our

---

[4]*Hū*: the pronoun of Divine Presence. All words in Arabic have a gender grammatically ascribed to them as they do in French and Spanish, etc. Although Allāh is referred to with the third person masculine pronoun *Hū* (*Huwa*), it is universally understood that Allāh's Essence is beyond gender or indeed any qualification. We should avoid the mistake of attributing human gender to That which is beyond all our attempts at definition, limitless in subtle glory.

present world that we have to be content with understanding that the only fit word by which we can name Him is "He": the pronoun standing for His name. His name—God or Allāh—is sometimes misused and applied to other beings or things; and we must emphatically repudiate any idea or suggestion that there can be any peer of God, the one true living God. He lives, but His life is self-subsisting and eternal: it does not depend upon other beings and is not limited to time and space. Perhaps the attribute of *Qayyūm* includes not only the idea of "Self-Subsisting" but also the idea of "Keeping up and maintaining all activity." His life is the source and constant support of all derived forms of life. Perfect life is perfect activity, in contrast to the imperfect life which we see around us, which is not only subject to death but to the need for rest or sloweddown activity (something which is between activity and sleep, commonly translated as "slumber"), and the need for full sleep itself. But God has no need for rest or sleep. His activity, like His life, is perfect and self-subsisting.

After we realize that His Life is absolute Life, His Being is absolute Being, while others are contingent and evanescent, our ideas of heaven and earth vanish like shadows. What is behind that shadow is He. Such reality as our heavens and our earth possess is a reflection of His absolute Reality. The pantheist places the wrong accent when he says that everything is He. The truth is better expressed when we say that everything is His. How then can any creatures stand before Him as of right, and claim to intercede for a fellow-creature? In the first place, both are His, and He cares as much for one as for the other. In the second place, they are both dependent on His will and command. But He in His Wisdom and Plan may grade his creatures and give one superiority over another. Then by His will and permission such a one may intercede or help according to the laws and duties laid on him. God's knowledge is absolute, and is not conditioned by Time or Space. To us, His creatures, these conditions always apply. His knowledge and our knowledge are therefore in different categories, and our knowledge only gets some reflection of Reality when it accords with His Will and Plan.

His throne could also be translated seat, power, knowledge, symbol of authority. In our thoughts we exhaust everything when we say *the heavens and the earth*. Well, then, in everything is the working of God's power and will and authority. Everything of course includes spiritual things as well as things of sense. Compare Wordsworth's fine outburst in "Tintern Abbey": "Whose dwelling is the light of setting sun, And the round ocean and the living air, And in the blue sky, and in the mind of man: A motion and a spirit that impels all thinking things, all objects of all thought, And rolls through all things."

He feels no fatigue in guarding and preserving them. A life of activity that is imperfect or relative would not only need rest for carrying on its own activities, but would be in need of double rest when it has to look after and guard, or cherish, or help other activities. In contrast with this is the Absolute Life, which is free from any such need or contingency. For it is supreme above anything that we can conceive. (A. Yusuf Ali, pp. 102-103)

No Coercion in Faith

Let there be no coercion in faith.
The right way now stands out from error:
and so whoever rejects the powers of evil
and believes in God has certainly taken hold of a reliable support,
which shall never give way,
for God is all-hearing, all-knowing.

[*Sūrah al-Baqarah* 2:256]

There are several stories associated with the revelation of this verse. Waḥīdi relates that on the authority of Ibn ʿAbbās, "When the children of a woman of the *Anṣār* (the helpers in Medina) all died in infancy, she vowed that if one lived, she would bring it up as a Jew. Thus, when the Jewish tribe of An-Nadir was banished from Medina (4/625), there were with them some children of the *Anṣār*. The *Anṣār* said, 'O Prophet of God, what will happen to our children!' And so God sent down this revelation." Ibn Jabayr thus said, "And so, whoever wished to join them, were free to do so, and whoever wished to enter Islam were also free." (Ayoub, pp. 252–253)

On a few other occasions that we know of, Muslims who tried to coerce people to accept Islam were dissuaded by the Prophet. In one case, two sons of Abū al-Ḥusayn were converted to Christianity by some Syrians and left Medina. When al-Ḥusayn heard of this, he went to the Prophet and asked whether he should pursue them. God then sent down: *There is no compulsion in religion.*

The word *dīn*, translated here as "religion," signifies religion in the widest sense of this term, pertaining to morality, worship, and beliefs regarding what is of ultimate value in life.

Muhammad Asad says:

The rendering of *dīn* as "religion," "faith," "religious law," or "moral law" depends on the context in which this term is used.

There shall be no coercion in matters of faith. On the strength of the categorical prohibition of coercion (*ikrāh*) in anything that pertains to faith or religion, all Islamic jurists (*fuqahā*), without any exception, hold that forcible conversion is under all circumstances null and void, and that any attempt at coercing a non-believer to accept the faith of Islam is a grievous sin: a verdict which disposes of the widespread fallacy that Islam places before the unbelievers the alternative of "conversion or the sword." (Asad, pp. 57-58)

(Helminski)

Out of the Darkness and into the Light

God is the Friend of those who have faith,
leading them out of the darkness toward the light.
Whereas those who are bent on denying the truth
have the powers of evil as their allies
that take them out of the light and deep into the darkness.
It is they who are destined for the Fire, there to abide.

[*Sūrah al-Baqarah* 2:257]

This passage contains both a promise from God and a description of how people of faith are guided toward the light, while those in denial will be guided by *powers of evil* toward darkness. In other words, we attract to ourselves certain powers or energies which will either guide and protect us, or ensure our descent into darkness. This should make us more aware of the significance of the power of choice we must exercise. Within the human being is this free will and power of choice, which not only governs us as individuals, but sets in motion powers outside of ourselves, whether for good or for evil.

God is the "Friend," the *Walī*, of those who possess *īmān*, faith. Faith is, therefore, a form of friendship with God. The word *Walī* implies being near to someone, as well as the protection such nearness offers. The result of this friendship is that we are brought toward the Light. Light, therefore, must have some inherent value, as opposed to darkness which is the reward of those who are *bent on denying the truth,* those who willfully turn away from spiritual reality to follow the selfish desires and negative impulses of their own egos. It may even be that certain people are perversely

41

attracted to this darkness, oblivious to the suffering they cause themselves and others.

It is said in *Sūrah an-Nūr: Allāh is the light of the heavens and the earth* [24:35]. Light is a phenomena that facilitates perception. Therefore Allāh is that power through which we see both in the visible world, the world of the physical senses, and also the invisible world of thoughts, emotions, and subtler perceptions. One attribute of Allāh, therefore, is this power of making perception possible. God is called *As-Samīʿ* (the hearing), *Al-Baṣīr* (the seeing), and *Al-ʿAlīm* (the knowing), and these are attributes shared to some extent by us human beings.

Our need for God, therefore, is also a need to grow in our ability to listen, see, and know through the power of His Light, while those who live in denial, in *kufr*, are actually chosing to become less aware, more oblivious. Such people, therefore, are less free and less alive. They have forfeited their essential human capacities, out of a perverse attachment to their own willfulness, denial, and separation from the Divine Reality.

Therefore the choice that confronts human beings is not only a choice between good and evil, but also a choice between awareness and heedlessness, conscious choice and compulsive habit. We can choose freedom within the broad margins allowed by the Divine Mercy or a compulsive slavery to the ego's whims and desires.

Whichever we choose, we will attract to ourselves either the powers of evil guiding us into ever more darkness or God the Friend, guiding us toward greater consciousness, freedom, and light. (Helminski)

Wisdom is the Greatest Wealth

O you who have faith!
Spend on others out of the good things which you may have acquired,
and out of that which We[5] bring forth for you out of the earth;
and do not choose for your spending
anything bad which you yourselves would not accept
without averting your eyes in disdain.
And know that God is the One Who is Rich,
the One Worthy of Praise.
Satan threatens you with the prospect of poverty
and bids you to be stingy,
while God promises you His forgiveness and abundance;
and God is infinite, all knowing,
He grants wisdom* [ḥikmah] *to whom He wills:
and whoever is granted wisdom
has indeed been granted abundant wealth,
but none are conscious of this
except those who are gifted with insight.

[*Sūrah al-Baqarah* 2:267-269]

Wisdom is explicitly called for in the verse we have cited above; and wisdom, by definition, is not something that can be laid down, in advance of

---

[5] In the revelation of the Qur'an, the Divine Being sometimes chooses to speak or refer to Itself from the first person singular, *I* or *Me*, sometimes as the third person singular, and sometimes as the first person plural, *We*. Some commentators suggest that the usage of *We* refers to the attributes of God.

all the concrete and unique situations in which wisdom needs to be applied, as if it were a formal rule or a blueprint. On the contrary, it is, on the one hand, a divine bestowal, and on the other, a quality that can be developed and cultivated through intellectual, moral, and spiritual effort. In Qur'anic terms, wisdom is described as a gift from God: *He gives wisdom to whom He will; and he to whom wisdom is given has been granted great good* [2:269]. And at the same time, it is a quality that can be cultivated, acquired, or learnt; this is implied in the following verse, where the Prophet is described as one who teaches and imparts, not just the formal message, but the wisdom required to understand and creatively apply that message:

He it is Who has sent among the unlettered ones a Messenger of their own, to recite to them His revelations and to make them grow in purity, and to teach them the Scripture and wisdom [62:2].

One of the most important aspects of wisdom taught by the scripture of the Qur'ān and the conduct of the Prophet is tolerance of those with belief-systems different from one's own; a tolerance grounded in a consciousness of the reality which transcends all systems of belief, one's own included, and yet is also mysteriously present in the depths of each human soul. Authentic dialogue emerges in the measure that this presence of God in all human beings is respected. For Muslims living at a time when the alternative to dialogue is not just diatribe but violent clash, the imperative of highlighting that which unites the different religions, of upholding and promoting the common spiritual patrimony of mankind, is of the utmost urgency. There is ample evidence in the Qur'anic text itself, and compelling commentaries on these verses by those most steeped in the spiritual tradition of Islam, to demonstrate that the Qur'ān not only provides us with a universal vision of religion, and thus with the means to contemplate all revealed religions as 'signs' (*āyāt*) of God; it also opens up paths of creative, constructive dialogue between the faithful of all the different religious communities, despite their divergent belief-systems. It provides us with the basis for dialogue and mutual enrichment on aspects of religious life and thought that go beyond the outward forms of belief, yielding fruit in the fertile fields of metaphysical insight, immutable values, contemplative inspiration, and spiritual realization. (Reza Shah-Kazemi)

Making No Distinction among His Messengers

The Messenger, and the faithful with him,
have faith in what has been revealed to him by his Sustainer:
they all have faith in God, and His angels,
and His revelations, and His messengers,
making no distinction between any of His messengers;
and they say: "We have heard, and we pay heed.
Grant us Your forgiveness, O our Sustainer,
for with You is all journeys' end!"

[*Sūrah al-Baqarah* 2:285]

Sūrah al-Baqarah started with the question of faith (2:3-4), showed us various aspects of faith and the denial of faith, and gave us ordinances for the new people of Islam as a community. It now completes the picture by returning to a confession of faith and its practical manifestation in conduct (*we have heard and we pay heed*), and closes on a note of humility, so that we may confess our sins, ask for forgiveness, and pray for God's help and guidance.

It is not for us to make any distinction between one and another of God's apostles: we must honor them all equally, though we know that God in His wisdom sent them with different kinds of mission and gave them different degrees of rank.

When our faith and conduct are sincere, we realize how far from perfection we are, and we humbly pray to God for the forgiveness of our sins. We feel that God imposes no burden on us that we cannot bear, and with this realization in our hearts and in the confession of our lips, we go

46

to Him and ask for His help and guidance. (A. Yusuf Ali, p. 116)

Literally, *we make no distinction between any of His apostles:* these words are put, as it were, in the mouths of the believers. Inasmuch as all the apostles were true bearers of God's messages, there is no distinction between them, albeit some of them have been *endowed more highly than others* [2:253]. (Asad, p. 64)

Let Not Our Hearts Swerve from the Truth

Step by step He has sent down to you this Book,
setting forth the truth which confirms
whatever remains of earlier revelations:
for it is He Who earlier bestowed from on high
the Torah and the Gospel, as a guidance to humankind,
and it is He Who has bestowed the standard for discernment. . .
He it is Who has bestowed upon you from on high this divine writ,
containing messages that are clear in and by themselves—
and these are the essence of the divine writ—
as well as others that are allegorical.
Now those whose hearts are given to swerving from the truth
go after that part of the divine writ which has been expressed in allegory,
seeking out [what is bound to create] confusion,
and seeking its final meaning;
but none except God knows its final meaning.
Hence, those who are deeply rooted in knowledge say:
"We believe in it; the whole of it is from our Sustainer—
although none takes this to heart
except those who are endowed with insight.
O our Sustainer!
Do not let our hearts swerve from the truth
after You have guided us;
and bestow on us Grace from Your presence:
for truly, You are the Generous Bestower."

[*Sūrah Āl ᶜImrān* 3:3-4,7-8]

48

Rabbanā lā tuzigh qulūbanā baʿda ʿidh hadaytanā
wa hab lanā mil-laduāka raḥmah;
ʿinnaka ʿAātal-Wahhāb.

The above passage may be regarded as a key to the understanding of the Qurʾān. Ṭabarī identifies the *āyāt muḥkamāt* (*messages that are clear in and by themselves*) with what the philologists and jurists describe as *naṣṣ*—namely, ordinances or statements which are self-evident (*ẓāhir*) by virtue of their wording. Consequently, Ṭabarī regards as *āyāt muḥkamāt* only those statements or ordinances of the Qurʾān which do not admit of more than one interpretation (which does not, of course, preclude differences of opinion regarding the implications of a particular *āyah muḥkamāh*). In my opinion, however, it would be too dogmatic to regard any passage of the Qurʾān which does not conform to the above definition as *mutashābih* ("allegorical"): for there are many statements in the Qurʾān which are liable to more than one interpretation but are, nevertheless, not allegorical—just as there are many expressions and passages which, despite their allegorical formulation, reveal to the searching intellect only one possible meaning. For this reason, the *āyāt mutashābihāt* may be defined as those passages of the Qurʾān which are expressed in a figurative manner, with a meaning that is metaphorically implied but not directly, in so many words, stated. The *āyāt muḥkamāt* are described as the "essence of the divine writ" (*umm al-kitāb*) because they comprise the fundamental principles underlying its message and, in particular, its ethical and social teachings: and it is only on the basis of these clearly enunciated principles that the allegorical passages can be correctly interpreted.

But none except God knows its final meaning. According to most of the early commentators, this refers to the interpretation of allegorical passages which deal with metaphysical subjects—for instance, God's attributes, the ultimate meaning of time and eternity, the resurrection of the dead, the

49

Day of Judgment, paradise and hell, the nature of the beings or forces described as angels, and so forth—all of which fall within the category of *al-ghayb*, i.e., that sector of reality which is beyond the reach of human perception and imagination and cannot, therefore, be conveyed to man in other than allegorical terms. This view of the classical commentators, however, does not seem to take into account the many Qur'anic passages which do *not* deal with metaphysical subjects and yet are, undoubtedly, allegorical in intent and expression. To my mind, one cannot arrive at a correct understanding of the above passage without paying due attention to the nature and function of allegory as such. A true allegory—in contrast with a mere pictorial paraphrase of something that could equally well be stated in direct terms—is always meant to express in a figurative manner something which, because of its complexity, *cannot* be adequately expressed in direct terms or propositions and, because of this very complexity, can be grasped only intuitively, as a general mental image, and not as a series of detailed "statements": and this seems to be the meaning of the phrase, *none except God knows its final meaning*. (Asad, pp. 66-67)

The Essential Religion is Submission

Indeed, with God the religion is submission,
And it was only because of envy that the People of the Book
developed other views, and only after knowledge had come to them,
but whoever denies the signs of God,
with God the reckoning is swift.

[*Sūrah Āl ʿImrān* 3:19]

Here we have one of the most important passages in the Qurʾān, one that deserves careful reflection. Its context, at the beginning of *Sūrah Āl ʿImrān*, is a discussion of the essential elements of faith.

Sūrah Āl ʿImrān begins with a confirmation of the authenticity of books revealed to Moses and Jesus, referring specifically to the Torah and the Gospel. These are called "guidance for mankind." The appropriateness and actuality of a diversity of religions is acknowledge in numerous places in the Qurʾān, for instance:

To every community We have appointed ways of worship, which they ought to observe. And so, do not let others draw you [O Muḥammad] into arguing about it, but invite them to your Sustainer: for you are indeed on the right way. And if they argue with you, say: "God knows best what you are doing." Indeed, God will judge between you on the Day of Resurrection concerning everything about which you would differ. [22:67-69]

Within the context of this acknowledgement of religious pluralism, humankind is given a clear warning: *Those who reject the signs of God will*

51

suffer the severest penalty [3:4]. What does it mean to reject the signs of God? It is said that various things distract us from recognizing the signs of God: women and sons, heaps of gold and silver, fine horses (or nowadays cars), and real estate. Our exclusive preoccupation with the things of the world (*dunya*) blinds us to the signs (*āyāts*).

Therefore, submission, here, should be understood as "islām" with a small "i," that is a state of being, a kind of relationship with God, rather than the specific forms of religion which we would understand as "Islam" with a capital "I."

An important unifying theme of these first nineteen *āyāts* of *Sūrah Āl ʿImrān* might be summarized by the supplication: *Our Sustainer, do not let our hearts deviate after you have guided us, but grant us Mercy from Your Presence* [3:8]. This deviation occurred among People of the Book and it can also occur among people who are nominally Muslim.

The people of true faith, of submission, *islām*, are described in this way:

> *Those who patiently persevere, who are sincere,*
> *who are worshipful, who share their resources,*
> *and who ask forgiveness from their innermost hearts before dawn.*

[*Sūrah Āl ʿImrān* 3:17]

These are the essential characteristics of "islam," which theoretically are possible for any human being in any divinely revealed form of religion. The fact that some Christians and Jews, out of *envy among themselves* (*bagyam baynahum*), invented beliefs beyond those which had been revealed to them, and claimed for their religion an exclusive validity, denying the validity of other approaches to God, is the way in which they negated their submission to God. Out of envy and denigration of others we fall into the sins of arrogance and self-righteousness. Then, instead of competing in the realm of virtue, there appears a competition based on adherence to beliefs and forms. Rather than true submission to God, and the

52

qualities that submission entails—patience, sincerity, worship, charity, and humility before God—human beings, distracted by their own false selves, become the source of conflict (*fitnah*).

If Muslims are to maintain their true alignment with God's Grace (*raḥmah*) and Guidance (*hudah*), we will have to realize the truth of: *Indeed with God the religion is submission* (islām). (Helminski)

Christ, the Word

Lo! The angels said:
"O Mary! Behold, God sends you the glad tiding,
*through **a Word from Him,***
who shall become known as the Christ Jesus, son of Mary,
of great honor in this world and in the life to come,
and of those who are near to God."

[*Sūrah Āl ʿImrān* 3:45]

Christ means literally "whose name shall be 'the Anointed' (*al-masīḥ*)." The designation *al-masīḥ* is the Arabicized form of the Aramaic *meshīḥā* which, in turn, is derived from the Hebrew *māhsīaḥ*, "the anointed"—a term frequently applied in the Bible to the Hebrew kings, whose accession to power used to be consecrated by a touch with holy oil taken from the Temple. This anointment appears to have been so important a rite among the Hebrews that the term "the anointed" became in the course of time more or less synonymous with "king." Its application to Jesus may have been due to the widespread conviction among his contemporaries that he was descended in direct . . . line from the royal House of David. . . . Whatever may have been the historical circumstances, it is evident that the honorific "the Anointed" was applied to Jesus in his own lifetime. In the Greek version of the Gospels—which is undoubtedly based on a now-lost Aramaic original—this designation is correctly translated as *Christos* (a noun derived from the Greek verb *chriein*, "to anoint"): and since it is in this form—"the Christ"— that the designation *al-masīḥ* has achieved currency in all Western languages, I am using it throughout in my translation.

As regards the expression *min al-muqarrabīn* (*of those who are near, i.e., to God*), the most excellent among the inhabitants of paradise are thus described in 56:10-12: *But the foremost shall be [they who in life were] the foremost [in faith and good works]: they who were [always] drawn close to God. In gardens of bliss [will they dwell].* (Asad, p. 73)

But the text continues to remind us not to take Jesus Christ as God:

It is not conceivable that a human being to whom God had granted
revelation, and sound judgment, and prophethood,
should thereafter have said to people, "Worship me beside God";
but rather:"Become men of God
by spreading the knowledge of the Book,
and by your own deep study of it."
And neither did he bid you
to take the angels and the prophets for your lords:
for would he bid you to deny the truth
after you have surrendered yourselves to God?

[*Sūrah Āl ʿImrān* 3:79-80]

Zamakhsharī regards the term "*ḥukm*" (*judgment* or *sound judgment*) occurring in the above sentence as synonymous, in this context, with *ḥikmah* ("wisdom"). According to Sībawayh (as quoted by Rāzī), a *rabbānī* is "one who devotes himself exclusively to the endavor to know the Sustainer (*ar-rabb*) and to obey Him": a connotation fairly close to the English expression "a man of God." (Asad, p. 79)

Hold Fast to the Rope of God

O you who have faith!
Be mindful of God with all the mindfulness that is due Him,
and do not allow death to overtake you
before you have surrendered yourselves to Him.
And hold fast, all together, to the rope of God,
and do not draw apart from one another.
And remember with gratitude the blessings
which God has bestowed on you:
how, when you were adversaries, He brought your hearts together,
so that through His blessings you became as though of one family;
and how when you were on the brink of a fiery abyss,
He saved you from it.
In this way, God makes clear His signs to you,
so that you might be guided,
and that there might grow out of you a community
that invites to all that is good, and encourages the doing of what is right
and forbids the doing of what is wrong:
and it is they who shall attain happiness!

[*Sūrah Āl ʿImrān* 3:102-104]

If anyone ever needed a beautiful reason to live, here it is. When so many people are so often lacking a sense of purpose, seeking happiness so unsuccessfully, there is a purpose to be recognized here in the possibility of human solidarity. This passage suggests the active role of the divine in offering guidance and establishing human togetherness.

To be mindful of God is our translation of *taqwāllah*, which Muḥammad Asad translates as "be conscious of God" and Yusuf Ali translates as "fear God."

Ibn Kathīr cites a *ḥadīth* reported on the authority of ʿAlī who said that "the Qurʾān is God's strong rope and the straight way." He cites another *ḥadīth* on the authority of Abū Saʿīd al-Khudrī in which the Prophet said, "The Book of God is God's rope stretched from heaven to earth." ʿAbd Allāh ibn Masʿūd reported that the Messenger of God said, "Surely this Qurʾān is God's strong rope, a manifest light, and a beneficial source of healing. It is protection for those who hold fast to it, and a means of salvation for those who abide by it." (Ayoub, p. 275)

According to Yusuf Ali:

The simile is that of people struggling in deep water, to whom a benevolent Providence stretches out a strong and unbreakable rope of rescue. If all hold fast to it together, their mutual support adds to the chance of their safety.

When you were adversaries, He brought your hearts together: Yathrib was torn with civil and tribal feuds and dissensions before the Apostle of God set his sacred feet on its soil. After that, it became the City of the Prophet, Medina, an unmatched brotherhood, and the pivot of Islam. This poor quarrelsome world is a larger Yathrib; can we establish the sacred feet on its soil, and make it a new and larger Medina? (A. Yusuf Ali, p. 149)

Furthermore, we are asked to *not draw apart from one another and remember with gratitude the blessings bestowed* on us. The result of these things, the blessing of it is that we will become "like one family." Adversaries become one in heart. When we are near the brink of the abyss, we are saved from it. Here is a clear picture of what God wishes to communicate to us. Through revelation we are not only offered inner peace and blessings on the individual level, but when the divine principles are embodied

57

in the life of a society, true well-being is increased for all.

The function of God's signs is to awaken us to true happiness and well-being. Signs are both of a universal nature, available to all sincere human beings. But in this passage the signs, or *āyāts*, have specifically established a community, the Muslim *ummah*, which *invites to all that is good, and forbids the doing of what is wrong*.

It is they who shall attain happiness. The word for happiness here (*muflih, aflaha, falāh*), suggests the attainment of happiness in this world and the next; success, prosperity, freedom from anxiety and inner conflict. Because it invites to all that is good, enjoins the right, and forbids the wrong, the ideal Muslim community is happy, self-confident, free of doubt and confusion, strong, united, and prosperous. (Rephrased from A. Yusuf Ali, p. 150) (Helminski)

Travel Through the World

Many ways of life have passed away before your time.
Go, then, travel through the world and see what happened
in the end to those who denied the truth:
here is a clear lesson for all human beings
and a guidance and a counsel for those who are mindful of God.
So do not lose heart, nor fall into despair:
for if you are faithful you are bound to ascend.

[*Sūrah Āl ʿImrān* 3:137-139]

Many ways of life (*sunan,* plural of *sunnah*) suggests the different value systems, economies, social structures by which human beings have organized their lives. Muḥammad Asad has this to say:

The word *sunnah* (of which *sunan* is the plural) denotes a "way of life" or "conduct" (hence its application, in Islamic terminology, to the way of life of the Prophet as an example for his followers). In the above passage, the term *sunan* refers to the "conditions (*aḥwāl*) characteristic of past centuries" (Rāzī), in which, despite all the continuous changes, an ever-recurring pattern can be discerned: a typically, Qurʾanic reference to the possibility, and necessity, of learning from man's past experiences. (Asad, p. 88)

The Qurʾān is offering us a grand perspective far above the narrow parochialisms which human beings tend to get caught up in. The first sentence expands our sense of time, while the second, which enjoins us to travel through the earth, widens our sense of place. Such travel could

59

even be heard as a Divine imperative, or at least an invitation. If we travel through the world we will inevitably see evidence of past communities and civilizations which have declined or have been destroyed. There is in this a "clear lesson" for everyone, but even more so, for those who are "mindful of God," those with *taqwā*, this will be a guidance and a counsel. The outer life that human beings create for themselves is inevitably a reflection of their inner lives. Their values and faith, or the lack thereof, will be evidenced in the societies they create.

But we are told not to fall into discouragement or despair, because if we are among those who keep the faith, we will ascend. Yusuf Ali offers this commentary:

Compare Tennyson (*In Memoriam*): "Our little systems have their day. They have their day and cease to be. They are but broken lights of You, and You, O Lord! art more than they." Only God's Truth will last, and it will gain the mastery in the end. If there is defeat, we must not be dejected, lose heart, or give up the struggle. Faith means hope, activity, striving steadfastly on to the goal. (A. Yusuf Ali, p. 158) (Helminski)

Facing Mortality

Do you think that you could enter paradise
unless God takes cognizance of your having striven hard ,
and of your having been patient in adversity?
For, indeed, you did long for death
until you came face to face with it;
and now you have seen it with your own eyes.
And Muḥammad is only a messenger;
all the messengers have passed away before him:
if, then, he dies or is slain, will you turn about on your heels?
But he that turns about on his heels does no harm to God—
whereas God will recompense all who are grateful.
And no human being can die except by God's permission,
at a term pre-ordained.
And if one desires the rewards of this world, We shall grant him thereof;
and if one desires the rewards of the life to come,
We shall grant him thereof;
and We shall recompense those who are grateful.

[*Sūrah Āl ʿImrān* 3:142-145]

It was this very passage of the Qurʾān which Abū Bakr, the first Caliph, recited immediately after the Prophet's death, when many faint-hearted Muslims thought that Islam itself had come to an end; but as soon as Abū Bakr added, "Behold, whoever has worshipped Muḥammad may know that Muḥammad has died; but whoever worships God may know that God is ever-living, and never dies" (Bukhārī), all confusion was stilled.

61

(Asad, p. 89)

This stress on the mortality of the Prophet—and that of all the other prophets who preceded him in time—connects, in the first instance, with the battle of Uḥud and the rumor of his death, which caused many Muslims to abandon the fight and even brought some of them close to apostasy. In its wider implications, however, the above verse re-states the fundamental Islamic doctrine that adoration is due to God alone, and that no human being—not even a Prophet—may have any share in it.

And we have need to remember this now and often for two reasons: (1) when we feel inclined to pay more than human honor to one who was the truest, the purest, and the greatest of men, and thus in a sense to compound for our forgetting the spirit of his teaching, and (2) when we feel depressed at the chances and changes of time, and forget that the eternal God lives and watches over us and over all His creatures now as in all history in the past and in the future.

And if one desires the rewards of this world, We shall grant him thereof: there is a slight touch of irony in this. As applied to the archers at Uḥud, who deserted their posts for the sake of plunder, they might have got some plunder, but they put themselves and the whole of their army into jeopardy. For a little worldly gain, they nearly lost their souls. On the other hand, those who took the long view and fought with staunchness and discipline—their reward was swift and sure. If they died, they got the crown of martyrdom. If they lived, they were heroes honored in this life and the next. (A. Yusuf Ali, pp. 159-160)

Free Will or Pre-Destination?

Then, after this woe, **He sent down upon you a sense of security,**
an inner calm which enfolded some of you,
whereas the others, who cared mainly for themselves,
entertained wrong thoughts about God—thoughts of pagan ignorance—
saying, "Did we, then, have any power of decision?"
Say: "Truly, all power of decision does rest with God"—
but they are trying to conceal within themselves
that which they would not reveal to you, [O Prophet] saying,
"If we had any power of decision,
we would not have left so many dead behind."
Say: "Even if you had remained in your homes,
those whose death had been ordained
would indeed have gone forth to the places
where they were destined to lie down."
And all this befell you so that God might put to a test
all that you harbor in your hearts,
and render your innermost hearts pure of all dross:
for God is aware of what is in the hearts.
Behold, as for those of you who turned away
on the day when the two hosts met in battle—
Satan caused them to stumble
only by means of something that they, themselves, had done.
But now God has effaced this sin of theirs:
For truly, God is much-forgiving, forbearing.
O you who have attained to faith,
be not like those who are intent on denying the truth

and say of their brethren
[who die] after having set out on a journey to faraway places
or gone forth to war,
"Had they but remained with us, they would not have died,"
or, "They would not have been slain"—
for God will cause such thoughts
to become a source of bitter regret in their hearts,
since it is God Who grants life and deals death.
And God sees all that you do.

[*Sūrah Āl ʿImrān* 3:154-156]

Did we, then, have any power of decision in this matter? i.e., in the matter of victory or defeat. The "thoughts of pagan ignorance" is obviously an allusion to the initial reluctance of those faint-hearted people at the battle of Uḥud to admit their moral responsibility for what had happened, and to their excusing themselves by saying that their failure to live up to their faith had been "predestined."

Satan caused them to stumble only by means of something that they themselves had done. This is an illustration of a significant Qurʾanic doctrine, which can be thus summarized: "Satan's influence" on man is not the primary *cause* of sin but its *first consequence:* that is to say, a consequence of a person's own attitude of mind which in a moment of moral crisis induces him to choose the easier, and seemingly more pleasant, of the alternatives open to him, and thus to become guilty of a sin, whether by commission or omission. Thus, God's "causing" a person to commit a sin is conditional upon the existence, in the individual concerned, of an attitude of mind which makes him prone to commit such a sin: which, in its turn, presupposes man's free will—that is, the ability to make, within certain limitations, a conscious choice between two or more possible courses of action. (Asad, p. 91)

64

The Prophet's Gentleness

And it was by God's grace that you [O Prophet]
dealt gently with your followers;
for if you had been harsh and hard of heart,
they would indeed have broken away from you.
Pardon them, then, and pray that they be forgiven.
And take counsel with them in all matters of public concern;
then, when you have decided upon a course of action,
place your trust in God:
for truly, God loves those who place their trust in Him.

[*Sūrah Āl ʿImrān* 3:159]

The commentator Rāzī connects this verse to the battle of Uḥud, which was a serious defeat for the outnumbered Muslims partly because they let themselves become distracted by the spoils of war and more importantly because they became faint-hearted when the Prophet was wounded. If there were a time when the Prophet could have shown anger and disappointment toward his followers, this would have been it. Nevertheless, he treated them with patience and kindness.

Yusuf Ali comments:

The extremely gentle nature of Muḥammad endeared him to all, and it is reckoned as one of the Mercies of God. One of the Apostle's titles is "A Mercy to all Creation." At no time was this gentleness, this mercy, this long suffering with human weakness, more valuable than after a disaster like that at Uḥud. It is a God-like quality, which then, as always, bound and binds the souls of countless men to him. (A. Yusuf Ali, p. 164)

65

Rāzī also quotes the following *hadīth*: "No clemency and compassion are more loved by God than those of a leader (*imām*), and no foolishness and harshness of character are more hateful to Him than his foolishness and harshness."

ʿĀʾishah reported that the Messenger of God Σ said, "God charged me with gentleness toward all human beings as He also charged me with the implementation of spiritual obligations (*farāʾiḍ*)."

Muḥammad Asad sees in this some important principles of governance:

This injunction, implying government by consent and council, must be regarded as one of the fundamental clauses of all Qurʾanic legislation relating to statecraft. The pronoun "them" relates to the believers, that is, to the whole community; while the word *al-amr* occurring in this context—as well as in the much earlier-revealed phrase *amruhum shūrā baynahum* in 42:38—denotes all affairs of public concern, including state administration. All authorities agree in that the above ordinance, although addressed in the first instance to the Prophet, is binding on all Muslims and for all times. (For its wider implications, see *State and Government in Islam*, by Muḥammad Asad, pp. 44 ff.) Some Muslim scholars conclude from the wording of this ordinance that the leader of the community, although obliged to take counsel, is nevertheless free to accept or to reject it; but the arbitrariness of this conclusion becomes obvious as soon as we recall that even the Prophet considered himself bound by the decisions of his council [as in the battle of Uḥud]. Moreover, when he was asked— according to a Tradition on the authority of ʿAlī ibn Abī Ṭālib—to explain the implications of the word *ʿazm* ("deciding upon a course of action") which occurs in the above verse, the Prophet replied, "[It means] taking counsel with knowledgeable people (*ahl ar-raʿy*) and thereupon following them [therein]." (Asad, p. 92)

The essence of these *āyāts* is that the Prophet Muḥammad Σ won the hearts of people through his kindness, patience, and humble willingness to consult others on practical matters. (Helminski)

Trials

You shall most certainly be tried in your possessions and in yourselves;
and indeed you shall hear much that will cause you grief
from those to whom revelation was granted before your time,
as well as from those
who have come to attribute divinity to others beside God.
But if you persevere and remain mindful
this is certainly a great resolve.

[*Sūrah Āl ʿImrān* 3:186]

During the Prophet's life, he and his companions suffered many hurtful and insulting incidents. Likewise, people of faith should not expect their lives to proceed without challenges, losses, and painful events, including from people who do not share their faith. This should not be a reason to lose heart, but, on the contrary, can be seen as an opportunity to strengthen one's resolve.

Life will inevitably present us with occasions when we are tested by challenges to our self-esteem, our beliefs, our possessions, and our security. The commentator Tabarsi writes: "This world is the realm of tests and afflictions. People of faith will face trials in order that they may develop patience and know spiritual blessings. God is telling us, 'You will encounter trials and hardships in what you possess by way of lessening and loss, and in your lives through death and injury, just as it was suffered on the day of Uḥud. God calls all afflictions a trial (*balwā*) metaphorically. God allows trials only in order that the people of truth may be distinguished from the people of falsehood." (Helminski)

Sustaining Remembrance

And to God belongs the dominion over the heavens and the earth;
and God has power over all things.
Truly, in the creation of the heavens and the earth,
and in the succession of night and day,
there are indeed signs for all who are endowed with insight,
*and **who remember God standing, and sitting,***
and lying on their sides,
and contemplate the creation of the heavens and the earth:
"O our Sustainer!
You have not created this without meaning and purpose.
Limitless are You in Your subtle glory!
Deliver us from the anguish of the Fire."

[*Sūrah Āl ʿImrān* 3:189-191]

It is characteristic of the Qurʾān that rather than offering human beings some complex theology or dogmatic proposition, it tells us instead to reflect with insight (*baṣira*) on the signs (*āyāts*) of the heavens and the earth. All natural processes are the evidence and reminder of the Divine power. We are asked to awaken to this, to open ourselves to the kind of perception which can witness the meaning and purpose behind everything, right down to the obvious fluctuation of night and day, darkness and light. By virtue of this we develop into people who "remember" or call God to mind in all conditions of life, and even as we lie down to sleep at night. This remembrance, in other words, is not to be identified with a special place or time, or any particular behavior; it is a continuous, sustained state

69

of awareness. And it is this state of awareness that develops into a deeper and deeper faith, the conviction that everything in existence is the manifestation of God's meaning and purpose.

This continual state of remembrance that we are called to will lead us to the awareness that everything has been created in accordance with a meaningful purpose: *You have not created this without meaning and purpose* (bāṭilan).

Nothing is accidental: *None of this has God created without [an inner] truth* [10:5]. *We have not created heaven and earth and all that is between them without meaning and purpose, as is the surmise of those who are bent on denying the truth* [38:27]. The state of those who remember God in all the conditions of life becomes a state of trust and surrender to the unfolding meaning of life. (Helminski)

Patience

O you who keep the faith!
Be patient, and encourage patience in each other,
and be strengthened by your connection,
and be mindful of God,
so that you might attain felicity.

[*Sūrah Āl ʿImrān* 3:200]

Yā ʿayyuhal-ladhīna ʿāmanuṣ-birū
wa ṣābirū wa rābiṭū
wat-taqul-lāha la-ʿallakum tufliḥūn

This short, deceptively simple exhortation contains an immense message
of guidance and hope. It calls upon those with *īmān*, those who *keep the
faith*. *Īmān* is not the state of belief, not the mental conviction in some
concept, but the active state of trusting in the Divine. Such people will
turn the noun, "patience," into a dynamic verb, represented here by
ṣābirū. We have no equivalent in the English language for the dynamic
activity of bearing all things with trust and acceptance. The word *rābiṭū*,
which we have translated as "be strengthened by your connection,"
means both to bond with something and to be strengthened by that bond.
The implication here is twofold: first that we should keep our conscious
connection with the Divine presence, and also that we should be actively
persevering in unity with other people of faith. The final word, which
comes from the root *f-l-ḥ*, is the same state that the *muezzin* calls us to in
the *aẓan*: *ḥayya ʿala falaḥ*, come to well-being, felicity, true prosperity.

Here is the essential message of Islamic spirituality: that faith in and conscious connection to the Beneficent, Divine Presence results in a state of inner strength, spiritual well-being, and true happiness. (Helminski)

Be patient: the full meaning of *ṣabr* is to be understood here: patience, perseverance, constancy, self-restraint, refusing to be cowed down. These virtues we are to exercise for ourselves and in relation to others: we are to set an example, so that others may vie with us, and we are to vie with them, lest we fall short. In this way, we strengthen each other and bind our mutual relations closer, in our common service to God.

Felicity or prosperity (*falāḥ*) here and in other passages is to be understood in a wide sense, including prosperity in our mundane affairs as well as in spiritual progress. In both cases it implies happiness and the attainment of our wishes, purified by the love of God. (A. Yusuf Ali, p. 176)

What God Wants for Us

God wants to bestow clarity upon you,
and guide you to the earlier, (sacred) ways of life,
and God turns to you:
for God is All-knowing, Wise.
And God wants to turn to you,
whereas those who follow their own lusts want you to drift far away.
God wants to lighten your burdens:
for man has been created weak.

[*Sūrah an-Nisāᶜ* 4:26-28]

The earlier, (sacred) ways of life: an allusion to the *genuine* religious teachings of the past, which aimed at bringing about a harmony between man's physical nature and the demands of his spirit—a harmony which is destroyed whenever asceticism is postulated as the only possible alternative to licentiousness. This allusion arises from the discussion of sexual morality in the preceding passages [earlier in this *sūrah*] devoted to marital relations.

God wants to lighten your burdens: i.e., to remove, by means of His guidance, all possibility of conflict between man's spirit and his bodily urges, and to show him a way of life in which these two elements of human nature can be harmonized and brought to full fruition.

And were it not that [with the prospect of boundless riches before them] all people would become one [evil] community, We might indeed have provided for those who deny the Most Gracious [huge wealth] [43:33]. Since *man has been created weak,* it is almost a "law of nature" that whenever he is exposed to

73

the prospect of great wealth, he is liable to lose sight of all spiritual and moral considerations, and to become utterly selfish, greedy, and ruthless.

And He does not demand of you [to sacrifice in His cause all of] your possessions: [for,] if He were to demand of you all of them, and urge you, you would niggardly cling [to them], and so He would [but] bring out your moral failings [47:36–37]. The implication is that since *man has been created weak*, the imposition of too great a burden on the believers would be self-defeating inasmuch as it might result not in an increase of faith but, rather, in its diminution. This passage illustrates the supreme realism of the Qur'ān, which takes into account human nature as it is, with all its God-willed complexity and its inner contradictions, and does not, therefore, postulate *a priori* an impossible ideal as a norm of human behavior.

And [always], O you believers—all of you—turn to God in repentance, so that you might attain to a happy state! [24:31]. The implication of this general call to repentance is that since *man has been created weak*, no one is ever free of faults and temptations—so much so that even the Prophet used to say, "Truly, I turn to Him in repentance a hundred times every day" (Ibn Ḥanbal, Bukhārī, and Bayhaqī, all of them on the authority of ʿAbd Allāh ibn ʿUmar). (Asad, pp. 108, 753, 783, 539)

Recompense

Truly, God does not wrong anyone by as much as an atom's weight;
and if there is a good deed, He will compound it
and will bestow out of His Presence an immense recompense.

[*Sūrah an-Nisāᶜ* 4:40]

Any little good of our own comes from the purity of our heart. Its results in the world are doubled and multiplied by God's grace and mercy: but an even greater reward comes, from His own Presence, His good pleasure, which brings us nearer to Him. (A. Yusuf Ali, p. 192)

A Beautiful Friendship

For all those who listen to God and the Messenger
are among those on whom God has bestowed His blessings:
the prophets, and those who never deviated from the truth,
and those who with their lives bore witness to the truth,
and the righteous ones; and what a beautiful friendship this is.
Such is the abundance of God—
and it suffices that God is All-Knowing.

[*Sūrah an-Nisāᶜ* 4:69-70]

This is a passage of the deepest spiritual meaning. Even the humblest man who accepts faith and does good becomes at once an accepted member of a great and beautiful spiritual fellowship. It is a company which lives perpetually in the sunshine of God's Grace. It is a glorious hierarchy, of which four grades are specified: (1) the highest is that of the prophets or apostles, who get plenary inspiration from God and who teach mankind by example and precept. That rank in Islam is held by Muḥammad Muṣṭafā. (2) The next are those whose badge is sincerity and truth; they love and support the truth with their person, their means, their influence, and all that is theirs. That rank was held by the special companions of Muhammad, among whom the type was that of Ḥaḍrat Abū Bakr Ṣiddīq. (3) The next are the noble army of witnesses, who testify to the truth. The testimony may be by martyrdom, as in the case of Imāms Ḥasan and Ḥusain. Or it may be by the tongue of the true preacher or the pen of the devoted scholar, or the life of the man devoted to service. (4) Lastly, there is the large company of righteous people, the ordinary folk who do their

76

ordinary business, but always in a righteous way. They are the rank and file of the beautiful fellowship, in which each has his place and yet all feel that they derive glory from the common association.

Such is the abundance of God—and it suffices that God is All-Knowing. If a generous General gives the private soldier the privilege of sitting with his comrades and officers, high and low, in one common brotherhood, people may perhaps wonder: how may this be? If we are admitted to that fellowship, we want to know more. It is enough to us that God knows our humility and our unworthiness, and with His full knowledge admits us to that glorious fellowship. (A. Yusuf Ali, pp. 200-201)

Courtesy to People of Other Faiths

O you who have faith! When you go forth in God's cause
use your discernment and do not—
out of a desire for the fleeting gains of this worldly life—
say to anyone who offers you a greeting: "You are not of the faithful!"
for with God are abundant benefits.
You, too, were once in the same condition—
but God has been gracious to you:
so use your discernment: truly, God is well-aware of all that you do.

[*Sūrah an-Nisāᶜ* 4:94]

You are not of the faithful, that is to say, "and therefore one of the enemies." This verse prohibits the treating of noncombatants as enemies and using their supposed unbelief as a pretext for plundering them. The injunction *use your discernment* (*tabayyanū*) imposes on the believers the duty of making sure, in every case, whether the persons concerned are actively engaged in hostilities or not.

You, too, were once in the same condition is literally *thus have you been aforetime.* Since the preceding injunction refers to the *whole community*, it would seem that the above clause, too, bears the same implication: namely, a reference to the time when the Muslim community was, because of its weakness and numerical insignificance, at the mercy of enemies endowed with greater power. Thus, the believers are told, as it were: "Remember your erstwhile weakness, and treat the peacefully-minded among your enemies with the same consideration with which you yourselves were once hoping to be treated." (Asad, p. 123)

78

God's Evidence and Promise

O humankind!
Evidence has now come to you
from your Sustainer,
and We have sent to you a clear light.
And as for those who have attained to faith in Allāh[6]
and hold fast to Him—
He will cause them to enter into His compassion
and His abundant blessing,
and guide them to Himself by a straight way.

[*Sūrah an-Nisāᶜ 4:174-5*]

First of all, this verse is addressed to all of humanity, announcing that "evidence" (*burhān*) and clear light (*nūram mubīn*) have come to us. In verses 164-166 it is said: *Of some messengers We have already told you the story, and of others We have not, and to Moses Allāh spoke directly. Messengers who brought both good news and warning, so that humanity, after their coming, should have no complaint against God, for God is the Powerful and the Wise. But God bears witness that what He has sent to you, He has sent with His knowledge.*

---

[6]The Arabic word for God: used by Arabic-speaking Christians as well as Muslims.

79

Bear Witness to the Truth

O you who have attained to faith!
Stand firmly in your devotion to God,
bearing witness to the truth in complete fairness;
and never let hatred of anyone
lead you to make the mistake of deviating from justice.
Be just: this is the closest to being God-conscious.
And remain conscious of God:
truly, God is well-aware of all that you do.

[*Sūrah al-Māʿidah* 5:8]

Justice is God's attribute, and to stand firm for justice is to be a witness to God, even if it is detrimental to our own interests as we conceive them, or the interests of those who are near and dear to us. According to the Latin saying, "Let justice be done though heaven should fall." But Islamic justice is something higher than the formal justice of Roman Law or any other human law. It is even more penetrating than the subtler justice in the speculations of the Greek philosophers. It searches out the innermost motives, because we are to act as if in the presence of God, to Whom all things, acts, and motives are known.

To do justice and act righteously in a favorable or neutral atmosphere is meritorious enough, but the real test comes when you have to do justice to people who hate you or to whom you have an aversion. But no less is required of you by the higher moral law. (A. Yusuf Ali, pp. 223, 243)

80

Killing

If anyone slays a single soul—
unless it be in punishment for murder
or for spreading corruption on earth—
it shall be as though he had slain all humankind;
whereas, if anyone saves a life,
it shall be as though he had saved the lives of all humanity.

[*Sūrah al-Māʿidah* 5:32]

To kill or seek to kill an individual because he represents an ideal is to kill all who uphold the ideal. On the other hand, to save an individual life in the same circumstances is to save a whole community. What could be a stronger condemnation of individual assassination and revenge? (A. Yusuf Ali, p. 252)

Cultural Pluralism

And to you We have sent this Book
of the Truth, confirming the truth
of whatever remains of earlier revelations
and guarding what is true within.
Judge in accordance with what God has bestowed from on high,
and do not follow erring views,
forsaking the truth that has come to you.
For every one of you have
We designated a law and a way of life.
And if God had so willed,
He could surely have made you all one single community:
but He willed it otherwise in order to test you
by means of what He has bestowed on you.
Strive, then, with one another in doing good!
Your goal is God;
and then, He will make you understand
the truth of everything in which you have differed.

[*Sūrah al-Māʿidah* 5:48]

Confirming the truth of whatever remains of earlier revelations and guarding what is true within. The participle *muhaymin* is derived from the quadrilateral verb *haymana*, "he watched [over a thing]" or "controlled [it]," and is used here to describe the Qurʾān as the determining factor in deciding what is genuine and what is false in the earlier scriptures. *Judge in accordance with what God has bestowed from on high.* This apparently applies not

82

merely to judicial cases but also to opinions as to what is right or wrong in the ethical sense. As is evident from the mention of the "followers of the Gospel" and of the Torah in the verses just preceding this one, the people spoken of here are both the Jews and the Christians. The expression *for every one of you* denotes the various communities of which mankind is composed.

The term translated as "law" is *shir'ah* (or *shari'ah*) and signifies, literally, "the way to a watering-place" (from which men and animals derive the element indispensable to their life). It is used in the Qur'ān to denote a system of law necessary for a community's social and spiritual welfare. The term *minhāj*, on the other hand, denotes an "open road," usually in an abstract sense: that is, "a way of life." The terms *shir'ah* and *minhāj* are more restricted in their meaning than the term *dīn*, which comprises not merely the laws relating to a particular religion but also the basic, unchanging spiritual truths which, according to the Qur'ān, have been preached by every one of God's apostles, while the particular body of laws (*shir'ah* or *shari'ah*) promulgated through them, and the way of life (*minhāj*) recommended by them, varied in accordance with the exigencies of the time and of each community's cultural development. This "unity in diversity" is frequently stressed in the Qur'ān (2:148, 21:92-23, 23:52).

Because of the universal applicability and textual incorruptibility of its teachings—as well as of the fact that the Prophet Muḥammad is *the seal of all prophets,* i.e., the last of them [33:40]—the Qur'ān represents the culminating point of all revelation and offers the final, perfect way to spiritual fulfillment. This uniqueness of the Qur'ānic message does not, however, preclude all adherents of earlier faiths from attaining to God's grace: for—as the Qur'ān so often points out—those among them who believe uncompromisingly in the One God and the Day of Judgment (i.e., in individual moral responsibility) and live righteously *need have no fear, and neither shall they grieve.* (Asad, pp. 153-154)

Guarding what is true within: after the corruption of the older revelations, the Qur'ān comes with a twofold purpose: (1) to confirm the true and original message, and (2) to guard it, or act as check to its interpretations. For example, if people seek retaliation in a spirit of revenge, it holds forth mercy. If they glibly mask their cowardice or sentimentalism by empty talk of "turning of their cheek," it tests them by the practical test of forgiveness and mercy.

For every one of you have We designated a law and a way of life. Law is *shir'at*, the rules of practical conduct. Way of life or open way is *minhāj*, the finer things which are above the law, which are yet available to everyone, like a sort of open highway. The *light* in the verses just before this I understand to be something in the still higher regions of the spirit, which is common to mankind, though laws and rules may take different forms among different peoples. (*It was We Who revealed the Law (to Moses); therein was guidance and light* [5:47] and *in their footsteps We sent Jesus the son of Mary, confirming the Law that had come before him: we sent him the Gospel; therein was guidance and light and confirmation of the Law that had come before him* [5:49].)

And if God had so willed, He could surely have made you all one single community. By origin mankind were a single people or nation. (*O mankind! Be conscious of your Sustainer Who has created you out of a single soul, from that soul created its mate, and out of the two spread abroad a multitude of men and women* [4:1] and *All mankind were once one single community* [2:213].) That being so, God could have kept us all alike, with one language, one kind of disposition, and one set of physical conditions (including climate) to live in. But in His wisdom He gives us diversity in these things, not only at any given time but in different periods and ages. This tests our capacity for Unity (*waḥdāniyat*) still more, and accentuates the need of Unity and Islam.

Your goal is God; and then He will make you understand the truth of everything in which you have differed. As our true goal is God, the things that seem different to us from different points of view will ultimately be reconciled in Him. Einstein is right in plumbing the depths of Relativity in the world of physical science. It points more and more to the need of Unity in God in the spiritual world. (A. Yusuf Ali, pp. 258-259)

Ignorance, *Jāhiliyyah*

Do they, perchance, desire the law of pagan ignorance?
But for people who have inner certainty,
Who could be a better law-giver than God?

[*Sūrah al-Māʿidah* 5:50]

The days of ignorance were the days of tribalism, feuds, and selfish accentuation of differences in man. Those days are really not yet over. It is the mission of Islam to take us away from that false mental attitude, towards the true attitude of Unity. If our faith is certain, and not merely a matter of words, God will guide us to that Unity. (A. Yusuf Ali, p. 259)

By *pagan ignorance* (*jāhiliyyah*) is meant here not merely the time before the advent of the Prophet Muḥammad but, in general, a state of affairs characterized by a lack of moral perception and a submission of all personal and communal concerns to the criterion of "expediency" alone: that is, exclusively to the consideration as to whether a particular aim or action is useful or damaging (in the short-term, practical sense of these words) to the interests of the person concerned or of the community to which he belongs. Inasmuch as this "law of expediency" is fundamentally opposed to the concepts of morality preached by every higher religion, it is described in the Qurʾān as *the law* (ḥukm) *of pagan ignorance*. (Asad, p. 154)

86

Moderation in Pleasures

O you who have attained to faith!
Do not deprive yourselves of the good things of life
which God has made lawful to you,
but do not transgress the bounds of what is right:
truly, God does not love those who go beyond
the bounds of what is right.
And so partake of the lawful, good things
which God grants you as sustenance,
and be conscious of God, in whom you have faith.

[*Sūrah al-Māᶜidah* 5:87–88]

In pleasures that are good and lawful the crime is excess. There is no merit merely in abstention or asceticism, though the humility or unselfishness that may go with asceticism may have its value. In 5:85, Christian monks are praised for particular virtues (*Among these are men devoted to learning and men who have renounced the world, and they are not arrogant*), though here and elsewhere monasticism is disapproved of. Use God's gifts of all kinds with gratitude, but excess is not approved of by God. (A. Yusuf Ali, p. 270)

The implication is firstly, that what has been forbidden does *not* belong to the category of *the good things of life* (*aṭ-ṭayyibāt*), and, secondly, that all that has not been expressly forbidden is allowed. It is to be noted that the Qurʾān forbids only those things or actions which are injurious to man physically, morally, or socially. The term *aṭ-ṭayyibāt* comprises all that is good and wholesome in life—"the delightful things which human beings desire and towards which their hearts incline" (Ṭabarī): hence my rendering, *the good things of life*. (Asad, pp. 142, 161)

Intoxicants and Gambling

O you who have attained to faith! **Intoxicants, and games of chance,
and idolatrous practices, and the divining of the future
are but a loathsome evil of Satan's doing:**
*shun it, then, so that you might attain to a happy state!
By means of intoxicants and games of chance
Satan seeks only to sow enmity and hatred among you,
and to turn you away from the remembrance of God and from prayer.
Will you not, then, desist?*

[*Sūrah al-Māʿidah* 5:90-91]

According to all the lexicographers, the word *khamr* (derived from the verb *khamara*, "he concealed" or "obscured") denotes every substance the use of which obscures the intellect, i.e., intoxicates. Hence, the prohibition of intoxicants laid down in this verse comprises not merely alcoholic drinks, but also drugs which have a similar effect. The only exception from this total prohibition arises in cases of "dire necessity" (in the strictest sense of these words), as stipulated in the last sentence of verse 5:3 (*As for him, however, who is driven to what is forbidden by dire necessity and not by an inclination to sinning—behold, God is much-forgiving, a dispenser of grace.*): that is to say, in cases where illness or a bodily accident makes the administration of intoxicating drugs or of alcohol imperative and unavoidable. As regards the expression *idolatrous practices*, this term has, I believe, been used here metaphorically and is meant to circumscribe all practices of an idolatrous nature like personality worship, the attribution of "magic" properties to certain inanimate objects, the observance of all manner of supersti-

89

tious taboos, and so forth. (Asad, p. 162)

Gambling, *maisir*, means literally a means of getting something too easily, getting a profit without working for it. That is the principle on which gambling is prohibited. The form most familiar to the Arabs was gambling by casting lots by means of arrows, on the principle of a lottery: the arrows were marked and served the same purpose as a modern lottery ticket. Something, e.g., the carcass of a slaughtered animal, was divided into unequal parts. The marked arrows were drawn from a bag. Some were blank and those who drew them got nothing. Others indicated prizes, which were big or small. Whether you got a big share or a small share or nothing depended on pure luck, unless there was also fraud on the part of some persons concerned. The principle on which the objection is based is that, even if there is no fraud, you gain what you have not earned, or lose on a mere chance. Dice and wagering are rightly held to be within the definition of gambling. But insurance is not gambling when conducted on business principles. Here the basis for calculation is statistics on a large scale, from which mere chance is eliminated. The insurers themselves pay premiums in proportion to risks, exactly and statistically calculated.

Gambling and intemperance are social as well as individual sins. They may ruin us in our ordinary everyday worldly life, as well as spiritual future. In case it is suggested that there is not harm in a little indulgence, we are asked to think over all its aspects, social and individual, worldly and spiritual.

The idolatrous practices referred to *anṣāb,* stone altars or stone columns on which oil was poured for consecration, or slabs on which meat was sacrificed to idols. These were objects of worship, and were common in Arabia before Islam. Any idolatrous or superstitious practices are here condemned.

Besides the arrows used for the division of meat by a sort of lottery, arrows were also used for divination, i.e., for ascertaining lucky or unlucky moments, or learning the wishes of the heathen gods, as to whether men should undertake certain actions or not. All superstitions are condemned. We are asked to obey the commands of God, which are always reasonable, instead of following superstitions, which are irrational, or seeking undue stimulation in intoxicants or undue advantage in gambling. To some there may be temporary excitement or pleasure in these, but that is not the way either of prosperity or piety. (A. Yusuf Ali, pp. 86, 271)

Signs of Nature

Truly, God is the One Who splits the grain and the kernel apart,
bringing forth the living from the dead,
and He is the One Who brings forth the dead out of that which is alive.
This then, is God: how then can you be so deluded?
He is the One Who causes the dawn to break,
and Who has made the night to be a source of stillness,
and the sun and the moon for reckoning
by the order of the Almighty, the All-knowing.
And He it is Who has made the stars for you so that you might be guided by them
through the darknesses of land and sea:
clearly have We detailed Our signs for people of inner knowing.
And He it is Who has brought you all into being
out of a single soul,
and so designated for each of you a time-limit on earth
and a resting-place after death:
clearly have We detailed Our signs for people who can grasp the truth.
It is He Who sends down rain from the skies:
with it We produce vegetation of all kinds.
From some We produce green crops,
out of which We produce grain, heaped up.
Out of the date palm and its sheaths,
clusters of dates hanging low and near.
And gardens of grapes, and olives, and pomegranates,
each similar in kind yet different in variety: when they begin to bear fruit,
feast your eye with the fruit, and the ripeness thereof.
Behold! In these things there are signs for people who keep the faith.

[*Sūrah al-Anᶜām* 6:95-99]

92

Another beautiful nature passage, referring to God's wonderful artistry in His creation. In how few and how simple words the whole pageant of creation is placed before us! Beginning from our humble animal needs and dependence on the vegetable world, we are asked to contemplate the interaction of the living and the dead. Here is the mystic teaching, referring not only to physical life but to the higher life above the physical plane, not only to individual life but to the collective life of nations. Then we take a peep into the daily miracle of morning, noon, and night, and pass on to the stars that guide the distant mariner. We rise still higher to the mystery of the countless individuals from one human soul, their sojourn and their destiny. So we get back to the heaven: the description of the luscious fruits, which the "gentle rain from heaven" produces, leaves us to contemplate the spiritual truths which faith will provide for us, with the aid of the showers of God's mercy.

The seed grain and the date kernel are selected as types in the vegetable kingdom, showing how our physical life depends on it. The fruits mentioned later (in 6:99) start another allegory which we shall notice later. Botanists will notice that the seed grain includes the cereals (such as wheat, barley, rice, millet, etc.) which are monocotyledons, as well as the pulses (such as beans, peas, gram, etc.) and other seeds which are dicotyledons. These two represent the most important classes of good grains, while the date palm, a monocotyledon, represents for Arabia both food, fruit, confectionary, thatch, and pillars for houses, shady groves in oases, and a standard measure of wealth and well-being.

God is the One Who causes the grain and date kernel to split and sprout: the ideas of both "split" and "sprout" are included in the root *falqa*, and a third is expressed by the word "cleave" in the next verse: *He it is that cleaves the daybreak* (or *causes the dawn to break*), for the action of evolving daybreak from the dark. For vegetables, "split and sprout" represents a double process: (1) the seed divides, and (2) one part shoots up, seeking

93

the light and forming leaves and the visible parts of the future tree and the other part digs down into the dark, forming the roots and seeking just that sustenance from the soil which is adapted for the particular plant. This is just one small instance of the judgment and ordering of God, referred to in 6:96.

He is the One Who brings forth the dead out of that which is alive. This does not mean that in physical nature there are no limits between life and non-life, between the organic and the non-organic. In fact, physicists are baffled at the barrier between them and frankly confess that they cannot solve the mystery of Life. If there is such a barrier in physical nature, is it not all the more wonderful that God can create Life out of nothing? He has but to say "Be" and it is. He can bring Life from non-life and annihilate life. But there are two other senses in which we can contemplate the contrast between the living and the dead. (1) We have just been speaking of the botanical world. Take it as a whole, and see the contrast between the winter of death, the spring of revivification, the summer of growth, and the autumn of decay, leading back to the death of winter. Here is a cycle of living from dead, and dead from living. (2) Take our spiritual life, individual or collective. We rise from the darkness of spiritual nothingness to the light of spiritual life. And if we do not follow the spiritual laws, God will take away that life and we shall be again as dead. We may die many deaths. The keys of life and death are in God's hands. Neither life nor death are fortuitous things. Behind them both is the cause of causes, and only He.

He is the One Who causes the dawn to break, and Who has made the night to be a source of stillness, and the sun and the moon for reckoning by the order of the Almighty, the All-Knowing. And He it is Who has made the stars for you . . . . The night, the day, the sun, the moon, the great astronomical universe of God: how far, and yet how near to us! God's universe is boundless, and we can barely comprehend even its relations to us. But this last we must try to do if we want to be numbered with *the people of inner knowing.*

94

He it is Who has made the stars for you so that you might be guided by them through the darknesses of land and sea. At sea, or in deserts or forests, whenever we sweep over wide spaces, it is the stars that act as our guides, just as the sun and moon have already been mentioned as our measures of time.

He it is Who has brought you all into being out of a single soul: produced, *ansha'a,* made you grow, increase, develop, reach maturity: another of the processes of creation. It is one of the wonders of God's creation, that from one person we have grown to be so many, and each individual has so many faculties and capacities, and yet we are all one. In the next verse we have the allegory of grapes and other fruits; all grapes may be similar to look at, yet each variety has a distinctive flavor and other distinctive qualities, and each individual grape may have its own special qualities. So for man.

. . . and so designated for each of you a time-limit on earth and a resting-place after death. In the sojourn of this life, we must respond to God's hand in fashioning us by making full use of all our faculties, and we just get ready for our departure into the life that will be eternal.

Our allegory now brings us to maturity, the fruit, the harvest, the vintage. Through the seed we came up from nothingness to life; we lived our daily life of rest and work and passed the milestones of time; we had the spiritual experience of traveling through vast spaces in the spiritual world, guiding our course through the star of faith; we grew; and now for the harvest or the vintage! How satisfied the grower must be when the golden grain is harvested in heaps or the vintage gathered! So will man be if he has produced the fruits of faith!

Each similar, yet different: each fruit, whether it is grapes, or olives, or pomegranates, looks alike in its species, and yet each variety may be different in flavor, consistency, shape, size, color, juice or oil contents, proportion of seed to fruit, etc. In each variety individuals may be different. Apply the allegory to man, whose varied spiritual fruit may be equally

95

different and yet equally valuable!

When they begin to bear fruit, feast your eye with the fruit and the ripeness thereof. And so we finish this wonderful allegory. Search through the world's literature, and see if you can find another such song or hymn, so fruity in its literary flavor, so profound in its spiritual meaning!

There are signs for people who believe. There is a refrain in this song, which is subtly varied. In verse 97 it is *clearly have We detailed Our signs for people of inner knowing.* So far we were speaking of the things we see around us every day. Knowledge is the appropriate instrument for these things. In verse 98 we read: *clearly have We detailed Our signs for people who can grasp the truth (understand).* Understanding is a higher faculty than knowledge, and is necessary for seeing the mystery and meaning of this life. At the end of verse 99 we have *in these things there are signs for people who believe.* Here we are speaking of the real fruits of spiritual life. For them faith is necessary, as bringing us nearer to God. (A. Yusuf Ali, pp. 316-318)

God is Subtle

No vision can encompass Him,
but He encompasses all human vision:
for He alone is Subtle Beyond Comprehension, All-Aware.
Means of insight have now come to you
from your Sustainer through this divine Message.
Whoever, then, chooses to see,
does so for the benefit of His own soul;
and whoever chooses to remain blind,
does so to His own harm.

[*Sūrah al-Anᶜām* 6:102-104]

Here is an example of the deep and subtle metaphysics of the Holy Qur'ān. *No vision can encompass Him, but He encompasses all human vision* might be paraphrased as "no seeing, no human mode of perception can fully grasp God, but God surrounds, encompasses, and enables human beings to perceive." We derive our seeing from His Seeing, but He is never the object of our perception, because He is not a thing.

This may seem to contradict the notion in *Sūrah al-Baqarah* 2:115 that *wherever you turn is the Face of God.* But this *āyah* tells us that God's essence can be witnessed in every particle of existence and not as an object or entity distinct from everything that exists.

This is made clear in the part of the *āyah* that says *He is the Subtle, the Aware.* It could be said that He is the subtlest state of everything and the final and most complete Awareness operating in the universes.

The practical meaning of this for us is that the human being as God's

97

khalīfah may share in this power of subtle awareness. Through *taqwā*, mindfulness of God, through *dhikrallāh*, remembrance of God, we are developing the spiritual side of our being, which is our capacity to bring God's subtle awareness into every detail of our lives. Elsewhere it is said, *God is the light of the heavens and the earth* [24:35]. In other words, Allāh enables perception in both the material world through the experience of our senses, and in the inner world through the heart and all our subtle faculties: self-awareness, insight, and inspiration. (Helminski)

Laṭīf as a name of God is as difficult to define in words as the idea it seeks to represent is difficult to grasp in our minds. It implies: (1) fine, subtle (the basic meaning); (2) so fine and subtle as to be imperceptible to human sight, so fine as to be imperceptible to the senses; (3) so pure as to be incomprehensible, above the mental or spiritual vision of ordinary men; (4) with sight so perfect as to see and understand the finest subtleties and mysteries; (5) so kind and gracious as to bestow gifts of the most refined kind; extraordinarily gracious and understanding. The active meaning (4) is expressed in 22:63: *Allāh is He Who understands the finest mysteries, and is well-acquainted with them.* (A. Yusuf Ali, pp. 868, 320)

He alone is Subtle Beyond Comprehension, All-Aware: the term *laṭīf* denotes something that is extremely subtle in quality, and therefore intangible and unfathomable. Whenever this term occurs in the Qurʾān with reference to God in conjunction with the adjective *khabīr* ("all-aware"), it is invariably used to express the idea of His inaccessibility to human perception, imagination, or comprehension, as contrasted with His Own all-awareness (see also 22:63, 31:16, 33:34, and 67:14). In the two instances where the combination of *laṭīf* and *khabīr* carries the definite article *al* (6:103 and 67:14), the expression *huwa'l-laṭīf* has the meaning of "He *alone* is unfathomable"—implying that this quality of His is unique and absolute. (Asad, p. 188)

Respect for Other Beliefs

Do not speak ill of those whom others invoke instead of God,
that they might not speak ill of God out of spite and ignorance:
*for, **We have made their own activities***
appear alluring to each community.
In time, to their Sustainer they must return;
and then He will make them understand
the truth of all that they were doing.

[*Sūrah al-Anᶜām* 6:108]

A man's actual personal religion depends upon many things: his personal psychology, the background of his life, his hidden or repressed feelings, tendencies, or history (which psychoanalysis tries to unravel), his hereditary dispositions or antipathies, and all the subtle influences of his education and his environment. The task before the man of God is (1) to use any of these which can serve the higher ends, (2) to purify such as have been misused, (3) to introduce new ideas and modes of looking at things, and (4) to combat what is wrong and cannot be mended: all for the purpose of leading to the truth and gradually letting in spiritual light where there was darkness before. If that is not done with discretion and the skill of a spiritual teacher, there may be not only a reaction of obstinacy, but an unseemly show of a dishonor to the true God and His truth, and doubts would spread among the weaker brethren whose faith is shallow and infirm. What happens to individuals is true collectively of nations or groups of people. They think in their self-obsession that their own ideas are right. God in His infinite compassion bears with them, and asks those

99

who have purer ideas of faith not to vilify the weaknesses of their neighbors, lest the neighbors in their turn vilify the real truth and make matters
even worse than before. Insofar as there are mistakes, God will forgive
and send His grace for helping ignorance and folly. In so far as there is
active evil, He will deal with it in His own way. Of course the righteous
man must not hide his light under a bushel, or compromise with evil, or
refuse to establish right living where he has the power to do so. (A. Yusuf
Ali, p. 321)

Waste

And do not be wasteful:
truly, He does not love those who are wasteful!

[*Sūrah al-Anᶜām* 6:141]

"Waste not, want not," says the English proverb. Here the same wisdom is preached from a higher motive. See what magnificent means God provides in nature for the sustenance of all His creatures, because He loves them all. Enjoy them in moderation and be grateful. But commit no excess and commit no waste: the two things are the same from different angles of vision. If you do, you take away something from other creatures and God would not like your selfishness. (A. Yusuf Ali, p. 331)

Beauty in Worship

O children of Adam!
Indeed, We have given you garments to cover your nakedness,
and as a thing of beauty;
but the garment of God-consciousness is the best of all.
This is one of God's messages—
that human beings might take it to heart . . . .
Say: "My Sustainer has but urged the doing of what is right;
and He wants you to put your whole being
into every act of worship,
and to call Him, sincere in your faith in Him alone.
As it was He Who brought you into being in the first instance,
so also you will return.
Some He will have graced with His guidance,
whereas for some a straying from the right path
will have become unavoidable:
for, behold, they will have taken evil impulses
for their masters in preference to God,
thinking all the while that they have found the right path!

O children of Adam! Beautify yourselves for every act of worship,
and eat and drink, but do not waste:
for truly, He does not love the wasteful!
Say: "Who is there to forbid the beauty
which God has brought forth for His creatures
and the good things from among the means of sustenance?"

[*Sūrah al-Aʿrāf* 7:26, 29-32]

102

Spiritually, God created man *bare and alone* [6:94]; the soul in its naked purity and beauty knew no shame because it knew no guilt. After it was touched by guilt and soiled by evil, its thoughts and deeds became its clothing and adornments, good or bad, honest or meretricious, according to the inner motives which gave them color. So in the case of the body: it is pure and beautiful as long as it is not defiled by misuse. Its clothing and ornaments may be good or meretricious, according to the motives in the mind and character. If good, they are the symbols of purity and beauty; but the best clothing and ornament we could have come from righteousness, which covers the nakedness of sin and adorns us with virtues.

He wants you to put your whole being (wajh) *into every act of worship, and to call Him, sincere in your faith in Him alone.* Our devotion should be sincere, not as in other men's sight, but by presenting our whole selves, heart and soul, to God. Even so, it may not be enough; for the sight of our heart and soul may be faulty. We should call upon God to give us the light, by which our sincerity may commend itself to Him as true sincerity "as in His sight" (with faith in Him alone). When we return to Him, we shall be stripped of all pretense, even such self-deception as may satisfy us in this life.

Some of you He will have graced with His guidance, whereas for some a straying from the right path will have become unavoidable: for, behold, they will have taken their own evil impulses for their masters in preference to God. Guidance is for all. But in some it takes effect; in others the doors are closed against it, because they have taken evil for their friend. If they have lost their way, they have richly deserved it, for they deliberately took their choice, even though, in their self-righteousness, they may think that their sin is their virtue, and that their evil is their good.

Beautify yourselves for every act of worship: zinat is beautiful apparel, adornments or apparel for beautiful living. This is construed to mean not only clothes that add grace to the wearer, but toilet and cleanliness, attention to hair, and other small personal details which no self-respecting man

103

or woman ought to neglect when going solemnly even before a great human dignitary, if only out of respect for the dignity of the occasion. How much more important it is to attend to these details when we solemnly apply our minds to the Presence of God, though He is always present everywhere! But the caution against excess applies: men must not go to prayer in silks or ornaments appropriate to women. Similarly sober food, good and wholesome, is not to be divorced from offices of religion; only the caution against excess applies strictly. Asceticism often means the negation of art and beauty. It has no necessary sanctity attached to it.

Who is there to forbid the beauty which God has brought forth for His creatures and the good things from among the means of sustenance? The beautiful and good things of life are really meant for, and should be the privilege of, those with faith in God. If they do not always have them in this life, and if there is sometimes the semblance of others having them who do not deserve them, let us at least consider the matter in another light. Our faith in God's wisdom is unshaken and we know that these are but fleeting and mixed types of the things in the spiritual world. Their pure counterparts in the spiritual world will be only for those who proved, in all the trials of this world, that they had faith. (A. Yusuf Ali, pp. 346-348)

We have given you garments . . . as a thing of beauty, literally, *as plumage*—a metaphorical expression derived from the beauty of bird's plumage.

Put your whole being into every act of worship. The term *wajh* (literally, *face*) occurring here is often used, in the abstract sense, to denote a person's entire being or entire attention—as, for instance, in the phrase *aslamtu wajhī li'llāhi, I have surrendered my whole being to God* [3:20]. The word *masjid*, which usually signifies the time or place of prostration in prayer (*sujūd*), evidently stands in this context for any act of worship. It is used as well in verse 7:31 (*Beautify yourselves for every act of worship*). *Beautify yourselves* is literally *take to your adornment* (*zīnah*). According to Rāghib, the proper meaning of *zīnah* is "a [beautifying] thing that does not disgrace or render unseemly . . . either in the present world or in that which is to come": thus, it signifies anything of beauty in both the physical and moral connotations of the word.

By declaring all good and beautiful things of life—i.e., those which are not expressly prohibited—are lawful to the believers, the Qur'ān condemns, by implication, all forms of life-denying asceticism, world-renunciation, and self-mortification. (Asad, pp. 206-207)

The Effects of Sin

Has it, then, not become obvious
to those who have inherited the earth
in the wake of former generations
that, if We so willed, We could punish them by means of their sins,
sealing their hearts so that they cannot hear?
Unto those communities—
some of whose stories We relate to you—
there had indeed come apostles of their own
with all evidence of the truth;
but they would not believe in anything
to which they had once given the lie:
thus it is that God seals the hearts of those who deny the truth.

[*Sūrah al-Aʿrāf* 7:100-101]

Here, again, we have an affirmation that what the Qurʾān describes as "God's punishment" (as well as "God's reward") is, in reality, *a consequence of man's own doings,* and not an arbitrary act of God: it is *by means of their sins* (*bi-dhunūbihim*) that God *sets a seal* upon the hearts of men.

But they would not believe in anything to which they had once given the lie, literally, *to which they had given the life aforetime;* an allusion to the instinctive unwillingness of most people to give up the notions, positive or negative, to which they are accustomed. (Asad, p. 218)

Stringency and Mercy

"Establish for us what is good in this world
as well as in the life to come:
see how we have turned to You in repentance!"
God answered: "With My stringency I try whom I will—
but My mercy overspreads everything,
and so I shall confer it upon those who are conscious of Me
and spend in charity, and who have faith in Our signs."

[*Sūrah al-Aʿrāf* 7:156]

God's mercy is in and for all things. All nature subserves a common purpose, which is for the good of all His creatures. Our faculties and our understanding are all instances of His grace and mercy. Each unit or factor among His creatures benefits from the others and receives them as God's mercy to itself; and in its turn, each contributes to the benefit of the others and is thus an instance of God's mercy to them. His mercy is universal and all-pervasive; while His justice and punishment are reserved for those who swerve from His plan and go out of His Peace.

The personal grace and mercy—and their opposite—are referred to in the singular pronoun "I," while the impersonal Law, by which God's signs operate in His universe, is referred to in the plural pronoun of authority and dignity, "We" ("Our" signs). (A. Yusuf Ali, p. 388)

The Heedless

He whom God guides, he alone is truly guided:
whereas those whom He lets go astray—
it is they, they who are the losers!
And most certainly have We destined for Hell
many of the invisible beings and men
who have hearts with which they fail to grasp the truth,
and eyes with which they fail to see,
and ears with which they fail to hear.
They are like cattle—no,
they are even less conscious of the right way:
it is they, they who are the truly heedless!
And God's alone are the attributes of perfection;
invoke Him, then, by these,
stand aloof from all who distort the meaning of His attributes.

[*Sūrah al-Aʿrāf* 7:178-180]

They are even less conscious of the right way is literally *they are farther astray*—inasmuch as animals follow only their instincts and natural needs and are not conscious of the possibility or necessity of a moral choice. *They who are truly heedless* are those who do not use their faculty of discernment in the way intended for it by God, and remain heedless of Him Who comprises within Himself all the attributes of perfection and represents, therefore, the Ultimate Reality. As regards the expression *al-asmā' al-ḥusnā* (literally, *the most perfect* [or *most goodly*] *names*), which occurs in the Qur'ān four times—i.e., in the above verse as well as in 17:110, 20:8, and

108

59:24—it is to be borne in mind that the term *ism* is, primarily, a word applied to denote the substance or the intrinsic attributes of an object under consideration, while the term *al-ḥusnā* is the plural form of *al-aḥsan* ("that which is best" or "most goodly"). Thus the combination of *al-asmā' al-ḥusnā* may be appropriately rendered as *the attributes of perfection*— a term reserved in the Qur'ān for God alone. (Asad, p. 231)

From a Single Soul

It is He Who has created you all out of one soul,
and out of it brought into being a mate,
so that man might incline with love towards woman.
And so, when he has embraced her, she conceives
a light burden, and continues to bear it.
Then, when she grows heavy [with child],
they both call to God, their Sustainer,
"If You indeed grant us a sound child,
we shall most certainly be among the grateful!"
And yet, as soon as He has granted them sound offspring,
they begin to ascribe to other powers beside Him
a share in bringing about what He has granted them!
Sublimely exalted, however, is God
above anything to which men may ascribe a share in His divinity!

[*Sūrah al-Aʿrāf* 7:189-190]

This selection suggests that we are all from one soul, one self. As Yusuf Ali suggests below, the Biblical notion that Eve was created from Adam's rib need not be assumed in Qurʾanic teaching. While we can never assume that we have a final understanding of the Divine Truth expressed in the Qurʾān, this *āyah* does seem to suggest that all human beings are related to each other through a common origin. (Helminski)

In reference to *It is He Who has created you all out of one soul* see 6:95. As regards the expression *zawjahā* ("its mate"), it is to be noted that, with

110

reference to animate beings, the term *zawj* ("a pair," "one of a pair," or "a mate") applies to the male as well as to the female component of a pair or couple; hence, with reference to human beings, it signifies a woman's mate (husband) as well as a man's mate (wife). Abū Muslim—as quoted by Rāzī—interprets the phrase *He created out of it* (minhā) *its mate* as meaning, *He created its mate* [*i.e., its sexual counterpart*] *out of its own kind* (min jinsihā)." The literal translation of *minhā* as *out of it* clearly alludes, in conformity with the text, to the biological fact that both sexes have originated from "one living entity."

They begin to ascribe to other powers beside Him a share in bringing about what He has granted them is literally *they attribute to Him partners with regard to that which He has granted them.* That is to say, many of them look upon the contributing factors of sound childbirth (like personal care during pregnancy, medical assistance, eugenics, etc.) as something *independent* of God, forgetting that all these contributing factors are—like the birth of the child itself—but an outcome of God's will and grace: a manifestation of what the Qur'ān calls "the way of God" (*sunnat Allāh*). Since this kind of mental association of "other" factors with God is not really intentional, it does not amount to the unforgivable sin of *shirk* ("the ascribing of divine qualities to powers other than God"); but it is close enough to it to warrant the subsequent discourse on *shirk* in the real meaning of this term in the following verses. (Asad, pp. 100, 233)

It is He Who has created you all out of one soul, and out of it brought into being a mate. Nafs may mean (1) soul, (2) self, (3) person, living person, (4) will, good pleasure. *Minhā*: I follow the construction suggested by Imām Rāzī. The particle *min* would then suggest here not a portion or a source of something else, but a species, a nature, a similarity. The pronoun *hā* refers of course to *nafs*. The Biblical story of the creation of Eve from a rib of Adam may be allegorical, but we need not assume it in Qur'anic teaching.

111

The mystery of the physical birth of man, as it affects the father and the mother, only touches the imagination of the parents in the later stages when the child is yet unborn and yet the life stirs within the body of the expectant mother. The coming of the new life is a solemn thing, and is fraught with much hope as well as much unknown risk to the mother herself. The parents in their anxiety turn to God. If this feeling of solemnity, hope, and looking towards God were maintained after birth, all would be well for the parents as well as for the rising generation. But the attitude changes, as the verses following show.

If You indeed grant us a sound child: ṣāliḥ includes the following ideas: sound in body and mind, healthy, righteous, of good moral disposition.

When the child is born, the parents forget that it is a precious gift of God, a miracle of creation, which should lift their minds up to the higher things of God. Instead, their gradual familiarity with the new life makes them connect it with many superstitious ideas or rites and ceremonies, or they take it as a matter of course, as a little plaything of the material world. This leads to idolatry or false worship, or the setting up of false standards, in derogation of the dignity of God. (A. Yusuf Ali, pp. 178, 398–399)

When Satan Stirs You Up, Remember

Make due allowance for human nature,
and urge the doing of what is right;
and leave alone all those who choose to remain ignorant.
And if it should happen that a prompting from Satan
stirs you up,
seek refuge with God: behold, He is all-hearing, all-knowing.
Truly, they who are conscious of God practice remembrance
whenever any dark suggestion from Satan touches them—
whereupon, lo! They begin to see clearly,
even though their brethren would draw them into error;
and then they cannot fail.

[*Sūrah al-Aʿrāf* 7:199-202]

God comforts the Apostle and directs his mind to three precepts: (1) to forgive injuries, insults, and persecution; (2) to continue to declare the faith that was in him, and not only to declare it, but to live up to it in all his dealings with friends and foes; (3) to pay no attention to ignorant fools who raised doubts or difficulties, hurled taunts or reproaches, or devised plots to defeat the truth: they were to be ignored and passed by, not to be engaged in fights and fruitless controversies, or conciliated by compromises.

If it should happen that a prompting from Satan stirs you up: even a man of God is but human. He might think that revenge or retaliation, or a little tactful silence when evil stalks abroad, or some compromise with ignorance, might be best for the cause. He is to reject such suggestions.

113

They begin to see things clearly: God protects His own as no one else can. He is the sure refuge—and the only one—for men of faith. If we are confused or angry, being blinded by this world, He will open our eyes.

Even though their brethren would draw them into error: the forces of evil never relax their efforts to draw their "brethren" (those who go into their family) deeper into the mire of sin and destruction. (A. Yusuf Ali, pp. 400–401)

Those who choose to remain ignorant is literally *the ignorant ones*—i.e., those who *willfully* remain deaf to moral truths, and not those who are simply unaware of them.

A prompting from Satan stirs you up [to blind anger]: the words "to blind anger" interpolated between brackets are based on a Tradition according to which the Prophet, after the revelation of the preceding verse calling for forbearance, exclaimed, "And what about [justified] anger, O my sustainer?" whereupon the above verse was revealed to him (Tabarī, Zamakhsharī, Rāzī, Ibn Kathīr).

Any dark suggestion from Satan: the noun *ṭā'if* (also forthcoming in the forms *ṭayf* and *ṭayyif*) denotes any ungraspable phantom, image, or suggestion, as in a dream, or "an imperceptible obsession which obscures the mind" (*Tāj al-'Arūs*). Since, in this context, it is described as coming from Satan, *a dark suggestion* seems to be the appropriate rendering. (Asad, pp. 234–235)

114

Don't Be Unaware

Say: "I only follow whatever is revealed to me by my Sustainer:
this revelation is a means of insight from your Sustainer,
and a guidance and grace to those who will have faith.
And so when the Qurᶜān is voiced, pay attention to it,
and listen in silence, so that you might be graced with God's mercy."
And remember your Sustainer humbly within yourself and with awe,
and without raising your voice,
in the morning and in the evening;
and don't allow yourself to be one of the unaware.
Those who are near to your Sustainer do not disdain to worship Him:
They celebrate His praises and bow down before Him

[*Sūrah al-Aᶜrāf* 7:204-205]

This revelation is a means of insight from your Sustainer: literally, *this is lights from your Sustainer.* Lights mean eyes, the faculty of spiritual insight. The revelation is for us (1) spiritual eyes, (2) guidance, and (3) mercy. Meaning (1) is the highest in degree, just as a blind man, if he is given eyes and the faculty of sight, is at once removed into an entirely new world, so those who can reach the stage of spiritual insight pass into and become citizens of a wholly new spiritual world. Meaning (2) is next in degree: the man of the world can act on the teaching about right conduct and prepare for the Hereafter. Meaning (3) is the Mercy of God, free to everyone, saint and sinner, who sincerely believe and puts his trust in God.

Those who are near to your Sustainer do not disdain to worship Him: the higher you are in spiritual attainment, the more is your desire and your

115

opportunity to serve and worship your Lord and Cherisher and the Lord and Cherisher of all the worlds.

They celebrate His praises and bow down before Him. At this stage a *sajdah* or prostration is indicated, as symbolical for our humble acceptance of the privilege of serving and worshipping God. This is a fitting close to a *sūrah* in which we are led, through a contemplation of the stories of the Messengers of God, to the meaning of revelation and its relation to our moral and spiritual progress. (A. Yusuf Ali, pp. 401-402)

Tremble with Awe

The faithful are those
whose hearts tremble with awe whenever God is mentioned,
and whose faith is strengthened
whenever His signs are conveyed to them,
and who place their trust in their Sustainer—
those who are constant in prayer
and spend on others out of what We provide for them as sustenance:
In truth, these are the faithful!
They shall have stations of dignity with their Sustainer,
and forgiveness, and a most generous provision.

[*Sūrah al-Anfāl* 8:2-4]

A most generous provision or *a most excellent sustenance*: i.e., in paradise. According to Rāzī, however, the *most excellent sustenance* is a metonym for "the spiritual raptures arising from the knowledge of God, the love of Him, and the self-immersion (*istighrāq*) in worshipping Him." In Rāzī's interpretation, this expression refers to the spiritual reward of faith in *this* world. Some commentators regard the above definition of true believers as the most important passage of this *sūrah*. (Asad, p. 238)

Inner Calm, Strengthened Heart

*[Remember how it was] when **He caused inner calm to enfold you**,*
as an assurance from Him,
and sent down upon you water from the skies,
so that He might purify you thereby
and free you from Satan's unclean whisperings
and strengthen your hearts and thus make firm your steps.
Lo! Your Sustainer inspired the angels
[to convey this His message to the believers]:
"I am with you!"

[Sūrah al-Anfāl 8:11-12]

This refers back to the battle at Uḥud, referenced in 3:154: *Then, after this woe, He sent down upon you a sense of security, an inner calm which enfolded some of you.* Calm (presence of mind) is essential in battle and in all posts of danger. If the mind is too much in a state of excitement, it cannot carry out a well-considered or well-concerted plan. The spirit of calm confidence on the part of the Muslims won against the blustering violence of the Quraish.

. . . *and sent down upon you water from the skies, so that He might purify you thereby and free you from Satan's unclean whisperings and strengthen your hearts and thus make firm your steps.* The rain was welcome for many reasons: (1) Water was scarce both for drinking and ablutions; (2) the Muslim band, without baggage or equipment or comforts, found that their thirst aggravated their fatigue; (3) the sand was loose, and the rain consolidated it and enabled them "to plant their feet firmly." In *Satan's un-*

118

clean whisperings, "unclean" is both literal and figurative. Dirt is physically a symbol of evil, and the Muslims were particular about ablutions before prayer. But the rain also refreshed their spirits and removed any lurking doubts in their minds (suggestions of the Evil One) that victory might be impossible in such adverse circumstances. (A Yusuf Ali, p. 417)

The word *nu'ās* translated as *inner calm* refers to the spiritual quiet and self-confidence of the believers in the face of overwhelming odds before the battle of Badr. Immediately from the beginning of the battle, the Meccan army invested the wells of Badr, thus depriving the Muslims of water; and under the influence of thirst, some of the latter fell prey to utter despair (here symbolized by *Satan's unclean whisperings*)—when, suddenly, abundant rain fell and enabled them to satisfy their thirst. (Asad, p. 239)

That Which Will Give You Life

O you who have faith!
Respond to the call of God and the Messenger
whenever he calls you to that which will give you life;
and know that God intervenes between man and his desires,
and that you shall be gathered back to Him.

[*Sūrah al-Anfāl* 8:24]

At the beginning of the *āyāts* we are told, *Respond to the call of God and the Messenger,* so the responsibility is placed on us, amidst the many things that call to us, to respond to the call of God and His Messenger.

That the Prophet Muḥammad Σ calls us to "life," echoes the words of Ḥaḍrati ʿIsā (Jesus), who gave as the purpose of his prophethood: "that you might have life and have it abundantly." Since answering the call of the prophets is no guarantee that one will live a longer life, it must be a spiritual life that is referred to here. "Life" is, after all, one of God's most beautiful names. It is a quality that turns mere material into something intelligent, responsive, capable of relationship.

Secondly, God has some intimate connection between ourselves and our desires. As Muḥammad Asad writes:

God intervenes between man and his desires, that is, between a man's desires and the outward action that may result from those desires: indicating that God can turn man away from what his heart urges him to do (Rāghib). In other words, it is God-consciousness alone that can prevent man from being misled by wrong desires and, thus, from becoming like *those deaf, those dumb ones who do not use their reason* [8:22]; and it is God-

120

consciousness alone that can enable man to follow the call *to that which gives life*—that is, spiritual awareness of right and wrong and the will to act accordingly. (Asad, p. 242)

Yusuf Ali writes:

Know that God intervenes between man and his desires (his heart). If the human heart is refractory and refuses to obey the call of God, that is not the end of the matter. God has to be reckoned with. The refusal may be because there was some pet human scheme which the heart of man was not willing to give up for God's cause. Will that scheme come to fruition by refusing to serve the higher cause? By no means. Man proposes, but God disposes. If the scheme or motive was perfectly secret from men, it was not secret from God. The heart is the innermost seat of man's affections and desires, but between this seat and man himself is the presence of the Omnipresent. (A. Yusuf Ali, p. 420)

The Divine Presence is with us always, even between ourselves and our most intimate desires. Responding to God's call, therefore, is what guides us to being more alive, whereas following the promptings of every desire is not necessarily the way to greater life. (Helminski)

Discernment

O you who have attained to faith!
If you remain conscious of God,
He will endow you with a standard by which to discern
the true from the false,
and will clear evil from you,
and will forgive you your mistakes:
for God is limitless in the abundance of His blessing.

[*Sūrah al-Anfāl* 8:29]

Discernment is the innate capacity within the human being to make distinctions, especially to discern the good and the true from the bad and the false.

In the realm of our own experience we can come to discern the qualities of the Spirit from the qualities of the compulsive ego. The ego is most concerned with its own survival, comfort, and vanity. The ego is the source of envy, resentment, pride, hypocrisy, guilt, and blame.

Spirit, on the other hand, is inwardly supportive, patient, forgiving, generous with no strings attached, humble without being weak, loving yet impartial.

The individualized Spirit, which we call the soul, can learn to see beyond its immediate identifications in the material and psychological worlds and resonate with Spirit.

Spirit possesses us; we don't possess It. We become aware of It and join with It. We become in Love with It. Eventually and incredibly, the ego, which had been such a tyrant, begins to lose its power and becomes

122

a willing servant.

As we become familiar with Spirit, the material world—with all its diversity, with all that can be gained and lost—becomes secondary. It is not less important, but secondary in priority. We become less dependent on circumstances for our sense of well-being. We feel connected to Life and Spirit.

What may appear as a loss, for instance, in the material world is seen differently in the world of Spirit where nothing can be lost. This does not mean that our grief just disappears—losses are still losses. The sorrows of life embitter some, and shatter others. Yet these same sorrows may set all of life against the backdrop of eternity, and become a fountain of refreshment, a living energy to draw on. The agony of Jesus, the pain of Mary, the submission of Muḥammad and ʿAlī are reminders that suffering cannot be avoided . . . and yet we are blessed.

The same Life that gave before will continue to give. We know and are aware that the Giver of Life, the Provider, the Generous One, the Beloved can take any shape. People and events do not lose their significance; they become witnesses and evidence of Spirit, transparent to the radiance of Spirit. We begin to see the qualities of the Creator in the creation. The heart is the manifesting part of the Spirit. It is activated through the unconditional love of life around us. Together with others we increase our life.

If it weren't for the presence of Spirit, this world would truly be a prison. But with Spirit and the faculty in humans that can perceive It, the world displays the infinite attributes of the One. (Helminski)

Inner Change

God would never change the blessings
with which He has graced a people
unless they change their inner selves:
and [know] that God is all-hearing, all-seeing.

[*Sūrah al-Anfāl* 8:53]

God bestows His grace freely, but He never withdraws it arbitrarily. Before He changes their state and circumstances, an actual state of rebellion and contumacy has arisen in their own souls, which brings about its inevitable punishment. (A. Yusuf Ali, p. 428)

This is related to 13:11: *God does not change men's condition unless they change their inner selves.* Please see the note there.

The Closeness of the Faithful

And as for those who embrace faith,
and who forsake the domain of evil
and strive hard together with you—
these are of you;
and they who are closely related
have the highest claim on one another according to God's decree.

[*Sūrah al-Anfāl* 8:75]

The classical commentators are of the opinion that this last clause refers to actual family relations, as distinct from the spiritual brotherhood based on a community of faith. According to these commentators, the above sentence abolished the custom which was prevalent among the early Muslims, whereby the *anṣār* ("the helpers"—i.e., the newly-converted Muslims of Medina) concluded, individually, symbolic ties of brotherhood with the *muhājirīn* ("the emigrants" from Mecca), who, almost without exception, arrived at Medina in a state of complete destitution: ties of brotherhood, that is, which entitled every *muhājir* to a share in the property of his "brother" from among the *anṣār*, and in the event of the latter's death, to a share in the inheritance left by him. The above verse is said to have prohibited such arrangements by stipulating that only actual close relations should henceforth have a claim to inheritance.

To my mind, however, this interpretation is not convincing. Although the expression *ūlu 'l-arḥām* is derived from the noun *raḥm* (also spelled *riḥm* and *raḥīm*), which literally signifies "womb," one should not forget that it is figuratively used in the sense of "kinship," "relationship,"

125

or "close relationship" *in general* (i.e., not merely blood-relationship). Thus, "in the classical language, *ūlu 'l-arḥam* means *any* relations: and in law, any relations that have no portion [of the inheritances termed *farā'iḍ*]" (Lane III, 1056, citing, among other authorities, the *Tāj al-'Arūs*). In the present instance, the reference to "close relations" comes at the end of a passage which centers on the injunction that the believers must be "the friends and protectors (*awliyā'*) of one another," and that all later believers shall, similarly, be regarded as members of the Islamic brotherhood. If the reference to "close relations" were meant to be taken in its *literal* sense and conceived as alluding to laws of inheritance, it would be quite out of tune with the rest of the passage, which stresses the bonds of faith among true believers, as well as the moral obligations arising from these bonds.

In my opinion, therefore, the above verse has no bearing on laws of inheritance, but is meant to summarize, as it were, the lesson of the preceding verses: All true believers, of all times, form one single community in the deepest sense of this word; and all who are thus closely related in spirit have the highest claim on one another in accordance with God's decree that *all believers are brethren* [49:10]. (Asad, p. 253)

The Religion of Truth

They would like to extinguish Allāh's light with their mouths,
*but **Allah insures that His light will be perfected,***
even though the deniers detest it.
He it is Who sent His Prophet with guidance and the religion of Truth,
uplifting it over all religion,
no matter how hateful this may be
to those who ascribe divinity to other than God.

[*Sūrah at-Tawbah* 9:33]

This *āyah* describes a dynamic between human beings' compulsion to talk down the truth and the inexorable power of the Divine Light to shine over everything. The Prophet Muḥammad was sent with guidance and the religion of truth (*Dīn al-Ḥaqq*) in order that it might stand out, manifest itself, be uplifted (*yuẓhirahū*) over all religion. Some have translated this word as prevail, implying domination, but in light of the Qurʾān's recognition of religious pluralism, this would not seem the most appropriate interpretation. It is possible to understand this as: *the Truth rises above all falsehood.* (Helminski)

Mutual Support of the Faithful

As for the faithful, both men and women—
they are protectors of one another:
they urge the doing of what is right
and forbid the doing of what is wrong,
and are constant in prayer, and render the charity that purifies,
and they heed God and His Messenger.
It is they on whom God will bestow His blessing:
truly, God is Almighty, Truly Wise!
God has promised the faithful, both men and women,
gardens beneath which running waters flow, there to abide
and fair dwellings in gardens of enduring bliss;
but God's good acceptance is the greatest bliss of all—
for this is the ultimate success!

[*Sūrah at-Tawbah* 9:71-72]

They are protectors of one another, "friends and protectors of one another" or "close to one another." Since the believers are here contrasted with the hypocrites (*the hypocrites, both men and women, are all of a kind* [9:67]), it is preferable to render the term *walī* (of which *awliyā'* is the plural) in its primary meaning of being "near" or "close" to one another.

In gardens of enduring bliss: in all the eleven instances in which the noun *ᶜadn* occurs in the Qur'ān, it is used as a qualifying term for the "gardens" (*jannāt*) of paradise. This noun is derived from the verb *ᶜadana*, which primarily denotes "he remained [somewhere]" or "he kept [to something]," i.e., permanently. In Biblical Hebrew, the closely related

128

noun *ᶜedûn* has also the additional connotation of "delight," "pleasure," or "bliss." Hence the combination of the two concepts in my rendering of *ᶜadn* as "perpetual bliss."] (Asad, pp. 272, 700)

God Has Purchased

See how God has purchased from the faithful
their lives and their possessions;
in return, theirs is the Garden,
and so they struggle in God's way.

[*Sūrah at-Tawbah* 9:111]

God has fixed a high price on you, as He has said: *Truly God hath purchased of the true believers their souls, and their substance, promising them the enjoyment of paradise* [9:111].

You surpass this world and the next in value. What am I to do if you do not know your own worth? Do not sell yourself short, for you are extremely valuable.

God says, "I have bought you, every breath you take, your substance and your life span. If they are spent on Me and given to Me, the price is eternal paradise. This is what you are worth to Me. If you sell yourself to hell, you will have done injustice to yourself, like the man who sticks a blade worth a hundred dinars in the wall and hangs a pot or a gourd on it." (Jalālu'ddin Rūmī, *Signs of the Unseen*, pp. 16-17)

No Refuge from God but in Him

After the earth in all its vastness had become too narrow for them,
and their souls had become utterly constricted,
they came to know with certainty that
There is no refuge from God, but in Him.

[*Sūrah at-Tawbah* 9:118]

The *Muhājirs* were the people who originally forsook their homes in Mecca and followed Muṣṭafā in exile to Medina. The *Anṣār* were the Medina people who received them with honor and hospitality into their city. Both these groups were staunch supporters of Islam, and proved their faith by great sacrifices. But in the difficult days of the Tabūk expedition some of them, not from contumacy or ill-will, but from slackness, thoughtlessness, and human weakness, failed to obey the holy Prophet's summons. They were naturally called on to explain and were excluded from the life of the community. Their mental state is here described graphically. Though the earth is spacious, to them it was constrained. In their own souls they had a feeling of constraint. In worldly affluence they felt poor in spirit. They realized that they could not flee from God, but could only find solace and refuge in coming back to Him. They freely repented and showed it in their deeds, and God freely forgave them and took them to His grace. Though illustrated by the particular examples of the *Anṣār*, the lesson is perfectly general and is good for all times. (A. Yusuf Ali, p. 476)

This verse makes it clear that God is inescapable; He is inescapable because He is One. All events, all inner states, are willed by God. It is

131

God's wish that we avail ourselves of His Mercy and avoid His Wrath; the whole of the *shari'ah* has this purpose. Yet if we choose not to grant Him that wish, if we pursue the illusion of autonomy and self-determination, then God's Wrath is His perfect response to that choice. If we show a snarling face to the Mirror, the Mirror will snarl back. We may not recognize the snarl for what it is; we may be so in love with our unlovely demeanor that it seems beautiful to us, as if it were God's reward for our cherished vanity. If so, God may decide to leave us alone with our illusions—and there is no greater misfortune than this. As God says in 7:182-183, *But as for those who are bent on giving the lie to Our messages—We shall bring them low, step by step, without their perceiving how it came about: for, behold, though I may give them rein for a while, My subtle scheme is exceedingly firm!*

If everything that happens is a part of God's Will, then all the things we pray that God will protect us from are also part of that Will. It is lawful to pray to God for protection; it is not lawful to blame the events and situations we wish to avoid on some power other than God. The *jinn*, as well as the actions of people who are inimical to us, may be involved in the negative things that happen to us, and in such cases we are called upon to do what we can to protect ourselves. But the *jinn*, powerful individuals opposed to us, criminal activities, destructive economic forces, disease, social chaos, war, and natural disaster are not independent powers which are fundamentally opposed to Him. I may rebel against God, yet everything I do in the course of that rebellion is a perfect and lawful part of the Divine economy. Tamarlane was an agent of God's Will—like every star and every atom—but this does not mean that he necessarily avoided the Fire. Those who make themselves agents of God's Wrath, the people to whom God's Wrath is more real than His Mercy, remain under the sign of that Wrath, unless God relents.

The Light of God out of which the universe is made can be compared to the light of the sun, which becomes dimmer and more dispersed the farther it travels from its source. In essence it never stops being sun-

132

light, but its manifestation fades and diminishes as it moves away from that radiant center. In the same way, the Light of God is stronger and more brilliant the closer we are to His Reality. In essence we can never depart from that Reality, since It alone is Real; light is always light; it is never anything else. But in terms of manifestation, we may be relatively far from, or relatively near to, the source of it. To be near to God is Mercy; to be far from Him is Wrath.

It is the passions which experience God's Wrath; fire calls to Fire. And when Wrath comes, we have only two choices. One, based on faith and humility, is to recognize in that Wrath the presence of those things in us which have summoned it, and be sincerely grateful to God for revealing them to us; true remorse is inseparable from gratitude. If a carpet is beaten to remove its dust, it is not to harm the carpet. Faith can recognize in Wrath the hard edge of Mercy, and thank God for whatever happens, trusting that He knows best.

The other choice, however, is to seek refuge from Wrath in Wrath itself—and this, in a way, is the essence of idolatry. How easy it is to make the fatal mistake of seeking refuge from lust in lust, refuge from anger in anger, refuge from cowardice in cowardice. The alcoholic takes refuge from the effects of alcohol in more alcohol; the opium addict turns to opium to save him from the effects of opium.

Idolatry is fundamentally an addiction to an object we pretend can be God for us; and here we can see exactly how an idol is an *inversion* of some aspect of God. The mercy of alcohol or opium is really wrath, whereas the Wrath of God is really Mercy. It is not really possible to take refuge from heroin in heroin, but it really *is* possible to take refuge from God in God. Wrath is a call to seek Mercy; distance is an invitation to draw near.

Wrath peels us to the core. The seat of God, in human experience, is the Heart, the center of our psyche which is potentially receptive to the Spirit. When the outer layers of our being start to burn—our anger, our lust, our cowardice, our frivolity, all the passions—our only refuge is the Heart. Who would not take refuge from the sun's punishing heat in the cool of the oasis?

If, by God's grace, we can sincerely accept Wrath as one face of Mercy—a face which is perfectly appropriate to our state, the very radical cure we need, and have in fact already asked for—then we can learn to use suffering to feed our remembrance of God instead of distracting us from it. And when suffering itself is experienced as Mercy, how great that Mercy is!

Even if this realization seems to be beyond us, still, it is a good thing to pray for. We have the right, and sometimes the duty, to pray to God to fulfil our needs and protect us from misfortune; to pretend otherwise is nothing but foolish pride. But to see the Mercy in Wrath, with real sincerity, is much greater: God loves above all those who can find no fault with Him. (Upton)

Nothing is Accidental

He it is Who has made the sun a source of radiant light
and the moon a light reflected, and has determined for it phases
so that you might know how to compute the years and to measure time.
None of this has God created without an inner truth.
Clearly does He spell out these messages to people of knowledge.
For, truly, in the alternating of night and day,
and in all that God has created in the heavens and on earth
there are messages indeed for people who are conscious of Him!

[*Sūrah Yūnus* 10:5-6]

Literally, *God has not created this otherwise than in accordance with truth*—i.e., to fulfill a definite purpose in consonance with His planning wisdom, implying that everything in the universe—whether existent or potential, concrete or abstract—is meaningful, and nothing is "accidental." Compare 3:191: *O our Sustainer! You have not created anything of this without meaning and purpose (bāṭilan)* and 38:27: *We have not created heaven and earth and all that is between them without meaning and purpose, as is the surmise of those who are bent on denying the truth.* (Asad, p. 289)

Human Delusions

When affliction befalls man, he cries out to Us,
whether he be lying on his side or sitting or standing;
but as soon as We have freed him of his affliction,
he goes on as though he had never invoked Us
to save him from the affliction that befell him!
Thus do their own doings seem fair
to those who waste their own selves.

[*Sūrah Yūnus* 10:12]

Even those who have a superficial belief in God call on Him in their trouble but forget Him when He has relieved their trouble. Their faith is not strong enough to make them realize that all good proceeds from God. But in moments of trouble they use every position, literally and figuratively, to appeal to Him.

Those without faith are selfish, and are so wrapped up in themselves that they think every good that comes to them is due to their own merits or cleverness. That is itself a cause of their undoing. They do not see their own faults. (A. Yusuf Ali, p. 486)

The expression *musrif*, which often (5:32, 7:81) denotes "one who is given to excesses" or "commits excesses" or (6:41) "one who is wasteful," has in this context the meaning of "one who wastes *his own self*" (Rāzī)—namely, destroys his spiritual potential by following only his base impulses and failing to submit to any moral imperative. The very similar expression *alladhīna khasirū anfusahum* occurs in many places and is rendered as *those*

136

who have squandered their own selves. In the sense in which it is used here, the term *isrāf* (literally, "wastefulness" or "lack of moderation in one's doings") is almost synonymous with the term *tughyān* ("overweening arrogance") occurring in the preceding verse, and relates to the same type of man. The phrase *goodly seem [to them] their own doings* describes the unthinking complacency with which *those who waste their own selves* go through life. (Asad, p. 290)

Friendship with God

And in whatever condition you may find yourself,
whatever discourse of this you may be reciting,
and whatever work you may do—
We are your witness when you enter upon it:
For not even the weight of an atom on the earth or in heaven
is beyond the awareness of Your Sustainer.
And there is neither the least nor the greatest of these things
but are clearly recorded.
Indeed, with the friends of God—
no fear need they have, and neither shall they grieve:
they who have attained to faith and have always been conscious of Him.
For them there is the glad tiding
in the life of this world and in the life to come;
nothing could ever alter God's promises,
this, this is the triumph supreme!

[*Sūrah Yūnus* 10:61-64]

There is nothing that men can do but God is a witness to it. We may be deeply engrossed in some particular thing and for the time being be quite unconscious of other things. But God's knowledge not only comprehends all things, but has all things actively before it. Nothing is hidden from Him. And His knowledge has another quality which human knowledge has not. Human knowledge is subject to time, and is obliterated by time. God's knowledge is like a Record and endures for ever. And His Record has a further quality which human records have not. The most permanent human record may be quite intelligible to those who make it but may be ambiguous to others and may become unintelligible with the progress of time, as happens almost invariably to the most enduring inscriptions from very ancient times. But in God's Record or knowledge there is no ambiguity, for it is independent of time, or place, or circumstance. This is the force of *mubīn*, "clear," here.

No fear need they have, and neither shall they grieve. God's all embracing knowledge and constant watchful care over all His creatures may be a source of fear to sinners, but there is no fear for those whom He honors with His love and friendship, neither in this world nor in the world to come. (A. Yusuf Ali, p. 500)

Muhammad Asad translates *awliyāᶜ* as *they who are close to God*:

In *they who are close to God*, the verb *waliya* (from which the noun *walī*, pl. *awliyāᶜ*, is derived) signifies, primarily, the nearness or closeness of one thing to another: thus, God is spoken of in the Qurʾān [2:257 and 3:68] as being *near to* (walī) *those who believe*. Although the term *walī*, when applied to God, as well as to the relationship between one created being and another, is often used in the Qurʾān in the sense of "helper," "friend," "protector," "guardian," etc., none of these secondary meanings can properly—i.e., without offending against the reverence due to God—describe *man's* attitude to, or relationship with, Him. Consequently, the above reference to the believers as *awliyā'* is best rendered as *they who are close to God*, in the sense of their being always conscious of Him. This rendering has the support of almost all the classical commentators. (Asad, p. 301)

Worship Repels Evil

And be constant in prayer at both ends of the day
and at the coming of the night,
for good deeds repel those that are evil.
Let this be a reminder to those who remember God.

[*Sūrah Hūd* 11:114]

This injunction circumscribes all the obligatory prayers without specifying either their form or the exact times of their performance, both of which are clearly laid down in the *sunnah* (i.e., the authenticated sayings and the practice) of the Prophet: namely, at dawn (*fajr*), shortly after mid-day (*ẓuhr*), in the afternoon (*ʿasr*), immediately after sunset (*maghrib*), and in the first part of the night (*ʿishāʿ*). Inasmuch as the above verse stresses the paramount importance of prayer in general, it is safe to assume that it refers not merely to the five obligatory prayers but to a remembrance of God at all times of one's wakeful life. (Asad, p. 333)

Stories of the Messengers

All that We relate to you of the stories of the messengers,
with it We strengthen your heart:
for through these Truth comes to you
as well as counsel
and a message of remembrance to those who have faith.

[*Sūrah Hūd* 11:120]

The Qur'ān does not intend to present those stories as such, but uses them (or, rather, the relevant parts of them) as illustrations of moral truths and as a means to strengthen the faith of the believer. "Narrative" as such is never the purpose of the Qur'ān. Whenever it relates the stories of earlier prophets, or alludes to ancient legends or to historical events that took place before the advent of Islam or during the lifetime of the Prophet, the aim is, invariably, a moral lesson; and since one and the same event, or even legend, has usually many facets revealing as many moral implications, the Qur'ān reverts again and again to the same stories, but every time with a slight variation of stress on this or that aspect of the fundamental truths underlying the Qur'ānic revelation as a whole. Only certain aspects of the relevant stories, and not the complete stories, are presented in the Qur'ān with the purpose being an illustration of an ethical principle or principles, and of men's varying reactions to the guidance which God offers them directly through His prophets and indirectly through the observable phenomena of His creation. (Asad, pp. 335, 321, 331)

The Commanding Self

Man's inner self does incite to evil,
and saved are only they upon whom my Sustainer bestows His grace.

[*Sūrah Yūsuf* 12:53]

This *āyah* from *Sūrah Yūsuf* conveys the words of the Prophet Joseph after he had been tempted by the wife of an Egyptian high official. This *āyah* became the source used by subsequent generations to describe how the human self, separated from divine grace and guidance, has a compulsion to evil. This state of the lower self has been named *an-nafs al-ammāra*, the commanding self. (Helminski)

Man's inner self does incite [him] to evil: literally, *is indeed wont to command [the doing of] evil*—i.e., is filled with impulses which often conflict with what the mind regards as a moral good. This is obviously a reference to the statement earlier in *Sūrah Yūsuf*, 12:24: *she desired him, and he desired her; [and he would have succumbed,] had he not seen [in this temptation] an evidence of his Sustainer's truth*—as well as to Joseph's prayer in verse 12:33: *unless You turn away their guile from me, I might yet yield to their allure.* Zamakhsharī, in his commentary on this verse, further points out that the moral significance of "virtue" consists in one's inner victory over a wrongful desire, and not in the *absence* of such a desire. Compare the well-known saying of the Prophet, recorded on the authority of Abū Hurayrah, by Bukhārī and Muslim: "God, exalted be He, says: 'If a servant of Mine [merely] desires to do a good deed, I shall count this [desire] as a good deed; and if he does it, I shall count it tenfold. And if he desires to commit a bad deed, but does not commit it, I shall count this as a good deed, seeing that he refrained from it only for My sake'," i.e., in consequence of a moral consideration (which, in the present instance, is described as "an evidence of God's truth"). Joseph's stress on the weakness inherent in human nature is a sublime expression of humility on the part of one who himself had overcome that very weakness; for, as the sequence shows, he attributes his moral victory not to himself but solely to the grace and mercy of God. (Asad, pp. 345, 340)

The Need for Real Change

Truly, God does not change men's condition
unless they change their inner selves.

[*Sūrah ar-Raᶜd* 13:11]

This *āyah* describes a relationship between God's will and our will. If people *change their inner selves*, literally, *that which is in themselves*, then God will change their outer circumstances. This is echoed in another important *āyah*:

God would never change the blessings
with which He has graced a people
unless they change their inner selves:
and [know] that God is all-hearing, all-seeing.

[*Sūrah al-Anfāl* 8:53]

These statements, taken together, have both positive and negative connotations: i.e., God supports people with His blessings unless their inner selves become depraved, and He withholds His blessings from wrongdoers until they change their inner disposition and make themselves receptive to His grace.

In actuality, this is an illustration of the divine law of cause and effect (*sunnat Allāh*) which governs the lives of both individuals and societies, and makes the rise and fall of civilizations dependent on people's spiritual qualities and the changes in *their inner selves*. (Asad, p. 360)

God is not intent on punishment. He created man virtuous and pure: He gave him intelligence and knowledge; He surrounded him with all sorts of instruments of His grace and mercy. If, in spite of all this, man distorts his own will and goes against God's Will, yet is God's forgiveness open to him if he will take it. It is only when he has made his own sight blind and changed his own nature or soul away from the beautiful mould in which God formed it, that God's wrath will descend on him and the favorable position in which God placed him will be changed. (A. Yusuf Ali, p. 606)

Prayer and Ultimate Reality

Unto Him is due all prayer aiming at the Ultimate Reality,
since those whom men invoke instead of God
cannot respond to them in any way.

[*Sūrah ar-Raᶜd* 13:14]

In these few simple words is the secret of Islam and of all true religion. The literal meaning could be rendered: *His is the call* [or *invocation*] *of the truth*; or *to Him* [*alone*] *is due all true supplication*. It should, however, be remembered that the term *al-ḥaqq* ("the Truth") is one of the Qurᵓanic attributes of God, signifying the Essential Reality (the *Urgrund* in German philosophical terminology): consequently, the expression *daᶜwat al-ḥaqq* may be understood to mean that *all prayer deserves to be directed towards Him Who is the Most Real*. Therefore to call upon any other being, power or principle is deluded and futile. (Asad, p. 361)

Ḥaqq means truth, right, what is due, befitting, proper. All these meanings are to be understood here. If we worship anything other than God—whether it is idols, stars, powers of nature, spirits, deified men, Self, power, wealth, science, art, talent, or our intellect—our worship is both foolish and futile. Worship and prayer are justified only to the One True God. (A. Yusuf Ali, p. 607)

Those Endowed with Insight

Can, then, he who knows that whatever has been bestowed
from on high upon you by your Sustainer is the truth
be deemed equal to one who is blind?
Only they who are endowed with insight are mindful:
they who are true to their bond with God
and never break their covenant;
and who keep together what God has bidden to be joined,
and stand in awe of their Sustainer
and fear the most evil reckoning;
and who are patient in adversity
out of a longing for their Sustainer's countenance,
and are constant in prayer,
and spend on others, secretly and openly,
out of what We provide for them as sustenance,
and repel evil with good.
It is these that shall find their fulfillment in the hereafter:
gardens of perpetual bliss,
which they shall enter together with the righteous
from among their parents, their spouses, and their offspring;
and the angels will come to them from every gate [and will say]:
"Peace be upon you, because you have persevered!"

[*Sūrah ar-Raᶜd* 13:19-24]

The central meaning of this passage is that some people have insight into
the essence of things and thus have faith, while others are simply blind.

147

Only they who are endowed with insight are mindful. Only those with ᶜ*albāb*, insight, seeing into the kernel (*lubb*) of things, can truly remember and be aware of God. Their fulfillment will be gardens of perpetual bliss. In other words, this state is not just blind belief or indoctrination, but a living insight into the way things truly are. (Helminski)

In this section the contrast between faith and righteousness on the one hand and infidelity and evil on the other is set out. The righteous man is known as one who (1) receives admonition; (2) is true to his covenants; (3) follows the universal religion of faith and practice joined together; (4) is patient and persevering in seeking God; and in practical matters he is known to be (5) regular in prayer; (6) generous in true charity, whether open or secret; and (7) not revengeful but anxious to turn off evil with good, thus breaking the chain of evil which tends to perpetuate itself.

Who keep together what God has bidden to be joined: that is, join faith with practice, love of God with love of man, and respect for all prophets alike, i.e., follow the universal religion, and not odd bits of it.

It is these that shall find their fulfillment in the hereafter: gardens of perpetual bliss, which they shall enter together with the righteous from among their parents, their spouses, and their offspring. The relationships of this life are temporal, but love in righteousness is eternal. In the eternal Gardens of Bliss the righteous will be reunited with all those near and dear ones whom they loved, provided only that they were righteous also; for in eternity nothing else counts. Blood relationships and marriage relationships create certain physical bonds in this life, which may lead to much good, and possibly also to evil. All that is physical or evil will go. But the good will come forth with a new meaning in the final reckoning. Thus ancestors and descendants, husbands and wives, brothers and sisters (for *zurrīyāt* includes them), whose love was pure and sanctified, will find new bliss in the perfecting of their love and will see a new and mystic meaning in the old and ephemeral bonds. (A. Yusuf Ali, pp. 610-611)

148

In *never break their covenant,* "covenant" is, in this context, a general term embracing the spiritual obligations arising from one's faith in God and the moral and social obligations, resulting from that faith, towards one's fellow-men (Zamakhsharī). Those *who keep together what God has bidden to be joined* refers to all ties arising from human relationships—e.g., the bonds of family, responsibility for orphans and the poor, the mutual rights and duties of neighbors—as well as the spiritual and practical bonds which ought to exist between all who belong to the brotherhood of Islam (see 8:75). In its widest sense, the phrase *what God has bidden to be joined* applies to the spiritual obligation, on the part of man, to remain conscious of the unity of purpose underlying all of God's creation, and hence—according to Rāzī—man's moral duty to treat all living beings with love and compassion.

In reference to those who *repel evil with good,* some of the commentators take this to mean that "if they have committed a sin, they repel it [i.e., its effect] by repentance" (Ibn Kaysān, as quoted by Zamakhsharī), while others think that the "repelling" connotes the doing of a good deed in atonement of a—presumably unintentional—bad deed (Rāzī), or that it refers to endeavors to set evil situations to rights by word or deed (an alternative interpretation mentioned by Zamakhsharī). But the great majority of the classical commentators hold that the meaning is "they *repay* evil with good." Thus Al-Ḥasan al-Baṣrī (as quoted by Baghawī, Zamakhsharī, and Rāzī): "When they are deprived [of anything], they give; and when they are wronged, they forgive." Tabarī's explanation is very similar: "They repel the evil done to them by doing good to those who did it," and "they do not repay evil with evil, but repel it by [doing] good." (See also 41:34-36.) (Asad, p. 363)

The Tranquility of Remembrance

He guides to Himself all who turn to Him—
those who have faith
and whose hearts find satisfaction in the remembrance of God—
for, truly, in the remembrance of God hearts find rest.

[*Sūrah ar-Raʿd* 13:28]

Here we have one of the foremost principles of the Qurʾān and one of the most essential truths for a human being to realize. Nothing can satisfy the heart as much as the remembrance of God. When we turn in the direction of Allāh, the ultimate reality, we will be guided to His Presence and our hearts will be satisfied, tranquil, still. The human heart was created restless, always searching for some object to devote itself to and love. In everyday life our hearts are likely to be distracted by various desires, attractions, and concerns. With the remembrance of God, however, we are reconnected to the divine center and all other desires and concerns fall into the proper perspective. (Helminski)

Just preceding this, the unbelievers ask "why is not a Sign sent down to him (Muḥammad) from his Lord?" God provides every guidance for those who turn to Him in penitence, but He will leave those to wander astray who deliberately close their eyes and their hearts to His grace and the comfort that comes from remembering Him and celebrating His praises. The Sign or miracle is not something external: it is something internal, something in your mind, heart, and soul. It depends on your inner spiritual experience. If you turn to God, that light, that experience will come. If you do not, God will not force you. (A. Yusuf Ali, p. 612)

150

A Book for All Mankind

This Book We have bestowed upon you from on high
in order that you might bring forth all mankind,
by their Sustainer's permission,
out of the depths of darkness into the light:
onto the way that leads to the Almighty,
the One to whom all praise is due . . . .
And never have We sent forth any Messenger otherwise than
in his own people's tongue,
so that he might make the truth clear to them,
but God lets go astray him that wills to go astray,
and guides him that wills to be guided—
for He alone is almighty, truly wise.
And, indeed, have We sent forth Moses with Our messages:
"Lead your people out of the depths of darkness into the light,
and remind them of the Days of God!"
Truly, in this there are messages
for those who are firmly patient and constant, grateful and appreciative

[*Sūrah Ibrāhīm* 14:1, 4-5]

These *āyāts* clarify the Prophetic mission of the Prophet Muḥammad Σ as one that goes beyond the tribal or ethnic messages of previous prophets whose message was in the language of their own people. Whereas Moses was commanded, *Lead your people out of the depths of darkness*, Muḥammad's message is *to bring forth all mankind, by their Sustainer's permission, out of the darkness.*

151

Imagine how unlikely this command might have seemed to the small band of people receiving it in the backwaters of Arabia at the time, and yet within one hundred and fifty years the message of Islam had been spread over the greater part of the known world.

The universality of the message should be understood, however, in the context of other verses which clearly recognize that the diversity of religions and ways of life are part of God's plan and that there shall be *no coercion in religion* [2:256]. The message of Islam stands out for all humanity to recognize, but must never become an oppressive system, dominating by sheer power. Its universality has been recognized in the fact that it has spread around the world, *by God's permission,* through people living in the beauty of Islam in their everyday lives. (Helminski)

By their Sustainer's permission: it is insisted on that every apostle speaks not from himself but from God. His leading into the light is but by the grace and mercy of God, not by any power of his own, or by any merit of those who hear him. Three qualities of God are mentioned: (1) His exalted position above all creation; (2) His goodness which entitles Him, and Him alone, to praise; and (3) His power in all heavens and earth.

Never have We sent forth any apostle other than with a message in his own people's tongue: if the object of a message is to make things clear, it must be delivered in the language current among the people to whom the apostle is sent. Through them it can reach all mankind. There is even a wider meaning for language. It is not merely a question of alphabets, letters, or words. Each age or people—or world in a psychological sense—casts its thoughts in a certain mould or form. God's message, being universal, can be expressed in all moulds and forms, and is equally valid and necessary for all grades of humanity, and must therefore be explained to each according to his or her capacity or receptivity. In this respect the Qur'ān is marvelous. It is for the simplest as well as the most advanced.

God lets go astray him that wills to go astray and guides him that wills to be guided. God's guiding *whom He pleases* is the usual expression for *mashīyat,* the universal Will and Plan, which is all-wise and on the highest plane of goodness and righteousness.

The Days of God: the days when God's mercy was specially shown to them. Every day and every hour and minute, God's grace flows to us abundantly, but there are special events in personal or national history which may be commemorated as red letter days. Those to the Israelites were set out in great detail in 2:40-61 and in other places.

Firmly patient and constant: *ṣabbār* is the intensive form, and includes all the ideas implied in *ṣabr*, which has many shades of meaning. It implies (1) patience in the sense of being thorough, not hasty; (2) patient perseverance, constancy, steadfastness, firmness of purpose; (3) systematic as opposed to spasmodic or chance action; (4) a cheerful attitude of resignation and understanding in sorrow, defeat, or suffering, as opposed to murmuring or rebellion, but saved from mere passivity or listlessness by the element of constancy or steadfastness. An additional meaning implied in *ṣabr* is self-restraint. Haqqānī defines it in his *tafsīr* as following reason and restraining fear, anger, and desire. What can be a higher reward for patience, perseverance, self-restraint, and constancy than that God should be with us? For this promise opens the door to every kind of spiritual well-being. Patient perseverance is not mere passivity. It is active striving in the way of Truth, which is the way of God.

Grateful and appreciative: *shakūr* and *shākir* have in them the idea of appreciation, recognition, gratitude as shown in deeds of goodness and righteousness. But these terms are applied to God as well as to men. A slight distinction in shades of meaning may be noted. *Shakūr* implies that the appreciation is even for the smallest favors and response on the other side; it is a mental attitude independent of specific facts. *Shākir* implies bigger and more specific things. (A. Yusuf Ali, pp. 619-620, 28, 61)

The Parable of a Good Word

Are you not aware how God sets forth the parable of a good word?
It is like a good tree, firmly rooted,
with its branches towards the sky,
yielding its fruit at all times by its Sustainer's permission.
And God propounds parables to men, so that they might
themselves reflect on the truth.
And the parable of a corrupt word is that of a corrupt tree,
torn up from its roots onto the face of the earth, wholly unable to endure.
God grants firmness to those who have attained to faith
through the word that is unshakably true
in the life of this world as well as in the life to come.

[*Sūrah Ibrāhīm* 14:24-27]

The *good word* is usually interpreted as the divine word, the divine message, the true religion. It may also be interpreted in a more general sense as a word of truth, a word of goodness or kindness, which follows from a true appreciation of religion. For religion includes our duty to God and our duty to man. The *corrupt word* is opposite to this: false religion, blasphemy, false speech, or preaching or teaching unkindness and wrongdoing. The word, in mystic language, is the root of the deed, and is identified with the deed.

The *good tree* is known for: (1) its beauty: it gives pleasure to all who see it; (2) its stability: it remains firm and unshaken in storms because its roots are firmly fixed in the earth; (3) its wide compass: its branches reach high, and it catches all sunshine from heaven and gives shade to countless birds in its branches and men and animals beneath it; and (4) its abundant

154

fruit, which it yields at all times. So is the *good word*. It is as beautiful as it is true. It abides in all the changes and chances of this life, and even beyond. It is never shaken by sorrow or what seems to us as calamity; its roots are deep down in the bedrock facts of life. Its reach is universal, above, around, below. It is illuminated by the divine light from heaven, and its consolation reaches countless beings of all grades of life. Its fruit—the enjoyment of its blessing—is not confined to one season or one set of circumstances. Furthermore, the fortunate man who is the vehicle of that word has no self-pride: he attributes all its goodness, and his act in spreading it, to the will and leave of God. (A. Yusuf Ali, p. 626)

This is the story of the destiny of a good word vs. a bad one. But whose word is it? Who, in these verses, is the speaker?

If *God grants firmness to those who have attained faith through the word that is unshakably true*, then the Speaker is God, and the unshakably true word is the Qur'ān. A word spoken by God is always true. Circumstances change, but God's word remains unshaken. When God's word takes root in the soul, it brings forth the firmly-rooted tree which yields good fruit. The earth in which the word takes root is the ground of virtue, particularly the virtues of spiritual poverty and humility. If we are willing to lower ourselves like the earth, we can receive God's word like the earth receives the seed. This lowness, this *humility* (from the Latin word *humus*, soil), is what allows our spiritual lives to grow toward the sun of the Spirit.

But if God is the One Who speaks the good word, then who speaks the corrupt word? We could say "Iblīs"; we could also say the *nafs al-ammāra*, the commanding self. The commanding self believes, or acts as if it believes, that it exists in its own right. It thinks it can create reality out of nothing through its lies, its fantasies, and its schemes. But such "co-creation" is simply not possible. *God created the heavens and the earth with truth* [64:3], but nothing whatever can be created out of lies and illusions,

155

no matter how much effort we expend. Lies and illusions can certainly destroy—though not without God's permission, so He can demonstrate to us their consequences—but they can never create. They are neither rooted in the ground of trust and sincerity, nor can their branches reach upward to receive Life and Truth and Mercy from the Sustainer.

But we ourselves are also speakers. When God speaks, He creates; when we speak, we either conform ourselves to His creative word, or we depart from it into a world of lies and illusions. To speak truth is to make truth our ally—both the simple factual truth of the situation, and that Truth which is one of the Names of God Himself, *Al-Ḥaqq*. The objective truth of any situation—not the lies we tell, or the way we hope it will be, or the way we fear it will be—is God's real presence in that situation. It may seem that liars have all power in this world, just as someone who has just jumped off a high cliff may feel that he is motionless and weightless. But truth will always have the final word, *in the life of this world as well as in the life to come.*

The human form stands upright like a tree. Only the human being is capable of being conscious of God's presence while remaining firmly rooted in this world. But if we fail to heed the true word, if we resort to lies and evasions, then we can depend neither upon the ground of the actual situation, nor upon the Truth and Mercy of God; we are *wholly unable to endure.* (Upton)

In its wider meaning, the term *kalimah* ("word") denotes any conceptual statement or proposition. Thus, a *good word* circumscribes any proposition (or idea) that is intrinsically true and—because it implies a call to what is good in the moral sense—is ultimately beneficent and enduring; and since a call to moral righteousness is the innermost purport of every one of God's messages, the term *good word* applies to them as well. Similarly the *corrupt word* mentioned in verse 26 applies to the opposite of what a divine message aims at: namely, to every idea that is intrinsically false or morally evil and, therefore, spiritually harmful. (Asad, p. 376)

God Always Grants a Part of Our Prayers

And always does He give you something
out of what you may be asking of Him,
and if you tried to count God's blessings,
you could never compute them.

[*Sūrah Ibrāhīm* 14:34]

I will never forget the day a friend of mine came to me and said, "Do you realize we always receive something of what we pray for?"

And I said, "Yes, and. . .?"

"Well, it says so in the Holy Qurʾān," and she proceeded to show me the above verse—one which, admittedly, I must have read at least several times before without being struck by its significance as she had been.

This is an example of how so much in the Qurʾān awaits a heart that is open to its truth. The promise of this verse had made my friend radiant with hope and gratitude. Hidden in this verse was one of the uncounted blessings.

Muḥammad Asad writes:

God satisfies every one of man's desires, provided that His unfathomable wisdom regards its satisfaction as ultimately beneficial to the human being concerned: this is the meaning of the preposition *min* (literally, *out of,* but in this context, "*something* out of") preceding the phrase *what you may be asking.* (Asad, p. 378)

But two things strike me in this selection: First, that we never know what will be or what has been granted from our prayers, and second, that we can never entirely reckon *all* the reasons we should be grateful. (Helminski)

God's Storehouses

And there is not a thing but its storehouses are with Us;
*but **We only send it down in appropriate measures.***

[*Sūrah al-Ḥijr* 15:21]

To understand this statement we must understand the nature of these *storehouses*. Yusuf Ali presents it this way:

Khazā-in: treasures, storehouses, places where valuable things are accumulated, from which supplies are distributed from time to time as need arises. All the wonderful gifts and forces and energies which we see in the world around us have their sources and fountainheads with God, the Creator and Sustainer of the Worlds. And what we see or perceive or imagine is just a small portion of what exists. That portion is sent out to us and to our world according to our needs or its needs from time to time as the occasion arises. It is strictly limited according to rule and plan. Its source is unlimited and inexhaustible. In the same way the forces which we see operating around us, in nature or in the spiritual world, according to laws which we can grasp and ascertain, are mere derived forces, in the 2nd, 3rd, or n^{th} degree. Their source and ultimate fountainhead is with God. (A. Yusuf Ali, pp. 640-641)

Classical commentators have proposed that all of creation is an expression of the treasury of Divine Names, which exist at another level of reality. This world of existence is the place of manifestation of the Divine Names or Attributes.

A very literal translation of this verse would be: *and We do not send it*

159

down [create it] otherwise than according to a measure known [to Us]: that is, in accordance with the needs of the Divine plan as such and according to the function which any particular thing or phenomenon is to have within that plan.

This idea of *appropriate measures* is evidenced in the principles of proportion by which the whole natural world seems to be created. In other words, all of nature seems to follow a pattern of organization which can be mathematically described. The golden mean (1:1.618) and other objective proportions, for instance, govern the growth of plants, the proportions of the human body, the nautilus shell, etc.

The principles of beautiful and orderly proportion is affirmed in other part of the Qur'ān as well:

> *In true proportions God created the heavens and the earth:*
> *truly, in that is a sign for those who have faith.*
>
> [*Sūrah al-ʿAnkabūt* 29:44]

> *He Who created the seven heavens in harmony;*
> *no lack of proportion will you see*
> *in that which the Most Compassionate has created—*
> *just look again: can you see any flaw?*
>
> [*Sūrah al-Mulk* 67:3]

> *Glorify the name of your Sustainer Most High*
> *Who has created and further given order and proportion;*
> *Who has determined the order, and gives guidance;*
>
> [*Sūrah al-Aʿlā* 87:2-3]

Given the evidence of these principles of proportion in the physical world, we might also suppose that some kind of appropriate measure governs all of existence, including even inner, psychological, and spiritual dimensions. That the human being was also created upon a beautiful model of proportion is affirmed in *Sūrah at-Tīn* 95:4: *The Human being was created upon the most beautiful model.* (Helminski)

Human Haughtiness

He creates the human being out of a drop of sperm
and lo! this same being shows himself endowed
with the power to think and to argue!

[*Sūrah an-Naḥl* 16:4]

The literal meaning of *endowed with the power to think and to argue,* according to Muḥammad Asad is: *He becomes an open contender in argument* (*kha-ṣīm*). Asad writes further:

According to Zamakhsharī and Rāzī, the above phrase is liable to two interpretations. In the words of Zamakhsharī, "one interpretation is that after having been a [mere] drop of sperm, a particle of matter without consciousness or motion, man becomes highly articulate (*minṭīq*), able to argue on his own [for or against a proposition], courageously facing disputes, and clearly formulating his arguments: [and herein lies] an indication of God's creative power. The other [interpretation] is that man is [prone to become] a contender in argument against his Sustainer, refusing to acknowledge his [very] Creator." Rāzī, on his part, gives his unqualified support to the first of these two interpretations, "because the above verses are meant to stress the evidence of the existence of a wise Creator, and not the fact of men's insolence and their proneness to blasphemy and ingratitude." The verses 36:77-78 were revealed at a considerably earlier period: *Is man, then, not aware that it is We Who create him out of a [mere] drop of sperm—whereupon, lo! he shows himself endowed with the power to think and to argue? And [now] he [argues about Us, and] thinks of Us in terms of comparison, and is oblivious of how he himself was created!* In view of those verses, I am of the opinion that the above two interpretations are not mutually

162

exclusive but, rather, complementary, inasmuch as this passage is meant to bring out man's unique quality as a rational being—a quality that may lead him to great heights of achievement, but may equally well lead him utterly astray: hence my free rendering of this profound, elliptic phrase. (Asad, p. 394)

Nature Prostrates Before God

For before God prostrates
all that is in the heavens and all that is on earth—
every creature that moves and the angels:
even these do not bear themselves with false pride:
they fear their Sustainer high above them,
and do whatever they are bidden to do.

[*Sūrah an-Naḥl* 16:49]

Every creature that moves and the angels, i.e., the lowest as well as the highest. The term *dābbah* denotes any sentient, corporeal being capable of spontaneous movement, and is contrasted here with the non-corporeal, spiritual beings designated as "angels" (Rāzī). *Do whatever they are bidden to do,* i.e., they must, by virtue of their nature, obey the impulses planted in them by God and are, therefore, incapable of what is described as "sinning." Man, however, is fundamentally different in this respect. In contrast with the natural sinlessness of *every beast that moves, and the angels,* man is endowed with free will in the moral sense of this term: he can *choose* between right and wrong—and therefore he can, and often does, sin. But even while he sins he is subject to the universal law of cause and effect instituted by God and referred to in the Qurʾān as *sunnat Allāh* ("God's way"): hence the Qurʾanic statement that "before God prostrate themselves, *willingly or unwillingly*, all [things and beings] that are in the heavens and on earth" [13:15]. (Asad, p. 401)

164

The Inspiration of the Bees

And consider how your Sustainer has inspired the bee:
"Prepare for yourself dwellings in mountains and in trees,
and in what men may build [for you by way of hives]:
and then eat of all manner of fruit,
and follow humbly the paths ordained for you by your Sustainer."
And there issues from within these a fluid of many hues,
wherein there is health for people.
In all this, behold, there is a message indeed for people who reflect!

[*Sūrah an-Naḥl* 16:68-69]

The expression *He has inspired* (*awḥā*) is meant to bring out the wonderful quality of the instinct which enables the lowly insect to construct the geometrical masterpiece of a honeycomb out of perfectly-proportioned hexagonal, prismatic wax cells—a structure which is most economical, and therefore most rational, as regards space and material. Together with the subsequently mentioned transmutation, in the bee's body, of plant juices into honey, this provides a striking evidence of "God's ways" manifested in all nature. (Asad, pp. 404-405)

Awḥā: waḥyun ordinarily means inspiration, the message put into the mind or heart by God. Here the bee's instinct is referred to God's teaching, which it undoubtedly is. In 99:5, this word is applied to the earth: *for your Lord will have given her [the earth] inspiration.* The honeycomb itself, with its hexagonal cells, geometrically perfect, is a wonderful structure, and is well called *buyūt*, homes. And the way the bee finds out inaccessi-

165

ble places, in the hills, in the trees, and even among the habitations of men, is one of the marvels of nature, i.e., of God's working in His creation.

The bee assimilates the juice of various kinds of flowers and fruit and forms within its body the honey which it stores in its cells of wax. The different kinds of food from which it makes its honey gives different col-·ors to the honey, e.g., it is dark-brown, light-brown, yellow, white, and so on. The taste and flavor also varies, as in the case of heather honey, the honey formed from scented flowers, and so on. As food it is sweet and wholesome, and it is used in medicine. Note that while the instinctive individual acts are described in the singular number, the produce of their bodies is described in the plural, as the result of their collective effort.

Follow humbly the paths ordained for you by your Sustainer: these paths are described as *zululan.* Two meanings are possible: (1) ways easy and spacious, referring to the unerring way in which bees find their way from long distances to their combs; and (2) the idea of humility and obedience in them. From both we can derive a metaphorical and spiritual meaning. (A. Yusuf Ali, p. 674)

Fair Treatment of Dependents, Employees, and Servants

And on some of you God has bestowed
more abundant means of sustenance than on others:
and yet, they who are more abundantly favored
are [often] unwilling to share their sustenance
with those whom their right hands possess,
so that they might be equal in this respect.
Will they, then, deny God's blessings?

[*Sūrah an-Naḥl* 16:71]

The phrase *to share their sustenance with* reads literally *to turn over their suste-nance to*. The expression *those whom their right hands possess* (i.e., *those whom they rightfully possess*) may relate either to slaves taken captive in a war in God's cause or, metonymically, to all who are dependent on others for their livelihood and thus become the latters' responsibility. The placing of one's dependents on an equal footing with oneself with regard to the ba-sic necessities of life is a categorical demand of Islam. Thus, the Prophet said: "They are your brethren, these dependents of yours (*khawalukum*) whom God has placed under your authority [literally, "under your hand"]. Hence, whoso has his brother under his authority shall give him to eat of what he eats himself, and shall clothe him with what he clothes himself. And do not burden them with anything that may be beyond their strength; but if you [must] burden them, help them yourselves." (This authentic Tradition, recorded by Bukhārī in several variants in his *Ṣaḥīḥ*, appears in the compilations of Muslim, Tirmidhī and Ibn Ḥanbal as

167

well.) However, men often fail to live up to this consciousness of moral responsibility: and this failure amounts, as the sequence shows, to a denial of God's blessings and of His unceasing care for all His creatures. (Asad, p. 405)

Justice

*Behold, **God enjoins justice**, and the doing of good,*
and generosity towards one's fellow-men;
and He forbids all that is shameful
and all that runs counter to reason,
as well as envy.

[*Sūrah an-Naḥl* 16:90]

Justice (*ʿadl*) is a comprehensive term, and may include all the virtues of cold philosophy. But religion asks for something warmer and more human, the doing of good deeds even where perhaps they are not strictly demanded by justice, such as returning good for ill, or obliging those who in worldly language "have no claim" on you; and of course the fulfilling of the claims of those whose claims are recognized in social life. Similarly, the opposites are to be avoided: everything that is recognized as shameful, and everything that is really unjust, and any inward rebellion against God's law or our own conscience in its most sensitive form. (A. Yusuf Ali, p. 681)

The term *al-munkar* (rendered in other places as "that which is wrong") has here its original meaning of *that which the mind* [or *the moral sense*] *rejects*, respectively *ought to reject*. Zamakhsharī is more specific, and explains this term as signifying in the above context *that which* [*men's*] *intellects disown* or *declare to be untrue* (*mā tunkiruhu al-ʿuqūl*): in other words, all that runs counter to reason and good sense (which, obviously, must not be confused with that which is *beyond* man's comprehension). This

169

eminently convincing explanation relates not merely to intellectually un-acceptable propositions (in the abstract sense of the term), but also to grossly unreasonable and, therefore, reprehensible actions or attitudes and is, thus, fully in tune with the rational approach of the Qur'ān to questions of ethics as well as with its insistence on reasonableness and moderation in man's behavior. Hence the rendering of *al-munkar*, in this and in similar instances, as *all that runs counter to reason*. (Asad, pp. 409-410)

Value the Bond with God

Do not trade the bond with God for a trivial reward:
for that which is with God is by far the best for you if only you knew.
What is with you must vanish; what is with God will endure.
And We will certainly bestow on those who patiently persevere
their reward according to the best of their actions.
Whoever works righteousness, man or woman, and has faith,
truly, to Him will We give a new life, a life that is good and pure,
and We will bestow on such their recompense
according to the best of their actions.

[*Sūrah an-Naḥl* 16:95-96]

This is similar to 20:112: anyone who will have done [whatever he could] of righteous deeds, and was a believer withal, need have no fear of being wronged or deprived [of any of his merit], literally, no fear of [any] wrong—i.e., punishment for any sin which he may have contemplated but not committed—and neither of diminution, i.e., of his merit; that the righteous shall be recompensed in the hereafter in accordance with the **best** that they ever did. (Asad, p. 482)

The Culmination of Revelation

And now that We replace one message by another—
since God is fully aware of what He bestows from on high, step by step—
they [who deny the truth] are wont to say, "You but invented it!"
Nay, but most of them do not understand it!
Say: "Holy inspiration has brought it down from your Sustainer by stages,
setting forth the truth,
so that it might give firmness to those who have attained to faith,
and provide guidance and a glad tiding
to all who have surrendered themselves to God."

[*Sūrah an-Naḥl* 16:101-102]

We replace one message by another: i.e., by substituting the message of the Qur'ān for the earlier dispensations—and not, as some Muslim scholars maintain, "abrogating" one Qur'anic verse and replacing it by another.

Step by step: the gradualness of revelation (implied in the verbal form *yunazzil*) corresponds to God's plan, according to which He has gradually unfolded His will to man, substituting one dispensation for another in the measure of mankind's intellectual and social development, bringing it to its culmination in the message of the Qur'ān.

Holy inspiration (*rūḥ al-qudus*) occurs in three other places in the Qur'ān (2:87, 2:253, 5:110). To my mind, it's a Qur'anic synonym for "divine revelation." However, a literal rendering, *spirit of holiness*—is also possible if one applies this term to the angel who communicates God's revelations to the prophets. (In 16:2: *He causes the angels to descend with this divine inspiration* where the word *rūḥ* is translated as divine inspiration.) (Asad, p. 412)

The Gentle Invitation

Invite to the way of your Lord
with wisdom and beautiful urging;
and discuss with them in the best and most gracious manner
for your Lord knows best who strays from His Path
and who receives guidance.

[*Sūrah an-Naḥl* 16:125]

In this wonderful passage are laid down principles of religious teaching, which are good for all time. But where are the teachers with such qualifications? We must invite all to the way of God, and expound His universal will; we must do it with wisdom and discretion, meeting people on their own ground and convincing them with illustrations from their own knowledge and experience, which may be very narrow or very wide. Our preaching must be not dogmatic, not self-regarding, not offensive, but gentle, considerate, and such as would attract their attention. Our manner and our arguments should not be acrimonious, but modeled on the most courteous and the most gracious example, so that the hearer may say to himself, "This man is not dealing merely with dialectics; he is not trying to get a rise out of me; he is sincerely expounding the faith that is in him, and his motive is the love of man and the love of God."

It may be that the person preaching sometimes says to himself, "What is the use of teaching these people? They have made up their minds, or they are obstinate, or they are only trying to trip me up." Let him not yield to such a thought. Who knows how the seed of the word of God may germinate in people's minds? It is not for man to look for results. Man's inner thoughts are known best to God. (A. Yusuf Ali, pp. 689-690)

173

This is similar to 29:46: *And do not argue with the followers of earlier revelation otherwise than in the most kindly manner.* This stress on kindness and tact and, hence, on the use of reason alone in all religious discussions with adherents of other creeds is fully in tune with the basic, categorical injunction, *There shall be no coercion in matters of faith* [2:256]. (Asad, p. 416)

Restraint in Retaliation

Hence, if you have to respond to an attack,
respond only to the extent of the attack levelled against you;
but to bear yourselves with patience is indeed far better for
those who are patient in adversity.
Then be patient, always remembering that your patience is from God;
and do not grieve over them,
and neither be distressed by the false arguments which they devise.
For God is with those who restrain themselves and those who do good.

[*Sūrah an-Naḥl* 16:126-128]

In the context this passage refers to controversies and discussions, but the words are wide enough to cover all human struggles, disputes, and fights. In strictest equity you are not entitled to give a worse blow than is given to you. But those who have reached a higher spiritual standard do not even do that. They restrain themselves and are patient. Lest you should think that such patience only gives an advantage to the adversary, you are told that the contrary is the case: the advantage is with the patient, the self-possessed, those who do not lose their temper or forget their own principles of conduct.

Then be patient: in the previous verse are laid down the principles of conduct in controversy for all Muslims. There patience was *recommended*. In this verse a command is directly addressed to the Prophet. It is a *command*: his standard as the great teacher is much higher, and he carried it out in his life. His patience and self-restraint were under circumstances of extraordinary provocation. In his human wisdom it may sometimes have

175

seemed questionable whether forbearance and self-restraint might not be human weaknesses: he had to defend his people as well as himself against the enemy's persecutions. He is told here that he need not entertain any such fears. Patience with constancy in those circumstances was in accordance with God's own command. Nor was he to grieve if they reject God's message; the Prophet has done his duty when he boldly and openly proclaimed it. Nor was his heart to be troubled if they hatched secret plots against himself and his people. God would protect them.

The *sūrah* ends with the highest consolation which the righteous can receive: the assurance that God is with them. A double qualification is indicated for so high an honor: (1) that they should not yield to human passion or anger or impatience, and (2) that they should go on with constancy doing good all around them. To attain to the Presence of God in the sense of "I am with you" is the culmination of the righteous man's aspiration. (A. Yusuf Ali, p. 690)

The believers are admonished to observe self-restraint while arguing with people of another persuasion, and never to offend against decency and intellectual equity. Although retaliation in argument is permissible if one's integrity is impeached by an opponent, the sequence makes it clear that it is morally preferable to renounce it altogether and to bear the unjust attack with patience. *And your patience in adversity* (ṣabr) *is due to* [or *rests with*] *none but God*—i.e., it must never be allowed to become a source of spiritual arrogance and false self-righteousness. (Asad, p. 416)

176

Misguided Prayers

As it is, human beings often pray for things that are harmful
as if they were praying for that which is good:
for people are inclined to be hasty.

[*Sūrah al-Isrāᶜ* 17:11]

Man in his ignorance or haste mistakes evil for good and desires what he should not have. The wise and instructed soul has patience and does not put its own desires above the wisdom of God. He receives with content-ment the favors of God, and prays to be rightly guided in his desires and petitions. (A. Yusuf Ali, p. 696)

Compare 2:216: *It may well be that you hate a thing the while it is good for you, and it may well be that you love a thing the while it is bad for you: and God knows, whereas you do not know.* In other words, divine guidance is the only objective criterion as to what is good and what is bad. (Asad, p. 419)

Personal Responsibility

Whoever chooses to follow the right path,
follows it but for his own good;
and whoever goes astray, goes but astray to his own hurt;
and no bearer of burdens
shall be made to bear another's burden.
And never would We chastise before sending a Messenger.

[*Sūrah al-Isrāᶜ* 17:15]

No bearer of burdens shall be made to bear another's burden: this basic ethical law appears in the Qurʾān five times: in 6:164, 35:18, 39:7 and 53:38 as well as here. It's implication is threefold: firstly, it expresses a categorical rejection of the Christian doctrine of the "original sin" with which every human being is allegedly burdened from birth; secondly, it refutes the idea that a person's sins could be "atoned for" by a saint's or a Prophet's redemptive sacrifice (as evidenced, for instance, in the Christian doctrine of Jesus' vicarious atonement for mankind's sinfulness, or in the earlier, Persian doctrine of man's vicarious redemption by Mithras); and, thirdly, it denies, by implication, the possibility of any "mediation" between the sinner and God. (Asad, p. 816)

178

The Wings of Humility

Your Lord has decreed that you worship none but Him,
and do good to your parents.
Should one of them, or both, reach old age in your care,
never speak with contempt to them or scold them,
but speak to them with reverence,
and tenderly lower to them the wings of humility,
and say: "O my Sustainer! Bestow Your grace upon them,
even as they cherished and nurtured me when I was but a child!"

[*Sūrah al-Isrāʾ* 17:23-24]

The spiritual and moral duties are now brought into juxtaposition. We are to worship none but God, because none but God is worthy of worship, not because "the Lord your God is a jealous God, visiting the iniquity of the fathers upon the children to the third and fourth generation of them that hate Me" (Exodus 20:5).

Note that the act of worship may be collective as well as individual, hence the plural *taʿbudū*. The kindness to parents is an individual act of piety, hence the singular *taqul, qul*, etc.

Tenderly lower to them the wings of humility: the metaphor is that of a high-flying bird which lowers her wing out of tenderness to her offspring. There is a double aptness. (1) When the parent was strong and the child was helpless, parental affection was showered on the child. When the child grows up and is strong and the parent is helpless, can he do less than bestow similar tender care on the parent? (2) But more: he must approach the matter with gentle humility: for does not parental love remind him of

179

the great love with which God cherishes His creatures? There is something here more than simple human gratitude: it goes up into the highest spiritual region.

Note that we are asked to honor our father and mother not "that your days may be long upon the land which the Lord your God giveth you" (Exodus 20:12) but upon much higher and more universal grounds, such as befit a perfected revelation. In the first place, not merely respect but cherishing kindness and humility to parents are commanded. In the second place, this command is bracketed with the command to worship the One True God: parental love should be to us a type of divine love. Nothing that we can do can ever really compensate for that which we have received. In the third place, our spiritual advancement is tested by this: we cannot expect God's forgiveness if we are rude or unkind to those who unselfishly brought us up. (A. Yusuf Ali, pp. 700-701)

Whereas God is the real, ultimate cause of man's coming to life, his parents are its outward, immediate cause: and so the call to God [in the preceding verses] is followed by the injunction to honor and cherish one's parents. Beyond this, the whole of the present passage—up to and including verse 39—is meant to show that kindness and just dealings between man and man are an integral part of the concept of "striving for the good of the life to come."

Tenderly lower to them the wings of humility is a metonymical expression evocative of a bird that lovingly spreads its wings over its offspring in the nest. (Asad, pp. 421-422)

Eight Moral Injunctions

And so, do not kill your children for fear of poverty:
it is We Who shall provide sustenance for them as well as for you.
Truly, killing them is a great sin.
And do not approach adultery—
for, behold, it is an abomination and an evil way.
And do not take any human being's life—
which God has willed to be sacred—
except in the pursuit of justice . . . .
And do not touch the substance of an orphan,
except to improve it, before he comes of age.
And be true to every promise—
for, truly, you will be called to account for every promise
which you will have made!
And give full measure whenever you measure,
and weigh with a balance that is true:
this will be for your own good, and best in the end.
And never concern yourself with anything
of which you have no knowledge:
truly your hearing and sight and heart—all of them—
will be called to account for it.
And do not walk upon the earth with proud self-conceit:
for, truly, you can never rend the earth asunder,
nor can you ever grow as tall as the mountains!
The evil of all this is odious in your Sustainer's sight:
this is part of that knowledge of right and wrong
with which your Sustainer has inspired you.

[*Sūrah al-Isrāᶜ* 17:31–39]

181

Do not kill your children for fear of poverty: historically, this may be a reference to the pre-Islamic Arabian custom of burying unwanted female children alive, as well as to the occasional—though much rarer—sacrifices of male children to some of their gods. Beyond this, however, the above prohibition has a timeless validity inasmuch as it relates also to abortions undertaken *for fear of poverty,* i.e., on purely economic grounds.

And do not commit adultery: literally, *do not come near adultery,* thus intensifying the prohibition. It is to be noted that the term *zinā* signifies all sexual intercourse between a man and a woman who are not husband and wife, irrespective of whether either of them is married to another partner or not; hence, it denotes both "adultery" and "fornication" in the English senses of these terms.

Do not take any human being's life . . . except in the pursuit of justice: i.e., in the execution of a legal sentence or in a just war, or in individual, legitimate self-defense.

Never concern yourself with anything of which you have no knowledge or *do not follow* [or *pursue*] *anything:* this would seem to relate to groundless assertions about events or people (and hence to slander or false testimony), to statements based on guesswork unsupported by evidence, or to interfering in social situations which one is unable to evaluate correctly.

This is part of that knowledge of right and wrong with which your Sustainer has inspired you or *which your Sustainer has revealed to you.* It is to be noted that the noun *ḥikmah,* usually signifying "wisdom," is derived from the verb *ḥakama* ("he prevented" or "restrained [him or it]," i.e., from acting in an undesirable manner). Hence, the primary meaning of *ḥikmah* is "that which prevents one from evil or ignorant behavior" (compare Lane II, 617). In its positive sense, it signifies "[conscious] insight into that which is most excellent" (*Lisān al-ʿArab, Tāj al-ʿArūs*). Inasmuch as this term refers here, in particular, to what is "odious in God's sight," it implies moral discrimination (or *the knowledge of right and wrong*) on the part of men; and this, in its turn, presupposes the existence of an absolute, God-willed standard of moral values. (Asad, pp. 423-424)

And give full measure whenever you measure, and weight with a balance that is true: this will be for your own good, and best in the end. Giving just measure and weight is not only right in itself but is ultimately to the best spiritual and material advantage of the person who gives it.

And never concern yourself with anything of which you have no knowledge: verify your hearing and sight and heart—all of them—will be called to account for it. Idle curiosity may lead us to nose into evil, through our ignorance that it is evil. We must guard against every such danger. We must only hear the things that are known to us to be of good report, and see things that are good and instructive, and entertain in our hearts feelings or in our minds ideas that we have reason to expect will be spiritually profitable to us. We shall be called to account for the exercise of every faculty that has been given to us. This goes a little farther than the famous sculpture on a Japanese temple in which three monkeys are shown as putting their hands to their ears, eyes, and mouths, respectively, to show that they were not prepared to hear any evil, or see any evil, or speak any evil. Here idle curiosity is condemned. Futility is to be avoided even if it does not reach the degree of positive evil.

And do not walk upon the earth with proud self-conceit: insolence, or arrogance, or undue elation at our powers or capacities is the first step to many evils. Besides, it is unjustified. All our gifts are from God. (A. Yusuf Ali, p. 704)

The Hidden Glorification

Limitless is He in His glory,
and sublimely, immeasurably exalted
above anything people may say.
The seven heavens acclaim His limitless glory,
and the earth, and all that they contain;
and there is nothing that does not celebrate
His immeasurable glory—
but you fail to grasp the manner of their glorifying Him!
Truly, He is forbearing, always ready to forgive!

[*Sūrah al-Isrāʿ* 17:44]

All creation, animate and inanimate, sings God's praises and celebrates His glory—animate with consciousness, and inanimate in the evidence which it furnishes of the unity and glory of God. The mystics believe that there is a soul in animate things also, which declares forth the glory of God. For all nature bears witness to His power, wisdom, and goodness. It is only those who reject the whole trend of nature and deny faith simply because they have been given a limited amount of choice and free will, it is only such as these who understand not what every other creature understands and proclaims with joy and pride. What must be their degradation! And yet God bears with them and forgives them. Such is His goodness! (A. Yusuf Ali, p. 706)

The seven heavens: the term *samāʿ* ("heaven" or "sky") is applied to anything that is spread like a canopy above any other thing. Thus, the

184

visible skies which stretch like a vault above the earth and form, as it were, its canopy, are called *samāᶜ*, and this is the *primary* meaning of this term in the Qurʾān. In a wider sense, it has the connotation of "cosmic system." As regards the "seven heavens," it is to be borne in mind that in Arabic usage—and apparently in other Semitic languages as well—the number "seven" is often synonymous with "several," just as "seventy" or "seven hundred" often means "many" or "very many." This, taken together with the accepted linguistic definition that "every *samāᶜ* is a *samāᶜ* with regard to what is below it" (Rāghib), may explain the "seven heavens" as denoting the multiplicity of cosmic systems.

But you fail to grasp the manner of their glorifying Him: i.e., although everything in creation bears witness to the existence of a conscious Creative Will, man is only too often blind and deaf to this overwhelming evidence of God's ever-present almightiness. (Asad, pp. 8, 425)

The High Standard of Human Speech

And tell my servants that they should speak in a kind manner,
for truly Satan is ready to stir up discord between people.

[*Sūrah al-Isrā* 17:53]

This command refers to two situations. (1) Even to your enemies and the enemies of God you should speak fair: who are you to judge others? Judgment belongs to God alone, for He knows you (i.e., all mankind) best, and your personal knowledge is at best imperfect. And Satan is always trying to divide mankind. (2) Amongst yourselves, also, you should not entertain suspicions, but speak politely according to the best standards of human speech. A false or unkind word may destroy all your efforts at building up unity, because the forces of disruption are more numerous than the forces of unity. (A. Yusuf Ali, p. 709)

Compare 29:46: *Do not argue with the followers of earlier revelations otherwise than in the most kindly manner.* This stress on kindness and tact and, hence, on the use of reason alone in all religious discussions with adherents of other creeds is fully in tune with the basic, categorical injunction, *There shall be no coercion in matters of faith* [2:256]. (Asad, p. 416)

186

Invoke God

Say: "Invoke God,
or invoke the Most Gracious:
by whichever name you invoke Him,
His are all the attributes of perfection."
And do not be too loud in your prayer
nor speak it in too low a voice, but follow a middle way.

[*Sūrah al-Isrāʿ* 17:110]

Raḥmān, the Most Gracious, describes one of the attributes of God—His Grace and Mercy which come to the sinner even before he feels conscious of the end of it—the preventive Grace which saves God's servants from sin. God can be invoked either by His simple name, which includes all attributes, or in the highest Sufi philosophy, rises above all attributes, or by one of the names implying the attributes by which we try to explain His nature to our limited understanding. The attribute of Mercy in *Raḥmān* was particularly repugnant to the pagan Arabs; that is why special stress is laid on it in the Qurʾān.

The beautiful names of Allāh are many. For devotional purposes a list of 99 is made out in *ḥadīth* literature; that in Tirmidhī is considered authoritative.

All prayer should be pronounced with earnestness and humility, whether it is congregational prayer or the private outpouring of one's own soul. Such an attitude is not consistent with an over-loud pronunciation of the words, though in public prayers the standard of permissible loudness is naturally higher than in the case of private prayer. In public prayers, of course, the *aẓān* or call to prayer will be in a loud voice to be heard near and far, but the chants from the sacred book should be neither so loud as to attract the hostile notice of those who do not believe nor so low in tone as not to be heard by the whole congregation. (A. Yusuf Ali, p. 726)

All that Glitters

That which is on earth
We have made but as a glittering show for the earth
in order that We may test them
as to which of them are best in conduct.

[*Sūrah al-Kahf* 18:7]

This world's goods—worldly power, glory, wealth, position, and all that men scramble for—are but a fleeting show. The possession or want of them does not betoken a man's real value or position in the spiritual world, the world which is to endure. Yet they have their uses. They test a man's sterling quality. He Who becomes their slave loses rank in the spiritual world. He Who uses them if he gets them, and does not fall into despair if he does not get them, shows his true mettle and quality. His conduct proclaims him. (A. Yusuf Ali, p. 729)

Inshāʾallāh!

Do not say of anything "I shall be sure to do so and so tomorrow"
without adding "If God wills!"
And call your Sustainer to mind when you forget,
and say: "I hope that my Lord will guide me
ever closer even than this to the right path."

[*Sūrah al-Kahf* 18:23-24]

We must never rely upon our own resources so much as to forget God. If by any chance we do forget, we must come back to Him and keep Him in remembrance. In our life there is always the hope of drawing closer and closer to God. (A. Yusuf Ali, p. 736)

If the Seas Were Ink . . .

Say: "If the sea were ink for the words of my Sustainer
the sea would be used up sooner
than would the words of my Sustainer,
even if we added to it sea upon sea."

[*Sūrah al-Kahf* 18:109]

The words and signs and mercies of God are in all creation, and can never be fully set out in human language, however extended our means may be imagined to be. (A. Yusuf Ali, p. 759)

Endow with Love

Truly, those who have faith and do righteous deeds
will the Most Gracious endow with Love:
and only to this end have We made this easy to understand,
in your own tongue, [O Prophet],
so that you might convey thereby a glad tiding to the God-conscious,
and warn thereby those who are given to contention.

[*Sūrah Maryam* 19:96-97]

Those who keep the faith and do righteous deeds: God will bestow on them His love and endow them with the capability to love His creation, as well as cause them to be loved by their fellow-men. This gift of love is inherent in the guidance offered to man through divine revelation. Since man is incapable of understanding the "word" of God as such, it has always been revealed to him in his own, human tongue (*Never have We sent forth any apostle otherwise than [with a message] in his own people's tongue* [14:4]), and has always been expounded in concepts accessible to the human mind. Hence the reference to the Prophet's revelations as "brought down *upon your heart*" [2:97] or "[divine inspiration] has alighted with it *upon your heart*" [26:193-194]. (Asad, p. 469)

Will the Most Gracious endow with Love: His own love, and the love of man's fellow creatures, in this world and in the Hereafter. Goodness breeds love and peace, and sin breeds hatred and contention. (A. Yusuf Ali, p. 786)

192

Increase My Knowing

Do not be hasty with the Qurᶜān
before its revelation to you is complete,
but say: "O my Sustainer! Increase me in knowledge."

[*Sūrah Ṭā Hā* 20:114]

God is above every human event or desire. His purpose is universal. But He is the Truth, the absolute Truth; and His kingdom is the true kingdom that can carry out His will. That Truth unfolds itself gradually, as it did in the gradual revelation of the Qurʾān to the holy apostle. But even after it was completed in a volume, its true meaning and purpose only gradually unfold themselves to any given individual or nation. No one should be impatient about it. On the contrary, we should always pray for increase in our own knowledge, which can never at any given moment be complete. (A. Yusuf Ali, p. 814)

Although it is very probable that—as most of the classical commentators point out—this exhortation was in the first instance addressed to the Prophet Muḥammad, there is no doubt that it applies to every person, at all times, who reads the Qurʾān. The idea underlying the above verse may be summed up thus: Since the Qurʾān is the Word of God, all its component parts—phrases, sentences, verses, and *sūrahs*—form one integral, coordinated whole. Hence, if one is really intent on understanding the Qurʾanic message, one must beware of a "hasty approach"—that is to say, of drawing hasty conclusions from isolated verses or sentences taken out of context—but should, rather, allow the *whole* of the Qurʾān to be re-

193

vealed to one's mind before attempting to interpret single aspects of its message. In 75:16-19, it says: *Move not your tongue in haste [repeating the words of the revelation]: for, behold, it is for Us to gather it [in your heart] and to cause it to be read [as it ought to be read]. Thus, when We recite it, follow you its wording [with all your mind]: and then, behold, it will be for Us to make its meaning clear."* This lays stress on the need to imbibe the divine writ slowly, patiently, to give full thought to the meaning of every word and phrase and to avoid the kind of haste which is indistinguishable from mechanical glibness, and which, moreover, induces the person who reads, recites, or listens to it to remain satisfied with the mere beautiful sound of the Qur'anic language without understanding—or even paying adequate attention to—its message. (Asad, pp. 483, 913)

The Tempting Lie

But Satan whispered to him, saying:
"O Adam! Shall I lead you to the tree of eternal life,
and thus to a kingdom that will never decay?
And so the two ate from it:
and thereupon they became conscious of their nakedness
and began to cover themselves
with pieced-together leaves from the garden.
And thus did Adam disobey his Sustainer,
and thus did he fall into grievous error.

[*Sūrah Ṭā Hā* 20:120-121]

Not only had the warning been given that Evil is an enemy to man and will effect his destruction, but it was clearly pointed out that all his needs were being met in the Garden of Happiness. Food and clothing, drink and shelter, were amply provided for. By these terms we must understand, if the Garden was a spiritual Garden, also spiritual good: the things that feed the soul and make it glad, that give it an aesthetic sense of beauty and afford it shelter from extremes of passion or emotion.

The suggestion of the Evil One is clever, as it always is: it is false, and at the same time plausible. It is false because (1) that felicity was not temporary, like the life of this world, and (2) they were supreme in the Garden, and a "kingdom" such as was dangled before them would only add to their sorrows. It was plausible, because (1) nothing had been said to them about Eternity, as the opposite of Eternity was not yet known, and (2) the sweets of power arise from the savor of Self, and Self's alluring (if false) attraction misleads the will. Hitherto they were clothed in the garb of innocence and knew no evil. Now when disobedience to God had sullied their soul and torn off the garment of their innocence, their sullied Self appeared to them in all its nakedness and ugliness, and they had to resort to external things (leaves of the Garden) to cover the shame of their self-consciousness.

Adam had been given the will to choose, and he chose wrong, and was about to be lost in the throng of the evil ones, when God's Grace came to his aid. His repentance was accepted, and God chose him for His mercy. (A. Yusuf Ali, pp. 815-816)

This symbolic tree is designated in the Bible as "the tree of life" and "the tree of the knowledge of good and evil" (Genesis 2:9), while, in the above Qur'anic account Satan speaks of it as *the tree of life eternal* (al-khuld). Seeing that Adam and Eve did not achieve immortality despite their tasting the forbidden fruit, it is obvious that Satan's suggestion was, as it always is, deceptive. On the other hand, the Qur'ān tells us nothing about the real nature of that "tree" beyond pointing out that it was *Satan* who described it—falsely—as *the tree of immortality,* and so we may assume that the forbidden tree is simply an allegory of the limits which the Creator has set to man's desires and actions: limits beyond which he may not go without offending against his own, God-willed nature. Man's desire for immortality *on earth* implies a wishful denial of death and resurrection, and thus of the ultimate reality of what the Qur'ān describes as "the hereafter" or "the life to come" (al-ākhirah). This desire is intimately connected with Satan's insinuation that it is within man's reach to become the master of *a kingdom that will never decay:* in other words, to become "free" of all limitations and thus, in the last resort, of the very concept of God—the only concept which endows human life with real meaning and purpose. (Asad, p. 484)

The Origin of Life and the Universe

Are, then, they who are bent on denying the truth
not aware that the heavens and the earth were once one single entity,
which We then parted asunder?—
*and that **We made every living thing out of water?***
Will they not, then, believe?

[*Sūrah al-Anbiyāᶜ* 21:30]

It is, as a rule, futile to make an explanation of the Qurʾān dependent on "scientific findings" which may appear true today, but may equally well be disproved tomorrow by new findings. Nevertheless, the above unmistakable reference to the unitary origin of the universe—metonymically described in the Qurʾān as *the heavens and the earth*—strikingly anticipates the view of almost all modern astrophysicists that this universe has originated as one entity from one single element, namely, hydrogen, which became subsequently consolidated through gravity and then separated into individual nebulae, galaxies, and solar systems, with further individual parts progressively breaking away to form new entities in the shape of stars, planets, and the latters' satellites.

The statement that God *made out of water every living thing* expresses most concisely a truth that is nowadays universally accepted by science. It has a threefold meaning: (1) water—and, specifically, the sea—was the environment within which the prototype of all living matter originated; (2) among all the innumerable—existing or conceivable—liquids, only water has the peculiar properties necessary for the emergence and development of life; and (3) the protoplasm, which is the physical basis of

197

every living cell—whether in plants or in animals—and which represents the only form of matter in which the phenomena of life are manifested, consists overwhelmingly of water and is, thus, utterly dependent on it. Read together with the preceding statement, which alludes to the unitary origin of the physical universe, the emergence of life from and within an equally unitary element points to the existence of a unitary *plan* underlying all creation and, hence, to the existence and oneness of the Creator. (Asad, pp. 491-492)

Permission to Fight

Permission is given to those who fight because they have been wronged.
Surely God is able to help them,
who were driven from their homes for no cause,
except for saying "Our Sustainer is God."
Had God not driven back some people
by means of others,
cloisters, churches, temples and mosques,
in which God's name is recollected,
would surely have been destroyed.
It is certain God will help whomever helps Him.
Surely God is All-Prevailing and Powerful.

[*Sūrah al-Ḥajj* 22:39-40]

Yūqatulūna is in the passive voice, *against whom war is made; those who fight because they have been wronged.* The wrong is indicated: *driven from their homes without cause except for saying "Our Sustainer is God."* This was the first occasion on which fighting—in self-defense—was permitted. This passage undoubtedly dates from Medina.

Had God not driven back some people by means of others: compare this to 2:251, where this expression is used in connection with David's fight against the Philistines, *By Allāh's will they routed them: and David slew Goliath, and Allāh gave him power and wisdom and taught him whatever He willed. And did not Allāh check one set of people by means of another, the earth would indeed be full of mischief. But Allāh is full of bounty to all the worlds.* To allow a righteous people to fight against a ferocious and mischief-loving people

199

was fully justified. But the justification was far greater here, when the little Muslim community was not only fighting for its own existence against the Meccan Quraish, but for the very existence of the faith in the one true God. They had as much right to be in Mecca and worship in the Ka'bah as the other Quraish: yet they were exiled for their faith. It affected not the faith of one peculiar people. The principle involved was that of all worship, Jewish or Christian as well as Muslim, and of all foundations built for pious use.

Surely God is All-Prevailing and Powerful: ʿazīz means exalted in power, rank, dignity, incomparable, full of might and majesty, able to enforce His will. The last signification is the one that predominates here. (A. Yusuf Ali, pp. 861–862)

Strive Hard

O you who have attained to faith!
Bow down and prostrate yourselves, and worship your Sustainer,
and do good, so that you might attain to a happy state!
And strive hard in God's cause with all the striving that is due to Him:
it is He Who has chosen you,
and has laid no hardship on you in religion,
the creed of your forefather Abraham.

[*Sūrah al-Ḥajj* 22:77-78]

And strive hard in God's cause with all the striving that is due to Him. The striving, or *jihād*, is outward in its narrow sense. In general, it may be said that Islam is the religion of peace, good will, mutual understanding, and good faith. But it will not acquiesce in wrong-doing, and its men will hold their lives cheap in defense of honor, justice, and the religion which they hold sacred. Their ideal is that of heroic virtue combined with unselfish gentleness and tenderness, such as is exemplified in the life of the Apostle. They believe in courage, obedience, discipline, duty, and a constant striving by all the means in their power—physical, moral, intellectual, and spiritual—for the establishment of truth and righteousness. War is only permissible in self-defense and under well-defined limits. When undertaken, it must be pushed with vigor but not relentlessly, but only to restore peace and freedom for the worship of God. In any case, strict limits must not be transgressed: women, children, old and infirm men should not be molested, nor trees and crops cut down, nor peace withheld when the enemy comes to terms. The *jihād* can also be considered more gen-

201

eral, applying to all true and unselfish striving for spiritual good.

He . . . has laid no hardship on you in religion, the creed of your forefather, Abraham. The Jews were hampered by many restrictions, and their religion was racial. Christianity, as originally preached, was a hermit religion: "sell whatsoever you have" (Mark 10:21); "take no thought for the morrow" (Matt. 6:34). Islam, as originally preached, gives freedom and full play to man's faculties of every kind. It is universal, and claims to date from Adam: father Abraham is mentioned as the great ancestor of those among whom Islam was first preached (Jews, Christians, and Arab Quraish). (A. Yusuf Ali, pp. 76, 75, 872)

The absence of any *hardship* in the religion of Islam is due to several factors: (1) it is free of any dogma or mystical proposition which might make the Qur'anic doctrine difficult to understand or might even conflict with man's innate reason; (2) it avoids all complicated ritual or system of taboos which would impose undue restrictions on man's everyday life; (3) it rejects all self-mortification and exaggerated asceticism, which must unavoidably conflict with man's true nature, and (4) it takes fully into account the fact that *man has been created weak* [4:28]. (Asad, pp. 517-518)

The Unity of Prophets

O you Prophets! Partake of the good things of life,
and do righteous deeds:
truly, I have full knowledge of all that you do.
And, truly, this community of yours is one single community,
since I am the Sustainer of you all: remain, then, conscious of Me!
But they have torn their unity wide asunder, piece by piece,
each group delighting in what they themselves possess.

[*Sūrah al-Muʿminūn* 23:51-53]

The men of God do not pose as ascetics but receive gratefully all God's gifts, and show their gratitude by their righteous lives.

All prophets form one brotherhood (see 21:92): their message is one, and their religion and teaching are one; they serve the one true God, Who loves and cherishes them; and they owe their duty to Him and Him alone. The people who began to trade on the names of the prophets cut off that unity and made sects, and each sect rejoices in its own narrow doctrine, instead of taking the universal teaching of unity from God. But this sectarian confusion is of man's making. It will last for a time, but the rays of truth and unity will finally dissipate it. (A. Yusuf Ali, pp. 883-884)

Partake of the good things of life, as a rhetorical apostrophe to all of God's apostles, is meant to stress their humanness and mortality, and thus to refute the argument of the unbelievers that God could not have chosen "a mortal like ourselves' to be His message-bearer: an argument which overlooks the fact that only human beings who themselves *partake of the good things of life* are able to understand the needs and motives of their fellow-men and, thus, to guide them in their spiritual and social concerns.

This community of yours is one single community is addressed to all who truly believe in God, whatever their historical denomination. By the preceding reference to *all* of God's apostles the Qur'ān clearly implies that all of them were inspired by, and preached, the same fundamental truths, notwithstanding all the differences in the ritual or the specific laws which they propounded in accordance with the exigencies of the time and the social development of their followers.

They have torn their unity wide asunder, literally, "in what they have [themselves]." In the first instance, this verse refers to the various religious groups as such: that is to say, to the followers of one or another of the earlier revelations who, in the course of time, consolidated themselves within different "denominations," each of them jealously guarding its own set of tenets, dogmas, and rituals and intensely intolerant of all other ways of worship. In the second instance, however, the above condemnation applies to the breach of unity *within* each of the established religious groups; and since it applies to the followers of *all* the prophets, it includes the latter-day followers of Muḥammad as well, and thus constitutes a prediction and condemnation of the doctrinal disunity prevailing in the world of Islam in our times. In regards to this, consider the well-authenticated saying of the Prophet quoted by Ibn Ḥanbal, Abū Dā'ūd, Tirmidhī and Dārimī: "The Jews have been split up into seventy-one sects, the Christians into seventy-two sects, whereas my community will be split up into seventy-three sects." (It should be remembered that in classical Arabic usage, the number "seventy" often stands for "many"— just as "seven" stands for "several" or "various"—and does not necessarily denote an actual figure; hence, what the Prophet meant to say was that the sects and divisions among the Muslims of later days would become many, and even more numerous than those among the Jews and Christians.) The Qur'ān impresses upon all who believe in God—Muslims and non-Muslims alike—that the differences in their religious practices should make them "vie with one another in doing good works" rather than lose themselves in mutual hostility. *Unto every one of you have We appointed a [different] law and way of life. And if God had so willed, He could surely have made you all one single community: but [He willed it otherwise] in order to test you by means of what He has vouchsafed to you. Vie, then, with one another in doing good works! Unto God you all must return; and then He will make you truly understand all that on which you were wont to differ.* [5:48]. (Asad, pp. 524, 154).

The Light of the Heavens and the Earth

God is the Light of the heavens and the earth.
The parable of His light is,
as it were, that of a niche containing a lamp;
the lamp is enclosed in glass, the glass like a radiant star;
lit from a blessed tree—an olive-tree
that is neither of the east nor of the west—
the oil of which would almost give light
even though fire had not touched it: light upon light!
God guides to His light the one whom He wills to be guided;
and God offers parables to human beings,
since God has full knowledge of all things.

[*Sūrah an-Nūr* 24:35]

The parable of *the light of God* is not meant to express His reality—which is inconceivable to any created being and, therefore, inexpressible in any human language—but only to allude to the illumination which He, who is the Ultimate Truth, bestows upon the mind and the feelings of all who are willing to be guided. In the above context, the particle *ka* ("as if" or "as it were") prefixed to a noun is called *kāf at-tashbīh* ("the letter *kāf* pointing to a resemblance [of one thing to another]" or "indicating a metaphor"). It alludes to the *impossibility* of defining God even by means of a metaphor or a parable—for, since *there is nothing like to Him* [42:11], there is also *nothing that could be compared with Him* [112:4]. Ṭabarī, Baghawī, and Ibn Kathīr quote Ibn 'Abbās and Ibn Mas'ūd as saying in this context: "It is the parable of His light *in the heart* of a believer."

206

The *lamp* is the revelation which God grants to His prophets and which is reflected in the believer's heart—the *niche* of the above parable (Ubayy ibn Ka'b, as quoted by Ṭabarī)—after being received and consciously grasped by his reason (*the glass [shining brightly] like a radiant star*): for it is through reason alone that true faith can find its way into the heart of man.

Neither of the east nor of the west: it would seem that this is an allusion to the organic continuity of all divine revelation which, starting like a tree from one "root" or proposition—the statement of God's existence and uniqueness—grows steadily throughout man's spiritual history, branching out into a splendid variety of religious experience, thus endlessly widening the range of man's perception of the truth. The association of this concept with the olive tree apparently arises from the fact that this particular kind of tree is characteristic of the lands in which most of the prophetic precursors of the Qur'anic message lived, namely, the lands to the east of the Mediterranean but since all true revelation flows from the Infinite Being, it is *neither of the east nor or the west*—and especially so the revelation of the Qur'ān which, being addressed to all mankind, is universal in its goal as well.

Light upon light: the essence of the Qur'anic message is described elsewhere as *clear [in itself] and clearly showing the truth* [12:1] and it is, I believe this aspect of the Qur'ān that the above sentence alludes to. Its message gives light because it proceeds from God; but *it would well-nigh give light [of itself] even though fire had not touched it*: i.e., even though one may be unaware that it has been *touched by the fire* of divine revelation, its inner consistency, truth, and wisdom ought to be self-evident to anyone who approaches it in the light of his reason and without prejudice.

God guides to His light him that wills [to be guided] is interpreted by most commentators as *God guides to His light whomever He wills*. Zamakhsharī gives it the sense adopted in my rendering, *God guides to His light him that wills [to be guided]* (both being syntactically permissible).

God propounds parables to men, since God [alone] has full knowledge of all things, i.e., because of their complexity, certain truths can be conveyed to man only by means of parables or allegories. (Asad, p. 541)

This glorious parable of light contains layer upon layer of allegorical truth about spiritual mysteries. No notes can do adequate justice to its full meaning. Volumes have been written on this subject, the most notable being Imām Ghazāli's *Mishkāt-ul-Anwar*. In these notes I propose to explain the simplest meaning of this passage, reserving a brief account of Ghazāli's exposition for the end.

The physical light is but a reflection of the true light in the world of reality, and that true Light is God. We can only think of God in terms of our phenomenal experience, and in the phenomenal world, light is the purest thing we know. But physical light has drawbacks incidental to its physical nature, e.g., (1) it is dependent upon some source external to itself; (2) it is a passing phenomenon; if we take it to be a form of motion or energy it is unstable, like all physical phenomena; (3) it is dependent on space and time; its speed is 186,000 miles per second, and there are stars whose light takes thousands of years before it reaches the earth. The perfect Light of God is free from any such defects.

The first three points in the parable center round the symbols of the niche, the lamp, and the glass. (1) The niche (*mishkāt*) is the little shallow recess in the wall of an Eastern house, fairly high from the ground, in which a light (before the days of electricity) was usually placed. Its height enabled it to diffuse the light in the room and minimize the shadows. The background of the wall and the sides of the niche helped to throw the light well into the room, and if the wall was whitewashed, it also acted as a reflector. The opening in front made the way for the light. So with the spiritual Light: it is placed high above worldly things; it has a niche or habitation of its own, in revelation and other signs of God; its access to men is by a special way, open to all, yet closed to those who refuse its rays. (2) The lamp is the core of the spiritual truth, which is the real illumination; the niche is nothing without it, the niche is actually made for it. (3) The glass is the transparent medium through which the light passes. On the one hand, it protects the light from moths and other forms of low life (lower motives in man) and from gusts of wind (passions) and on the other, it transmits the light through a medium which is made up of and akin to the grosser substances of the earth (such as sand, soda, potash, etc.) so arranged as to admit the subtle to the gross by its transparency. So the spiritual truth has to be filtered through human language or human intelligence to make it intelligible to mankind. The glass by itself does not shine. But when the light comes into it, it shines like a brilliant star. So men of God, who preach God's truth, are themselves illuminated by God's Light and become the illuminating media through which that Light spreads and permeates human life.

The olive tree is not a very impressive tree in its outward appearance. Its leaves have a dull, greenish-brown color, and in size it is inconspicuous. But its oil is used in sacred ceremonies and forms a wholesome ingredient of food. The fruit has a specially fine flavor. This mystic olive is not localized. It is neither of the East nor of the West. It is universal, for such is God's Light. As applied to the olive, there is also a more literal meaning, which can be allegorized in a different way. An olive tree with an eastern aspect gets only the rays of the morning sun; one with a western aspect, only the rays of the western sun. In the northern hemisphere the south aspect will give the sun's rays a great part of the day, while a north aspect will shut them out altogether, and *vice versa* in the southern hemisphere. But a tree in the open plain or on a hill will get perpetual sunshine by day: it will be more mature, and the fruit and oil will be of superior quality. So God's Light is not localized or immature: it is perfect and universal.

Pure olive oil is beautiful in color, consistency, and illuminating power. The world has tried all kinds of illuminants, and for economic reasons or convenience, one replaces another. But for coolness, comfort to the eyes, and steadiness, vegetable oils are superior to electricity, mineral oils, and animal oils. And among vegetable oils, olive oil takes a high place and deserves its sacred associations. Its purity is almost light itself: you may suppose it to be almost light before it is lit. So with spiritual truth: it illuminates the mind and understanding imperceptibly, almost before the human mind and heart have been consciously touched by it.

Light upon Light! Glorious, illimitable Light, which cannot be described or measured. And there are grades and grades of it, passing transcendently into regions of spiritual height, which man's imagination can scarcely conceive of. The topmost pinnacle is the true prototypical Light, the real Light of which all others were reflections, the Light of God. Hence the saying of the holy Prophet about God's "seventy thousands veils of light." (A. Yusuf Ali, pp. 907-908)

Undistracted Remembrance

In the houses which God has allowed to be raised
so that His name shall be remembered in them,
there are those who praise His limitless glory
morning and evening—
those whom neither business nor striving after gain
can turn from the remembrance of God,
and from constancy in prayer, and from charity:
who are filled with awe
of the Day on which all hearts and eyes will be transformed,
who only hope that God will give them recompense
in accordance with the best of their actions,
and give them even more out of His blessing:
for God grants sustenance to whom He wills, beyond all reckoning.

[*Sūrah an-Nūr* 24:36-38]

This selection informs us of places where *God's name is remembered* and people who praise God's majesty, undistracted by business and gain. Since Islam does not promote monasticism, these are not people who have no business in the world, but people who are not distracted by the business they have. This is an example of being "in the world but not of it," which is so characteristic of Islamic spirituality. It suggests the possibility of reaching the highest level of spirituality while still accepting the responsibililities of everyday life.

These *āyāts* end with an eschatological statement, i.e., a proposal regarding how these lives will measure up in the light of eternity. While

211

they would hope that the Ruler of the Day of Reckoning would at least reward them in accordance with the "best of their actions," God's promise is even more generous: God will bestow blessings *beyond all reckoning*. (Helminski)

The Praise of Nature

Are you not aware that it is God whose limitless glory
all creatures in the heavens and on earth praise,
even the birds as they outspread their wings?
Indeed, each of them knows how to pray to Him and glorify Him;
and God has full knowledge of all that they do:
for God's is the sovereignty of the heavens and the earth,
and with God is all journeys' end.

[*Sūrah an-Nūr* 24:41-42]

Here a question is posed: *Are you not aware?* Can't you see that all of nature praises God in its own way, or are you so confined to your own limited point of view that you cannot see the natural world for what it is? What we take to be "normal" human consciousness, especially in this modern, technological age, may actually be a kind of blindness. We are encouraged to observe nature and see the glorification of a spiritual reality even in the outspread wings of birds. (Helminski)

The Blessing of Discernment

Blessed is the One Who
sent down Discernmentn to His servant
that it might be a counsel to all the world.

[*Sūrah al-Furqān* 25:1]

Blessed, or *tabāraka;* comes from the root meaning of "increase" or "abundance." Here that aspect of God's dealing with His creatures is emphasized which shows His abundant goodness to all His creatures, in that He sent the Revelation of His Will, not only in the unlimited book of nature, but in a definite book in human language, which gives clear direction and admonitions to all. The English word *blessed* hardly conveys that meaning, but I can find no other without departing far from established usage. To emphasize the meaning I have explained, I have translated *Blessed is . . .* , but *Blessed be . . .* is also admissible, as it brings out another shade of meaning, that we praise and bless His holy name.

The Criterion (or Discernment) is that by which we can judge clearly between right and wrong. Here the reference is to the Qur'ān, which has already been symbolized by Light. The symbol is continued here, and many contrasts are shown, in the midst of which we can distinguish between the true and the false by God's Light, especially the contrast between righteousness and sin.

That it might be a counsel: the pronoun "it" in *yakūna* may refer either to *Furqān* (the Criterion) or to *ᶜabd* (the holy Prophet). In either case, the ultimate meaning is the same. The Qur'ān is the standing Criterion for judgment between right and wrong. (A. Yusuf Ali, p. 926)

214

Walk in Humility upon the Earth

Blessed is He Who made constellations in the skies
and placed there a lamp and a moon giving light;
And it is God Who made the night and the day to follow each other,
for such as have the will to celebrate God's praises
or to show their gratitude.
And the servants of the Infinitely Compassionate
are those who walk on the earth in humility
and when the ignorant address them they say, "Peace!"—
those who spend the night in adoration of their Sustainer
in prostration and standing upright.

[*Sūrah al-Furqān* 25:61-64]

When the ignorant address them, they say, "Peace!". "Ignorant" is used in a spiritual sense; "address" in the aggressive sense. Their humility is shown in two ways: (1) to those in real search of knowledge, they give such knowledge as they have and as the recipients can assimilate; (2) to those who merely dispute, they do not speak harshly, but say *Peace!* as much as to say, "May it be well with you, may you repent and be better," or "May God give me peace from such wrangling," or "Peace and good-bye; let me leave you!"

Those who spend the night in adoration of their Sustainer in prostration and standing upright: humble prayer brings them nearer to God. (A. Yusuf Ali, pp. 941-942)

215

A Sound Heart

And let me not be in disgrace on the Day when we will be raised up,
the Day when neither wealth nor children will be of use,
but only the one who brings to God a sound heart.
(Prayer of Abraham)

[*Sūrah ash-Shuʿarāʾ* 26:87-89]

Now we have a vision of the Day of Judgment. Nothing will then avail except a pure heart; all sorts of the so-called "good deeds" of this world, without the motive of purity, will be useless. The contrast of the Garden of Bliss with the Fire of Misery will be plainly visible. Evil will be shown in its true colors—isolated, helpless, cursing, and despairing—and all chances will then have been lost. (A. Yusuf Ali, p. 957)

Turn Aside from Idle Talk

Twice will they be given their reward
because they have persevered:
they have turned aside evil with good,
and they give to others from what We have given to them.
And when they hear vain talk they turn away from it and say:
"To us our deeds and to you yours;
peace be with you: we do not seek the ignorant."

[*Sūrah al-Qaṣaṣ* 28:54-55]

The righteous do not encourage idle talk or foolish arguments about things sacred. If they find themselves in some company in which such things are fashionable, they leave politely. Their only rejoinder is: "We are responsible for our deeds, and you for yours. We have no ill-will against you; we wish you well, and that is why we wish you to know of the knowledge we have received. After that knowledge you cannot expect us to go back to the ignorance which we have left." (A. Yusuf Ali, p. 1017)

Everything is Perishing except His Face

And let nothing inhibit you from the signs of God
after they have been revealed to you;
and invite to your Sustainer,
and do not be among those who join gods with God.
And do not call on another god besides God.
There is no god but He.
Everything is perishing except His Face.
To Him belongs the Command,
and to Him will you all return.

[*Sūrah al-Qaṣaṣ* 28:87-88]

This sums up the lesson of this whole *sūrah*. The only Reality is God. His "Face" or self, personality, or being is what we should seek, knowing that it is the only enduring thing of which we can have any conception. The whole phenomenal world is subject to flux and change and will pass away, but He will endure for ever. If we think of an impersonal God, an abstract force of good, we cannot reconcile it with the vital Self or Being, of which we have a faint echo or reflection in our most intense moments of spiritual exaltation. We know then that what we call our own self has no meaning, for there is only one true Self, and that is God. This is also the Advaita doctrine of Shrī Shankara in his exposition of the *Brihadaranyaka Upanishad* in Hindu philosophy. (A. Yusuf Ali, p. 1027)

218

Travel

Say: "Travel through the earth
and see how God originated creation.
Even so will God create again,
for God has power over all things."

[*Sūrah al-ʿAnkabūt* 29:20]

Travel through the earth: literally as well as symbolically. If we actually go through this wide earth, we shall see the wonderful things in His creation: the Grand Canyon and the Niagaras in America, beautiful harbors like that at Sydney in Australia, mountains like Fujiyama, the Himalayas, and Elburz in Asia, the Nile with its wonderful cataracts in Africa, the fjords of Norway, the geysers of Iceland, the city of the midnight sun in Tromsoe, and innumerable wonders everywhere. But wonders upon wonders are disclosed in the constitution of matter itself, the atom, and the forces of energy, as also in the instincts of animals, and the minds and capacities of man. And there is no limit to these things. Worlds upon worlds are created and transformed every moment, within and presumably beyond man's vision. From what we know we can judge of the unknown. (A. Yusuf Ali, p. 1033)

The Spider

The parable of those who take protectors other than God
is that of the Spider who builds itself a house;
but truly, the Spider's house is the flimsiest of houses
if they only knew.
Truly, your Sustainer knows what they call upon besides Him
and He is Most Exalted, the All-Wise.
And such are the parables We offer humankind
but only those of inner knowing understand them.
In accordance with [an inner] truth
God created the heavens and the earth:
truly, in that is a sign for those who have faith.

[*Sūrah al-ᶜAnkabūt* 29:41-44]

The spider's house is one of the wonderful signs of Allāh's creation. It is made up of fine silk threads spun out of silk glands in the spider's body. There are many kinds of spiders and many kinds of spider's houses. Two main types of houses may be mentioned. There is the tubular nest or web, a silk-lined house or burrow with one or two trap doors. This may be called his residential or family mansion. Then there is what is ordinarily called a spider's web, consisting of a central point with radiating threads running in all directions and acting as tie-beams to the quasi-circular concentric threads that form the body of the web. This is his hunting box. The whole structure exemplifies economy in time, material, and strength. If an insect is caught in the net, the vibration set up in the radiating threads is at once communicated to the spider, who can come

220

and kill his prey. In case the prey is powerful, the spider is furnished with poison glands with which to kill his prey. The spider sits either in the center of the web or hides on the underside of a leaf or in some crevice, but he always has a single thread connecting him with his web, to keep him in telephonic communication. The female spider is much bigger than the male, and in Arabic the generic gender of ʿankabūt (the name of this sūrah) is feminine.

The facts describing the spider can be read into the parable. For their thickness, the spider's threads are very strong from the point of view of relativity, but in our actual world they are flimsy, especially the threads of the gossamer spider floating in the air. So is the house and strength of the man who relies on material resources, however fine or beautiful relatively; before the eternal Reality they are as nothing. The spider's most cunning architecture cannot stand against a wave of a man's hand. His poison glands are like the hidden poison in our beautiful worldly plans which may take various shapes but have seeds of death in them. Men, out of spiritual ignorance, build their hopes on flimsy unsubstantial things (like the spider's web) which are broken by a thousand chance attacks of wind and weather or the actions of animals or men. If they cannot fully grasp their own good, they should seek His Light. To Him everything is known: men's frailty, their false hopes, their questionable motives, the false gods whom they enthrone in their midst, the mischief done by the neglect of truth, and the way out for those who have entangled themselves in the snares of evil. He is All-Wise and is able to carry out all He wills, and they should turn to Him.

Such are the parables We offer humankind, but only those of inner knowing understand them. Parables seem simple things, but their profound meaning and application can only be understood by those who seek knowledge and by Allāh's grace attain it.

In true proportions God created the heavens and the earth: truly, in that is a sign for those who have faith. Do not stop short at the wonders of nature, but penetrate "from nature up to nature's God." God not only created the heavens and the earth: with every increase of knowledge we see in what true and perfect proportions all creation is held together. Creatures are subject to time, but the Creator is not; His word is the key that opens the door of existence. In all Allāh's creation, not only is there evidence of intelligent purpose, fitting all parts together with wisdom, but also of supreme goodness and cherishing care, by which all needs are satisfied and all the highest and truest cravings fulfilled. These are like beckoning signals to lead on those who pray and search in faith. (A. Yusuf Ali, p. 1040)

Remembrance is the Greatest

Recite what is sent of the Book by inspiration to you
and establish regular prayer:
for prayer restrains from shameful and unjust deeds,
and remembrance of God is surely the greatest of all.
And God knows that which you do.

[*Sūrah al-ᶜAnkabūt* 29:45]

The *tilawat* of the Qurʾān implies: (1) rehearsing or reciting it, and publishing it abroad to the world; (2) reading it to ourselves; (3) studying it to understand it as it should be studied and understood: *Those to whom We have sent the book study it as it should be studied; they are the ones that believe in it; those who reject it, they are the losers* [2:121]; (4) meditating on it so as to accord our knowledge and life and desires with it. When this is done, it merges into real prayer, and prayer purges us of anything (act, plan, thought, motive, words) of which we should be ashamed or which would work injustice to others. Such prayer passes into our inmost life and being, for then we realize the presence of Allāh, and that is true *zikr* (or remembrance), for remembrance is the bringing to mind of things as present to us which might otherwise be absent to us. And that is the greatest thing in life. It is subjective to us: it fills our consciousness with Allāh. For Allāh is in any case always present and knows all. (A. Yusuf Ali, pp. 1041)

223

Self–Destructiveness

Do they not travel through the earth
and see what was the end of those before them?
They were superior to them in strength; they tilled the soil
and populated it more extensively than these have done;
there came to them their messengers with clear signs.
It was not God Who wronged them
but they who wronged their own souls.

[*Sūrah ar-Rūm* 30:9]

Let not any generation think that it is superior to all that went before it.
We may be "heirs to all ages, in the foremost files of times." That is no
reason for arrogance, but on the contrary adds to our responsibility.
When we realize what flourishing cities and kingdoms existed before,
how they flourished in numbers and prosperity, what chances they were
given, and how they perished when they disobeyed the law of Allāh, we
shall feel a sense of humility, and see that it was rebellion and self-will that
brought them down. Allāh was more than just; He was also merciful. But
they brought about their own ruin. (A. Yusuf Ali, p. 1053)

Life and Death

So glorify God when you reach the evening
and when you rise in the morning;
for all praise belongs to Him in the heavens and on earth,
and also in the late afternoon and when the day passes its zenith.
It is He Who brings out the living from the dead
and Who brings out the dead from the living,
and Who gives life to the earth after it has died,
and even so shall you all be brought forth.

[*Sūrah ar-Rūm* 30:17-19]

The special times for Allāh's remembrance are so described as to include all our activities in life: when we rise early in the morning, and when we go to rest in the evening; when we are in the midst of our work, at the decline of the sun, and in the late afternoon. It may be noted that these are all striking stages in the passage of the sun through our terrestrial day, as well as stages in our daily working lives. On this are based the hours of the five canonical prayers afterwards prescribed in Medina; namely, (1) early morning before sunrise (*fajr*); (2) when the day begins to decline, just after noon (*ẓuhr*); (3) in the late afternoon, say midway between noon and sunset, (*ᶜaṣr*); and (4) and (5) the two evening prayers, one just after sunset (*maghrib*) and the other after the evening twilight has all faded from the horizon, the hour indicated for rest and sleep (*ᶜishāᶜ*). *Therefore be patient with what they say and celebrate the praises of your Lord before the rising of the sun and before its setting; celebrate them for part of the hours of the night and at the sides of the day; that you may have spiritual joy* [20:130]. We must pray

225

to Allāh and commune with Him, so that our patience and faith may be strengthened, and we may be able the better to grapple with evil. For we thus not only get strength in this world but pleasure of Allāh in the Hereafter as well.

It is He Who brings out the living from the dead and Who brings out the dead from the living, and Who gives life to the earth after it has died, and even so shall you all be brought forth. Compare this to part of 2:164: *In the rain which Allāh sends down from the skies and the life which He gives to an earth that is dead.* From dead matter Allāh's creative act produces life and living matter, and even science has not yet been able to explain the mystery of life. Life and living matter again seem to reach maturity and again die, as we see every day. No material thing seems to have perpetual life. But again we see the creative process of Allāh constantly at work, and the cycle of life and death seems to go on. The earth itself, seemingly so inert, produces vegetable life at once from a single shower of rain, and in various ways sustains animal life. Normally it seems to die in the winter in northern climates, and in a drought everywhere, and the spring revives it in all its glory. Metaphorically, many movements, institutions, organizations, seem to die and then to live again, all under the wonderful dispensation of Allāh. So will our personality be revived when we die on this earth, in order to reap the fruit of this our probationary life. (A. Yusuf Ali, pp. 818, 1054-1055)

He Created for You Mates

Among the signs of God is this: that He created you from dust,
and then, see how you become human beings ranging far and wide!
And among His Signs is this: that He created for you mates
from among yourselves
that you may dwell in tranquillity with them,
and He engenders love and compassion between you;
truly in that are signs for those who reflect.

[*Sūrah ar-Rūm* 30:20-21]

Do you deny Him Who created you out of dust, then out of a drop of sperm, then fashioned you into a man? [18:37]. In spite of the lowly origin of man's body, Allāh has given him a mind and soul by which he can almost compass the farthest reaches of time and space. Is this not enough for a miracle or sign? From a physical point of view, see how man, a creature of dust, scatters himself over the farthest corners of the earth!

And among His signs is this: that He created for you mates from among yourselves that you may dwell in tranquility with them, and He engenders love and compassion between you. This refers to the wonderful mystery of sex. Children arise out of the union of the sexes. *It is He Who has created you all out of one soul, and out of it brought into being a mate, so that man might incline with love towards woman. And so, when he has embraced her, she conceives a light burden, and continues to bear it. Then, when she grows heavy with child, they both call to God, their Sustainer, "If You indeed grant us a sound child, we shall most certainly be among the grateful"*[7:189]. It is always the female sex that brings forth the offspring, whether female or male. But the father is as

227

necessary as the mother for bringing forth offspring.

Unregenerate man is pugnacious in the male sex, but rest and tran-quility are found in the normal relations of a father and mother dwelling together and bringing up a family. A man's chivalry to the opposite sex is natural and God-given. The friendship of two men between each other is quite different in quality and temper from the feeling which unspoilt na-ture expects as between men and women. There is a special kind of love and tenderness between them. And as woman is the weaker vessel, that tenderness may from a certain aspect be likened to mercy, the protecting kindness which the strong should give to the weak. (A. Yusuf Ali, pp. 1055-1056)

Variations in Your Languages and Colors

And among His signs is the creation of the heavens and the earth
and the variations in your languages and your colors:
truly in that are signs for those who know.
And among His signs is your sleep by night and by day
as well as your quest for provision from His Bounty:
truly, in that are signs for those who pay attention.
And among His Signs He shows you the lightning
by way both of fear and of hope
and He sends down rain from the sky
and with it gives life to the earth after it is dead:
truly, in that are signs for those who are wise.

[*Sūrah ar-Rūm* 30:22-24]

And among His signs is the creation of the heavens and the earth and the varia-
tions in your languages and your colors. The variations in languages and colors
may be viewed from the geographical aspect or from the aspect of periods
of time. All mankind were created of a single pair of parents, yet they
have spread to different countries and climates and developed different
languages and different shades of complexions. And yet their basic unity
remains unaltered. They feel in the same way, and are all equally under
Allāh's care. Then there are the variations in time. Old languages die out
and new ones are evolved. New conditions of life and thought are constantly evolving new words and expressions, new syntactical structures,
and new modes of pronunciation. Even old races die, and new races are
born.

229

And among His signs is your sleep by night and by day as well as your quest for provision from His Bounty. If we consider deeply, sleep and dreams, the refreshment we get from sleep to wakefulness as well as from wakefulness to sleep, as also the state of our thoughts and feelings and subconscious self in these conditions, are both wonderful and mysterious. Normally we sleep by night and do our ordinary work *in quest of the bounty of Allāh* by day. But sleep and rest may come and be necessary by day, and we may have to work by night. And our work for our livelihood may pass by insensible transitions to our work or thought or service of a higher and spiritual kind. These processes suggest a background of things which we know but vaguely, but which are as much miracles as other signs of Allāh.

These verses, 30:20-30:27 [see the next selection], mention a series of signs or miracles which should awaken our souls and lead us to true reality if we try to understand Allāh. (1) There is our own origin and destiny, which must necessarily be our subjective starting point: "I think, therefore I am." No particular exertion of our being is here necessary (30:20). (2) The first beginnings of social life arise through sex and love (4:1). To understand this in all its bearing, we must *reflect* (30:21). (3) The next point is to understand our diversities in speech, color, etc., arising from differences of climate and external conditions; yet there is unity beneath that diversity, which we shall realize by extended knowledge (30:22). (4) Next we turn to our psychological conditions, sleep, rest, visions, insight, etc.; here we want teaching and guidance, to which we must hearken (30:23). (5) Next, we must approach the higher reaches of spiritual hopes and fears, as symbolized by such subtle forces of nature as lightning and electricity, which may kill the foolish or bring prosperity in its train by rain and abundant harvest; to understand the highest spiritual hopes and fears so symbolized, we want the highest wisdom (30:24). (6) And lastly, we may become so transformed that we rise above all petty, worldly, ephemeral things: Allāh calls to us and we rise, as from our dead selves to a height which we can only describe as the heaven of stability: here no human processes serve, for the call of Allāh Himself has come

(30:25-27).

And among His signs He shows you the lightning by way both of fear and of hope and He sends down rain from the sky and with it gives life to the earth after it is dead. Compare 13:12: *It is He Who shows you the lightning by way both of fear and of hope: it is He Who raises up the clouds heavy with rain!* To cowards, lightning and thunder appear as terrible forces of nature: lightning seems to kill and destroy where its irresistible progress is not assisted by proper lightning-conductors. But lightning is also a herald of rain-bearing clouds and showers that bring fertility and prosperity in their train. This double aspect is also symbolical of spiritual fears and hopes: fears lest we may not be found receptive or worthy of the irresistible perspicuous message of Allāh, and hopes that we may receive it in the right spirit and be blessed by its mighty power of transformation to achieve spiritual well-being. Note that the repetition of the phrase *gives life to the earth after it is dead* connects this verse with verse 30:19 above. In other words, the Revelation, which we must receive with wisdom and understanding, is a sign of Allāh's own power and mercy and is vouchsafed in order to safeguard our own final future. (A. Yusuf Ali, pp. 1056-1057)

The Essence of the Most Sublime

And among His signs is this:
that heaven and earth stand by His Command.
Then, when He calls you from the earth by a single call,
witness, you will emerge.
To Him belongs every being that is in the heavens and on earth:
all devoutly obey Him.
It is He Who begins the unfolding of creation,
then repeats it; and it is most easy for Him.
For His is the essence of all that is most sublime
in the heavens and the earth:
for He is Exalted in Might, All-Wise.

[*Sūrah ar-Rūm* 30:25-27]

And among His signs is this: that heaven and earth stand by His Command. Then, when He calls you from the earth by a single call, witness, you will emerge. In the physical world, the sky and the earth, as we see them, stand unsupported, by the artistry of Allāh. They bear witness to Allāh, and in that our physical life depends on them—the earth for its produce and the sky for rain, the heat of the sun, and other phenomena of nature—they call to our mind our relation to Allāh Who made them and us. How can we then be so dense as not to realize that our higher future, our *maᶜād*, is bound up with the call and mercy of God?

To Him belongs every being that is in the heavens and on earth: all devoutly obey Him. All nature in creation not only obeys Allāh, but devoutly obeys Him, i.e., glories in its privilege of services and obedience. Why should

232

we not do likewise? It is part of our original unspoilt nature, and we must respond to it, as all beings do, by their very nature.

It is He Who begins the unfolding of creation, then repeats it; and it is most easy for Him. Compare to 30:11, where the same phrase began the argument about the beginning and end of all things being with Allāh: *It is Allāh Who begins the unfolding of creation, then repeats it; then shall you be brought back to Him.* This has been illustrated by reference to various signs in creation, and now the argument is rounded off with the same phrase. Allāh's glory and Allāh's attributes are above any names we can give to them. Human language is not adequate to express them. We can only form some idea of them at our present stage by means of similitudes and parables. But even so, the highest we can think of falls short of the true reality. For Allāh is higher and wiser than the highest and wisest we can think of. (A. Yusuf Ali, pp. 1057-1058)

The Primordial Religion

Turn your face with purity toward the primordial religion (dīn ḥanīfā),
according to the innate nature (fiṭrah)
with which He has made humankind;
do not allow what God has made to be corrupted.
That is authentic religion,
but most people do not understand.
Turn in repentance to Him and remain conscious of Him:
be constant in prayer
and do not be among those
who confuse other powers with God,
those who split apart their religion and create sects—
each group separately rejoicing in what it has!

[*Sūrah ar-Rūm* 30:30-32]

Truly, this community of yours is one single community, since I am the Sustainer of you all: remain, then, conscious of Me! [23:52, very similar to 21:92]. These verses are addressed to all who truly believe in God, whatever their historical denomination. By the reference to *all* of God's apostles, the Qurʾān clearly implies that all of them were inspired by, and preached, the same fundamental truths, notwithstanding all the differences in the ritual or the specific laws which they propounded in accordance with the exigencies of the time and the social development of their followers.

In reference to creating sects, this refers to the various religious groups, the followers of one or another of the earlier revelations who, in the course of time, consolidated themselves within different "denomina-

234

tions," each of them jealously guarding its own set of tenets, dogmas, and rituals and intensely intolerant of all other ways of worship. The above condemnation also applies to the breach of unity *within* each of the established religious groups; and since it applies to the followers of *all* the prophets, it includes the latter-day followers of Muḥammad as well, and thus constitutes a prediction and condemnation of the doctrinal disunity prevailing in the world of Islam in our times. [See 23:51-53.] (Asad, p. 524)

Ḥanīf means inclined to right opinion, firm in faith, sound and well-balanced, true. Perhaps the last word, true, sums up most of the other shades. Here, "true" is used in the sense in which we say "the magnetic needle is true to the north." Those who have been privileged to receive the Truth should never hesitate or swerve, but remain constant, as men who know. The pure, *ḥanīf* doctrine of Abraham was to live and die in faith in the One True God.

As turned out from the creative hand of God, man is innocent, pure, true, free, inclined to right and virtue, and endued with true understanding about his own position in the universe and about God's goodness, wisdom, and power. That is his true nature, just as the nature of a lamb is to be gentle and of a horse is to be swift. But man is caught in the meshes of customs, superstitions, selfish desires, and false teaching. This may make him pugnacious, unclean, false, slavishly hankering after what is wrong or forbidden, and deflected from the love of his fellow men and the pure worship of the One True God. The problem before spiritual teachers is to cure the crookedness and to restore human nature to what it should be under the Will of God.

Authentic religion or *dīn qaiyīm,* includes the whole life, thoughts, and desires of men. The "standard religion" or "straight way" is thus contrasted with the various human systems that conflict with each other and call themselves separate "religions" or "sects." God's standard religion is one, as God is One.

Repentance does not mean sackcloth and ashes, or putting on a gloomy pessimism. It means giving up disease for health, crookedness (which is abnormal) for the straight way, the restoration of our nature as God created it from the falsity introduced by the enticements of evil. To revert to the simile of the magnetic needle, if the needle is held back by obstructions, we must restore its freedom, so that it points true again to the magnetic pole. (A. Yusuf Ali, pp. 55, 1059-1060)

Illusory Time

And when the Last Hour dawns, those who had been lost in sin
will swear that they had not tarried on earth longer than an hour:
thus were they used to deluding themselves [all their lives]!

[*Sūrah ar-Rūm* 30:55]

The illusory character of man's earthbound concept of "time" is brought out in the Qur'ān in several places. In the above context, stress is laid, firstly, on the *relativity* of this concept—i.e., on the infinitesimal shortness of our life on earth as compared with the timeless duration of life in the hereafter (compare, for instance, 10:45 or 17:52)—and, secondly, on the resurrected sinners' self-deluding excuse that their life on earth had been too short to allow them to realize their errors and mend their ways. It is to this second aspect of the problem that the Qur'ān alludes in the words *thus were they wont to delude themselves* (literally, *to be turned away*, i.e., from the truth). The verb *yuʿfikūn* is related to the verb *afaka* which signifies "he turned [someone or something] away"; in an abstract sense it often denotes "he uttered a lie" (because it implies a turning away from the truth). The passive form *ufika* has frequently the meaning of "he was turned away from his opinion" (or "from his judgment") and thus, "his mind became perverted" or "deluded." (Asad, pp. 625-626, 159)

For Our Own Good

"Be grateful to God.
Anyone who gives thanks does so to the profit of his own soul;
but if anyone is ungrateful, truly God is free of all needs,
and ever to be praised."

[*Sūrah Luqmān* 31:12]

The sage Luqmān, after whom this *sūrah* is called, belongs to Arab tradition. Very little is known of his life. He is usually associated with a long life, and his title is *Muʿammar* (the long-lived). He is referred by some to the age of the ʿĀd people. Their eponymous ancestor ʿĀd was fourth in generation from Noah, having been a son of ʿAus, the son of Aram, the son of Sām, the son of Noah. They occupied a large tract of country in Southern Arabia, extending from ʿUmmān at the mouth of the Persian Gulf to Ḥadhramaut and Yemen at the southern end of the Red Sea.

Luqmān is the type of perfect wisdom. It is said that he belonged to a humble station in life, being a slave or carpenter, and that he refused worldly power and a kingdom. Many instructive apologues are credited to him, similar to Aesop's Fables in Greek tradition. The identification of Luqmān and Aesop has no historical foundation, though it is true that the traditions about them have influenced each other.

God is free of all needs. The basis of the moral law is man's own good, and not any benefit to God, for God is above all needs, and *worthy of all praise,* i.e., even in praising Him, we do not advance His glory. When we obey His Will, we bring our position into conformity with our own nature as made by Him. Compare 14:8: *If you show ingratitude—you and all*

238

on earth together—yet is Allāh free of all wants, worthy of all praise. Ingratitude is not only in feelings or words, but in disobedience, and willful rejection and rebellion. If the whole of you band together against God, you do not detract from God's power one atom, because God does not depend upon you for anything, and His goodness and righteousness and praiseworthiness cannot be called into question by your contumacy. (A. Yusuf Ali, pp. 1082, 358, 621)

Goodness Toward Parents

Witness, Luqmān counseled his son:
"O my dear son! Do not ascribe divine power to any beside God:
for such false worship is indeed a profound wrong-doing."
And We have enjoined upon the human being
goodness towards his parents;
in travail upon travail did his mother bear him
and in two years was his weaning.
Be grateful to Me and to your parents:
with Me is all journey's end.
But if they strive to make you ascribe divinity, side by side with Me,
to something which is contrary to your knowing,
do not obey them;
yet bear them company in this life with kindness,
and follow the way of those who turn to Me:
in the end you will all return to Me
and I will make clear to you the truth of all that you were doing.

[*Sūrah Luqmān* 31:13-15]

Luqmān is held up as a pattern of wisdom because he realized the best in a wise life in this world, as based upon the highest home in the inner life. To him, as in Islam, true human wisdom is also divine wisdom; the two cannot be separated. The beginning of all wisdom, therefore is conformity with the Will of God. That means that we must understand our relations to Him and worship Him aright. Then we must be good to mankind, beginning with our own parents. For the two duties are not diverse but one. Where they appear to conflict, there is something wrong with the human will.

But if they strive to make you ascribe divinity, side by side with Me, to something which is contrary to your knowing, do not obey them; yet bear them company in this life with kindness. Where the duty to man conflicts with the duty to God, it means that there is something wrong with the human will, and we should obey God rather than man. But even here, it does not mean that we should be arrogant or insolent. To parents and those in authority, we must be kind, considerate, and courteous, even where they command things which we should not do and therefore disobedience becomes our highest duty.

The worship of things other than God is the worship of false things, things which are alien to our true knowledge, things that go against our own pure nature as created by God.

In any apparent conflict of duties, our standard should be God's Will, as declared to us by His command. That is the way of those who love God; and their motive in disobedience to parents or human authority where disobedience is necessary by God's Law is not self-willed rebellion or defiance, but love of God, which means the true love of man in the highest sense of the word. And the reason we should give is: "Both you and I have to return to God; therefore not only must I follow God's Will, but you must command nothing against God's Will."

In the end you will all return to Me and I will make clear to you the truth of all that you were doing. These conflicts may appear to us strange and puzzling in this life. But in God's Presence we shall see their real meaning and significance. It may be that that was one way in which our true mettle could be tested: for it is not easy to disobey and love man at the same time. (A. Yusuf Ali, pp. 1082-1083)

241

Be Modest in Your Bearing

"O my dear son!" continued Luqman,
"If there were anything the weight of even a mustard-seed,
and it were within a rock or in the heavens or on earth,
God will bring it to light:
for God comprehends the subtlest mysteries and is All-Aware.
O my dear son! Be constant in prayer,
encourage what is just, and forbid what is wrong,
and bear with patient perseverance whatever comes to you;
witness, this is something upon which to set one's heart.
And do not turn away from people with pride
nor walk in insolence on the earth;
for God does not love the arrogant boaster.
And be modest in your bearing and lower your voice;
for without a doubt, the harshest of sounds
is the braying of the ass."

[*Sūrah Luqmān* 31:16-19]

The mustard seed is proverbially a small, minute thing, that people may ordinarily pass by. Not so God. Further emphasis is laid by supposing the mustard seed to be hidden beneath a rock or in the cleft of a rock, or to be lost in the spacious expanse of the earth or of the heavens. To God everything is known, and He will bring it forth, i.e., take account of it.

God comprehends the subtlest mysteries: Laṭīf, as a name of God, is as difficult to define in words as the idea it seeks to represent is difficult to grasp in our minds. It implies: (1) fine, subtle (the basic meaning); (2) so

242

fine and subtle as to be imperceptible to human sight; (3) so pure as to be incomprehensible; (4) with sight so perfect as to see and understand the finest subtleties and mysteries; (5) so kind and gracious as to bestow gifts of the most refined kind; extraordinarily gracious and understanding.

Do not turn away from people with pride nor walk in insolence on the earth. The Arabic usage means arrogance or effrontery, including smug self-satisfaction and a sense of lofty superiority.

And be modest in your bearing . . . . The Golden Mean is the pivot of the philosophy of Luqmān as it is of the philosophy of Aristotle and indeed of Islam. And it flows from a true understanding of our relation to God and His universe and to our fellow creatures, especially man. In all things be moderate. Do not go the pace, and do not be stationary or slow. Do not be talkative and do not be silent. Do not be loud and do not be timid or half-hearted. Do not be too confident, and do not be cowed down. If you have patience, it is to give you constancy and determination that you may bravely carry on the struggle of life. If you have humility, it is to save you from unseemly swagger, not to curb your right spirit and your reasoned determination. (A. Yusuf Ali, pp. 1084, 868)

The Most Trustworthy Hand-Hold

Whoever submits his or her whole self to God
and is a doer of good
has indeed grasped the most trustworthy hand-hold:
for with God rests the final outcome of all endeavors.

[*Sūrah Luqmān* 31:22]

A hand-hold is something which the hands can grasp for safety in a moment of danger. It may be a loop or a handle or an anchor. It is without flaw, so that there is no danger of breaking; our safety is absolutely assured so long as we hold fast to it. Our safety then depends on our own will and faith: God's help and protection will always be unfailing if we hold firmly to God and trust in Him. (A. Yusuf Ali, p. 103)

The Excellence of God's Creation

Such is He Who knows all
that is beyond the reach of a created being's perception,
as well as all that can be witnessed by a creature's senses or mind:
the Almighty, the Dispenser of Grace,
Who makes most excellent everything that He creates.
Thus, He begins the creation of man out of clay,
then He causes him to be begotten out of the essence of a humble fluid;
and then He forms him in accordance with what he is meant to be,
and breathes into him of His spirit:
and He endows you with hearing, and sight, and feelings as well as minds:
how seldom are you grateful!

[*Sūrah as-Sajdah* 32:6-9]

God's attributes may be summed up with reference to knowledge, power, and mercy. Where our knowledge is partial and uncertain, His is complete and certain. Where our power often falls short of the carrying out of our will, or needs the help of time, His is complete and coterminous with His Will. Where our mercy seems to be bounded by or opposed to justice, His is absolute and unconditioned.

God's creation in itself is good: it is beautiful, in proper proportions, and adapted for the functions it has to perform. There is no evil or disorder in it. Such evil or disorder as creeps in is due to man's will (as far as the world of man is concerned), and spiritual teaching is directed to train and cure that will and bring it into conformity with the universal order and plan.

245

Man is asked to contemplate his own humble beginning. His material body (apart from life) is a piece of earth or clay, which is another term for primeval matter. Matter is therefore the first stage, but even matter was not self-created. It was created by God.

Then comes life and the reproduction of life. We are still looking at the purely physical aspect, but it is now a stage higher, it is an animal. Its reproduction is through the sperm or semen, which is a quintessence of every part of the body of man. Yet it issues from the same part of his body as the urine, and is therefore despicable in man's sight. It is a living cell or cells, summing up so much ancestral life history.

The third stage is being formed *in accordance with what he is meant to be*. Compare 15:29, where Allāh says to the angels about the creation of Adam: *When I have fashioned him in due proportion and breathed into him of My spirit, fall down in obeisance to him*. After fertilization of ovum by the sperm, an individual life comes into existence, and it is gradually fashioned into shape: its limbs are formed, its animal life begins to function, all the beautiful adaptations come into play. The fourth stage here mentioned is that of distinctive man, into whom God's spirit is breathed. Then he rises higher than animals. As a complete man he gets the higher faculties. The five animal senses I understand to be included in the third stage. But in the fourth stage he rises higher and is addressed in the second person, *you,* instead of the third person *him*. He has now the spiritual counterpart of hearing (i.e., the capacity of hearing God's Message) and seeing (i.e., the inner vision), and feeling the nobler heights of love and understanding the bearings of the inner life (both typified by the heart). Yet with all these gifts, what thanks does unregenerate or corrupted man give to God? (A. Yusuf Ali, pp. 1093-1094)

God's *breathing of His spirit into man* is a metaphor for the divine gift of life and consciousness, or of a "soul" (one of the meanings of *rūh*). Consequently, "The soul of every human being is of the spirit of God" (Rāzī).

246

The verb *sawwāhu* is rendered as *He forms him in accordance with what he is meant to be.* He endows everything with inner coherence and with qualities consistent with the functions which it is meant to perform, and thus adapts it *a priori* to the exigencies of its existence. (Asad, pp. 634, 946)

Straight Speaking

O you who have faith! Stand in awe of God
and always speak a word on behalf of that
which is right and true:
that He may make your behavior whole and sound
and forgive you your mistakes.
The one who heeds God and His Messenger
has already attained a mighty success.

[*Sūrah al-Aḥzāb* 33:70-71]

We must not only speak the truth as far as we know, but we must always try to hit the right point: i.e., we must not speak unseasonably, and when we do speak, we must not beat about the bush, but go straight to that which is right, in deed as well as in word. Then God will make our conduct right and cure any defects that there may be in our knowledge and character. With our endeavor directed straight to the goal, we shall be forgiven our errors, shortcomings, faults, and sins of the past.

The one who heeds God and His Messenger has already attained a mighty success. This is salvation, the attainment of our real spiritual desire or ambition, as we are on the highway to nearness to God. (A. Yusuf Ali, p. 1129)

Always speak a word on behalf of that which is right and true: the expression *qawl sadīd* signifies, literally, *a saying that hits the mark*, i.e., is truthful, relevant, and to the point. In the only other instance where this expression is used in the Qurʾān (at the end of 4:9) it may be appropriately rendered as *speaking in a just manner*. In the present instance, however, it obviously relates to speaking *of others* in a manner devoid of all hidden meanings, insinuations and frivolous suspicions, aiming at no more and no less than the truth. (Asad, p. 652)

The Covenant of Trust

Truly, We offered the Trust
to the heavens, and to the earth, and to the mountains;
but they refused to undertake it, as they were afraid of it—
but the human being undertook it
though he was indeed unjust and foolish,
so that God must chastise the hypocrites, men and women,
and the deniers, men and women,
yet God turns in mercy to the faithful, men and women:
for God is Ever-ready to Forgive, Infinitely Merciful.

[*Sūrah al-Aḥzāb* 33:72-73]

We offered the Trust: the Trust is something given to a person, over which he has a power of disposition; he is expected to use it as directed or expected, but he has the power to use it otherwise. There is no trust if the trustee has no power, and the trust implies that the giver of the trust believes and expects that the trustee would use it according to the wish of the creator of the trust, and not otherwise.

What is the meaning of *the offer of the Trust to the heavens, the earth, and the mountains*? Compare 59:21, where the hypothetical sending down of the Qurʾān to the mountains is mentioned (*Had We sent down this Qurʾān on a mountain, truly you would have seen it humble itself and break asunder from awe of God.*) and it is mentioned that such parables are put forth in order to aid men to reflection. We may therefore take the mountains, the earth, and the heavens as symbolical. The mountains stand for firmness and stability; they have been created for this quality, and they are

250

always true to that quality. An earthquake or a volcano has to be with movements within the earth's crust; it has nothing to do with the mountain's will. In fact, it has no free will of any kind: there is no question of any Trust here. If we take the earth as a whole, as a part of the solar system or a compendium of the terrestrial nature we see around us, it obeys the fixed laws of God, and there is no will or Trust. If we take the heavens either as celestial space or as symbolical of the angels they absolutely obey God's Will and law; they have no will of their own.

The heavens, the earth, and the mountains, i.e., other creatures of God besides man, refused to undertake a Trust or a responsibility and may be imagined as happy without a choice of good or evil being given through their will. In saying that they refused, we imply a will, but we limit it by the statement that they did not undertake to be given a choice between good and evil. They preferred to submit their will entirely to God's Will, which is All-Wise and Perfect, and which would give them far more happiness than a faculty of choice, with their imperfect knowledge. Man was too audacious and ignorant to realize this, and the result has been that man as a race has been disrupted: the evil ones have betrayed the Trust and brought punishment on themselves, though the good have been able to rise far above other creation, to be the *muqarrabīn,* the nearest ones to God (56:11 and 56:88). What can be higher than this for any creature?

Read 2:30-34 for the Qurʾān's account of the creation of Adam. God intended a very high destiny for man, and placed him in his uncorrupted state even above the angels, but in his corruption he made himself even lower than the beasts. What was it that made man so high and noble? The differentiating quality which God gave man was that God breathed something of His own spirit into man (32:9, 15:29). This meant that man was given a limited choice of good and evil, and that he was made capable of forbearance, love, and mercy. And in himself man summed up God's great world: man is in himself a microcosm.

251

That man should undertake the God-like attributes (in however small a degree) of will, forbearance, love, and mercy brought him nearer to God than was possible for any other creature of God. This was part of God's Will and plan, but little did man realize then what a tremendous task he was undertaking or question himself whether he would be equal to it. *Zalūm* (translated "unjust") and *jahūl* (ignorant) are both in the Arabic intensive form; as much as to say, "man *signally* failed to measure his own powers or his own knowledge." But God's Grace came to his assistance. Where man did his best, he won through by God's Grace, even though man's best was but a poor good.

How did man generally undertake this great responsibility which made him *representative of God* [2:30]? Here comes in the mystic doctrine of a covenant, express or implied, between God and humanity. *When your Lord drew forth from the children of Adam, from their loins, their descendants, He made them testify concerning themselves, saying "Am I not your Lord?" to which they answer "Yes! we bear witness that You are!" This We did lest you mankind should say on the Day of Judgment, "Truly, we were unaware of this."* [7:172]. *O you who have attained to faith! Be true to your covenants!* [5:1]. A covenant (*mithāq*) necessarily implies trust, and its breach necessarily implies punishment. Man's generic covenant, which flowed from his exercising the option given him, choosing will, forbearance, love, and mercy, made it necessary that breach of it should carry its own punishment. Breach of it is here classed under two heads: those who betray their trust act either as hypocrites or as unbelievers. Hypocrites are those who profess faith but bring not forth the fruits of faith. Unbelievers are those who openly defy faith, and from whom therefore no fruits of faith are to be expected. Those who remain firm to their faith and their covenant will receive the aid of God's Grace; their faults and weaknesses will be cured, and they will be made worthy of their exalted destiny. For God is *Ever-ready to Forgive, Infinitely Merciful.* So ends a *sūrah* which deals with the greatest complications and misunderstandings in our throbbing life here below, and points upwards to the great achievements, the highest salvation. (A. Yusuf

Ali, pp. 1130–1131)

But the human being undertook it, that is to say, *and then failed to measure up to the moral responsibility arising from the reason and the comparative free will with which he has been endowed* (Zamakhsharī). This obviously applies to the human race as such, and not necessarily to all of its individuals.

God must chastise the hypocrites, men and women, and the deniers, men and women: in other words, God imposes suffering on those who offend against what their own reason and conscience would have them do. This suffering, whether in this world or in the hereafter, is but a causal consequence—as the *lām al-ʿāqibah* at the beginning of this sentence shows—of man's moral failure, and not an arbitrary act of God. (See 2:7.) (Asad, p. 653)

Spend on Others

Say: "Truly my Sustainer grants abundant sustenance
or bestows it in meager measure
to such of His servants as He wills;
and whatever you spend on others, He replaces it:
for He is the Best of Providers."

[*Sūrah Sabā* 34:39]

Compare to 34:36: *Truly my Lord enlarges and restricts the provision to whom He pleases, but most men understand not.* Provision or sustenance includes the good things of all kinds in this life, material goods as well as power, opportunities, influence, mental gifts, etc. These do not necessarily all go to the good, nor is their denial to be interpreted to mean that it is a withdrawal of God's favor. Very often the contrary is the case. Their distribution is in accordance with the universal plan and purpose, which is all-wise and all-good. But ignorant people cannot understand this.

Even in the seeming inequality of distribution of the good things of life, God has a wise and merciful purpose; for nothing arises by chance. He is the best to give us, now and evermore, just those things which serve our real needs and advance our inner development. (A. Yusuf Ali, pp. 1145, 1146)

A Prophet Asks for No Reward

Say: "I counsel you one thing only:
be ever conscious of standing before God—
whether you are in the company of others or alone
and reflect: your companion is not possessed:
he is only a warner to you of an intense suffering to come."
Say: "No reward do I ask of you; it is in your own interest.
My reward is with God alone, and to all things He is Witness."

[*Sūrah Sabāᶜ* 34:46-47]

A crowd mentality is not best for the perception of the final spiritual truths. For these, it is necessary that each soul should commune within itself with earnest simplicity as before God: if it requires a teacher, let it seek out one, or it may be that it wants the strengthening of the inner conviction that dawns on it, by the support of a sympathizer or friend. But careful and heartfelt reflection is necessary to appraise the higher truths.

In these verses, arguments are suggested to the Prophet by which he can convince any right-thinking man of his sincerity and truth. Here the argument is that he is not possessed or out of his mind. If he is different from ordinary men, it is because he has to give a warning of a terrible spiritual danger to the men whom he loves but who will not understand His message. The second argument is that he has nothing to gain from them. His message is for their own good. He is willing to suffer persecution and insult, because he has to fulfill his mission from God.

God's Truth is so vast that no man in this life can compass the whole of it. But God in His Mercy selects His servants on whom it is cast like a mantle. They see enough to be able to teach their fellow men. It is through that mantle—that mission received from God—that an apostle can speak with authority to men. He cannot explain the exact mystery of inspiration, but he *knows* it is from God, and this is his third argument.

The fourth argument is that the Truth is final: it does not come and go. It creates new situations and new developments, and if by any chance it *seems* to be defeated for a time, it comes back and restores the true balance, unlike *falsehood which by its very nature is doomed to perish* [17:81]. The Prophet's credentials are known by the test of time. This was already becoming apparent to discerning eyes when this *sūrah* was revealed in Mecca, but it became clear for the whole world with the story of Islam's progress in Medina.

If it could possibly be supposed that the Prophet was a self-deceived visionary, it would affect him only and could not fail to appear in his personality. But in fact he was steady in his constancy and faith, and he not only went from strength to strength, but won the enduring and wholehearted love and devotion of his nearest and dearest and of those who most came into contact with him. How was this possible, unless he had the Truth and inspiration of God behind him? This is the fifth and last argument in the passage. (A Yusuf Ali, pp. 1148-1149)

Spiritually We Bear Only Our Own Burden

Nor can one who bears burdens bear the burden of another.
If one weighed down by his load
should call another to help him carry it
not the least portion of it could be carried
even if he is one's close relation.
You can counsel only those who stand in awe of their Sustainer,
though He is unseen,
and are constant in prayer,
and whoever purifies himself does so for the benefit of his own soul;
and all are journeying to God.

[*Sūrah al-Fāṭir* 35:18]

Natural relationship may be considered as a reasonable cause or opportunity for bearing each other's burdens. For example, a mother or a father might offer to die for her or his child, and *vice versa*. But this does not apply to spiritual matters. There the responsibility is strictly personal and cannot be transferred to another.

Those who stand in awe of their Sustainer, though He is unseen: the man, who, though he does not see God, so realizes God's Presence in himself as if he saw Him, is the man of genuine faith, and for him God's revelation comes through many channels and is always truthful. *And are constant in prayer*: prayer is one of the means of purifying ourselves of lower motives in life, for in prayer we seek the Presence of God. But the purity which we seek is for our own souls: we confer no favor on God or on any power in the spiritual world, as some imagine who make "gifts" to God. In any case the destination of all is to God. (A. Yusuf Ali, p. 1158)

257

The Blind and the Seeing

The blind and the seeing are not alike,
nor are the depths of darkness and the light,
nor are the shade and the heat of the sun;
nor are alike those that are living and those that are dead.
God can make any that He wills to hear;
but you cannot make those hear who are buried in graves.
You are nothing but a warner.
Truly, We have sent you with truth as a bearer of joyous news
and as a warner;
and never has there been a people
without a warner having lived among them.

[*Sūrah al-Fāṭir* 35:19-24]

The blind and the seeing are not alike: now we are offered some contrasts between those who obey God's Law and are thus citizens of the Kingdom of Heaven and those who are rebels against God's kingdom and are thus outlaws. How can they be considered alike? The godly are like those who see, as contrasted with those who are blind; and their motives and actions are like the purest and highest Light, contrasted with the depths of darkness; or, to take another metaphor, their lives are like the genial and warmth-giving heat of the sun, which benefits all who come within its influence, contrasted with the chilly shadows of gloom in which no vegetation flourishes.

Nor are alike those that are living and those that are dead. The final contrast is between the Living and the Dead; those whose future has in it the promise of growth and fulfillment, and those who are inert and on the road to perish. With God everything is possible: He can give Life to the Dead. But the human teacher should not expect that people who are (spiritually) dead and buried will by any chance hear his call.

You are nothing but a warner: the function of a Prophet is to preach God's Truth, to point out the right Way, to show men the need of repentance, and to warn them against the dangers which they incur by living a life of evil. He cannot compel them to accept the Truth or listen to the Message. It is God Who sends the Revelation. While there is warning in it for the heedless, there is good news for those who listen and repent. The warning always came to all peoples before punishment. (A. Yusuf Ali, p. 1159)

Pairs of Opposites

Limitless in His glory is He Who has created opposites
in whatever the earth produces, and in men's own selves,
and in that of which [as yet] they have no knowledge.

[*Sūrah Yā Sīn* 36:36]

The literal meaning of the above *āyah* is: *Who has created all the pairs out of whatever the earth produces, and out of themselves, and out of that of which they have no knowledge,* a reference to the polarity evident in all creation, both animate and inanimate, which expresses itself in the existence of antithetical and yet complimentary forces, like the sexuality in human beings, animals, and plants, light and darkness, heat and cold, positive and negative magnetism and electricity, the positive and negative charges (protons and electrons) in the structure of the atom, and so forth. It is to be borne in mind that the noun *zawj* denotes both "a pair" and "one of a pair." The mention of that of which they have no knowledge evidently relates to things or phenomena not yet understood by man but potentially within the range of his comprehension: hence my interpolation, between brackets, of the words "as yet." (Asad, pp. 676-677)

The Companions of the Garden

Thus, when they are told, "Spend on others
out of what God has provided for you as sustenance,"
those who are bent on denying the truth say to those who have faith,
"Shall we feed anyone whom, if God had so willed, He could have fed?
Clearly, you wander in error!"
And they add, "When is this promise of resurrection to be fulfilled?
Answer this if you are people of truth!"
Nothing awaits them beyond a single burst of God's power,
which will overtake them while they are still arguing:
and then no chance will they have to order their affairs,
nor to their own people will they return!
And the trumpet will be blown—and see!
Out of their graves towards their Sustainer will they all rush forth!
They will say: "Oh, woe to us! Who has roused us from our sleep?"
They will be told: "This is what the Most Gracious has promised!
And His message-bearers spoke the truth!"
Nothing will there have been but one single burst—
Witness! Before Us will all of them be gathered:
then on that Day, no soul shall be wronged in the least,
and you shall be recompensed only for that which you have done.
Truly, the companions of the garden
shall that Day be wholly immersed in Joy;
in shady groves they and their spouses will rest on couches;
fruits will be there for them, and theirs shall be all that they could ask for:
"Peace!"—-a word from a Most Merciful Sustainer.

[*Sūrah Yā Sīn* 36:47-58]

261

To selfish men, the good may make an appeal, and say: "Look! God has given you wealth, or influence, or knowledge, or talent. Why not spend some of it in charity, i.e., for the good of your fellow-creatures?" But the selfish only think of themselves and laugh at such teaching with scorn. They are too full of themselves to have a corner in their heart for others. "If," they say, "God gave them nothing, why should we?" There is arrogance in this as well as blasphemy: arrogance in thinking that they are favored because of their merits, and blasphemy in laying the blame of other people's misfortunes on God. They further try to turn the tables on the Believers by pretending that the Believers are entirely on a wrong track. They forget that all men are on probation and trial: they hold their gifts on trust: those apparently less favored, in that they have fewer of this world's goods, may be really more fortunate, because they are learning patience, self-reliance, and the true value of things ephemeral which is apt to be very much exaggerated in men's eyes.

In addition to their arrogance and blasphemy, they not only refuse Faith, but they taunt the men of Faith as if the men of Faith were dealing in falsehood: "If there is a Hereafter, tell us when it will be!" The answer is: "It will come sooner than you expect: you will yet be disputing about things of Faith and neglecting your opportunities in Life, when the Hour will sound, and you will have no time even to make your dispositions in this life; you will be cut off from everyone whom you thought to be near and dear to you, or able to help you!"

When the Day comes, men will be taken aback. The dead will rise as in a stupor, and they will be confused in the new conditions. They will gradually regain their memory and their personality. They will be reminded that God in His grace and mercy had already announced the Hereafter in their probationary lives, and the word of God's apostles, which then seemed so strange and remote, was true and was now being fulfilled. Time and space, as we know them here, will be no more. The whole gathering will be as in the twinkling of an eye. The Judgment will be on the highest standard of Justice and Grace. Not the least merit will go unrewarded, though the reward will be for the righteous far more than their desserts. No penalty will be exacted but that which the doer himself by his past deeds brought on himself.

Truly, the companions of the garden shall that Day be wholly immersed in Joy: We now have the symbolism for the indescribable Bliss of the Hereafter, in the four verses 55-58. Notice the subtle gradation in the description. First, in this verse, we have the nature of the *mise en scène* and the nature of the joy therein. It will be a Garden, i.e., everything agreeable to see and hear and feel and taste and smell; our bodily senses will have been transformed, but we can imagine something corresponding to them in our spiritual being: delightfully green lawns and meadows, trees and shrubs: the murmur of streams and the songs of birds; the delicate texture of flowers and leaves and the shapes of beauty in clouds and mist; the flavors of fruits; and the perfumes of flowers and scents. The joy in the Garden will be an active joy, without fatigue: whatever we do in it, every employment in which we engage, there will be a source of joy without alloy.

In shady groves they and their spouses will rest on couches. Secondly, the joy or happiness is figured to be not solitary but shared, shared by associates like those we imagine in spiritual Love or Marriage, in whose fair faces "some ray divine reflected shines" (Jāmī), whose society is enjoyed in homes of happiness, situated in soothing shade, and furnished with thrones (couches) of dignity and peace.

Fruits will be there for them, and theirs shall be all that they could ask for." Thirdly, besides external conditions of Bliss, the Bliss of the Hereafter has an inner quality, expressed by the word *fākihatun.* The root *fākiha* means "to rejoice greatly," "to be full of merriment." The ordinary meaning of "fruit" attached to *fākihat* is derived from the idea that the flavor of choice, ripe fruit delights the heart of man. Just as *akala* (to eat) is used for "enjoyment" (also in 5:69 and 13:35), so *fākihat,* "fruit" stands here for that specially choice enjoyment which goes with a fastidious and well-cultivated taste. In other words, it suggests that highest kind of joy which depends upon the inner faculty rather than any outward circumstance. This is further emphasized by the second clause, *they shall have whatever they call for.* Again using the language of this life, the musician's heaven will be full of music; the mathematician's will be full of mathematical symmetry and perfection; the artist's will be full of beauty of form, and so on.

Peace! A word from a Most Merciful Sustainer. Fourthly, we reach the highest grade of bliss, the mystic salutation *Peace!* from God Most Merciful. That word sums up the attainment of the final Goal. For it explains the nature of the Most High: He is not only a Lord and Cherisher, but a Lord Whose supreme glory is Mercy, Peace, and Harmony! (A. Yusuf Ali, pp. 1180-1183)

The Book of Blessings

This Book of blessings We have sent down to you—
so that they may meditate on its signs[7]
and that people of insight might take them to heart.

[*Sūrah Ṣād* 38:29]

Revelation is not a mere chance or haphazard thing. It is a real blessing—among the greatest that God has bestowed on man. By meditation on it in an earnest spirit man may learn of himself, and his relation to nature around him and to God the Author of all. Men of understanding may, by its help, resolve all genuine doubts that there may be in their minds, and learn the true lessons of spiritual life. (A. Yusuf Ali, p. 1224)

---

[7] Signs: *āyāts* mean verses, as well as "significations."

Our Servant Job

And call to mind Our servant Job,
how it was when he cried out to his Sustainer,
"Behold, Satan has afflicted me with utter weariness and suffering!"—
and thereupon was told: "Strike the ground with your foot:
here is cool water to wash with and to drink!"
And We bestowed upon him new offspring, doubling their number
as an act of grace from Us,
and as a reminder to all who are endowed with insight.
And finally We told him:
"Now take in your hand a small bunch of grass,
and strike therewith, and you will not break your oath!"—
for, truly, We found him full of patience in adversity:
how excellent a servant, who, behold,
would always turn to Us!

[*Sūrah Ṣād* 38:41-44]

Satan has afflicted me with utter weariness and suffering, i.e., with life-weariness *in consequence of* suffering. As soon as he realizes that God has been testing him, Job perceives that his utter despondency and weariness of life—eloquently described in the Old Testament (The Book of Job, 3)—was but due to what is described as "Satan's whisperings": this is the moral to be drawn from the above evocation of Job's story.

According to the classical commentators, the miraculous appearance of a healing spring heralded the end of Job's suffering, both physical and mental.

In the words of the Bible (The Book of Job 2:9) at the time of his seemingly hopeless suffering, Job's wife reproached her husband for persevering in his faith: "Do you still retain your integrity? Curse God and die." According to the classical Qur'ān commentators, Job swore that, if God would restore him to health, he would punish her blasphemy with a hundred stripes. But when he did recover, he bitterly regretted his hasty oath, for he realized that his wife's "blasphemy" had been an outcome of her love and pity for him; and thereupon he was told in a revelation that he could fulfill his vow in a symbolic manner by striking her *once* with *a bunch of grass containing a hundred blades or more.* (Compare 5:89: *God will not take you to task for oaths which you may have uttered without thought.*) (Asad, pp. 699–700)

A Book Consistent Within Itself

Are you not aware that it is God Who sends down water from the skies,
and then causes it to travel through the earth in the shape of springs?
And then He brings forth thereby herbage of various hues;
and then it withers, and you can see it turn yellow;
and in the end He causes it to crumble to dust.
Truly, in this there is indeed a reminder
to those who are endowed with insight!
Is one whose heart God has opened to surrender
so that he is illumined by a light from his Sustainer
no better than one who is hard-hearted?
Woe to those whose hearts are hardened
against remembrance of God!
They obviously wander astray!
God has revealed the most beautiful message
in the form of a Book consistent within itself,
repeating its teaching in various guises—
the skins of those who stand in awe of their Lord
tremble with it;
then their skins and their hearts soften
with the remembrance of God.
Such is God's guidance:
with it He guides the one who wills to be guided,
but those whom God lets stray have none to guide them.

[*Sūrah az-Zumar* 39:21-23]

Those who listen to God's Message find at each stage God's Grace helping them more and more to expand their spiritual understanding and to receive God's Light, so that they travel farther and farther to their Goal in the Path of Truth and Righteousness. They are not to be compared to those who shut out God's Light from their hearts. Just as there is spiritual progress for those who seek God, so there is more and more spiritual retrogression for those who close their hearts to God. Their hearts get hardened, and they allow less and less of God's Grace to penetrate within. But it is obvious that they flounder on the Way and cannot walk with the firm steps of those of assured Faith.

In the form of a Book consistent within itself, repeating its teaching in various guises. The word *mutashābih* [consistent within itself] is here to be understood in the same sense as in 3:7, where it can be translated as "allegorical." There is a slightly different shade of meaning here, as suggested by the context. In the earlier passage, it was opposed to *muhkam* ("verses of established meaning"). Here it is contrasted or compared to *mathānī*, whose root meaning is "having something similar," "working by analogy, or allegory, or parable," "having its parts consistent with each other." The last meaning I adopt here. The Qur'ān was revealed in parts at different times. And yet its parts all conform to each other. There is no contradiction or inconsistency anywhere.

The skins of those who stand in awe of their Lord tremble with it: the skin is the outer integument of the body. It receives the first shock from the impact of anything unusual, and it trembles and its hair stands on end under excitement. So in spiritual matters the first stimulation from God's Message is external. Those who receive Faith do it as it were with tremor and not with apathy. But the next stage is that it penetrates their outer nature and goes right into their hearts. Their whole nature is "softened" to receive the beneficent Message, and it transforms them through and through.

Such is God's guidance: with it He guides the one who wills to be guided. God's Will and Plan, in allowing limited free will to man, is not to force

269

man's will, but to give all guidance, and leave alone those who reject that guidance, in case they should repent and come back into Grace. But in all cases, in so far as we are given the choice, we shall be called to account for all our actions. "Leaving to stray" does not mean that we can do what we please. Our personal responsibility remains. *If Allāh so willed, He could make you all one People, but He leaves straying whom He pleases, and He guides whom He pleases: but you shall certainly be called to account for all your actions* [16:93]. (A. Yusuf Ali, pp. 1243-1244, 123, 682)

As in many other instances, this Qur'anic reference to the endless transformations and the miraculous cycle of life and death in all nature serves to emphasize God's almightiness and, specifically, His power to resurrect the dead—thus alluding, indirectly, to the statement at the end of the preceding verse that *never does God fail to fulfill His promise.*

God has revealed: literally, *has been bestowing from on high*, i.e., *step by step*. The verbal form *nazzala* indicates both gradualness and continuity in the process of divine revelation.

Repeating its teaching in various guises: another possible meaning, preferred by Rāzī, is "pairing its statements," i.e., referring to the polarity stressed in all Qur'anic teachings (e.g., command and prohibition, duties and rights, reward and punishment, paradise and hell, light and darkness, the general and the specific, and so forth). (Asad, p. 708)

270

One Master or Many?

God offers a parable:
a person belonging to many partners at variance with each other
and a person belonging entirely to one master:
are those two equal in state?
All praise belongs to God! But most of them do not comprehend.

[*Sūrah az-Zumar* 39:29]

The difference between the creed of polytheism and the gospel of unity is explained by the analogy of two men. One belongs to many masters: the masters disagree among themselves, and the poor man of many masters has to suffer from the quarrels of his many masters; it is an impossible and unnatural position. The other serves only one master; his master is good, and does all he can for his servant. The servant can concentrate his attention on his service, he is happy himself, and his service is efficiently performed. Can there be any doubt as to which of them is the happier and which of them is in a more natural position? No man can serve two, still less numerous, masters. (A. Yusuf Ali, p. 1246)

271

This Present Life

The one who had faith said further: "O my People!
Follow me: I will lead you to the right path.
O my people! This present life is just a brief convenience;
it is the Hereafter that is the enduring Home.
The one who does evil will only be requited with its like;
and anyone who does that which is good, whether man or woman,
and who has faith, these will enter the Garden—
there they will have infinite abundance."

[*Sūrah Ghāfir* 40:38-40]

Faith makes him see the contrast between vanities, even though they may glitter temporarily, and the eternal Good that is destined for man. The spiritual Good will not only last. It will be a most liberal reward, far above any merits of the recipient. *The life of this world is alluring to those who reject faith, and they scoff at those who believe. But the righteous will be above them on the Day of Resurrection; for Allāh bestows His abundance without measure on whom He will* [2:212]. God's gifts in this world seem unequal, and sometimes those get them who seem to deserve them least. God's bounty is unlimited, to the just as well as the unjust. In His wisdom He may give to whomsoever He pleases. The account is not taken now, but will be taken in the end, when the balance will be redressed. (A. Yusuf Ali, pp. 1274, 83)

Call on Me

And your Sustainer says: ***"Call on Me; I will answer you."***

[*Sūrah Ghāfir* 40:60]

As this life is not the end of all things, and we are to have its fulfillment in the Hereafter, we have only to pray to the Lord of the Present and the Hereafter, and He will hear us, forgive us, guide us, and make our Path smooth. (A. Yusuf Ali, p. 1279)

We Will Show Them Our Signs

We will show them Our signs on the farthest horizons
and within their own selves
until it becomes manifest to them that this is the Truth.
Is it not enough that your Lord is witness to all things?
Indeed! Are they in doubt concerning the Meeting with their Lord?
Ah, truly! it is He Who encompasses all things!

[*Sūrah Fuṣṣilat* 41:53-54]

When God acts, He does not act only through situations, nor only through His speech to us in the secrecy of our own souls. He is neither outside us, that He could be identified exclusively with events, nor inside us, that He could be identified exclusively with our own states of consciousness. He is beyond both the inner and the outer worlds; heaven and earth cannot contain Him.

Every object in the outer world, every thing, person, or situation, the earth below our feet, our society and the natural world around us, the sun, moon, stars, and all the distant galaxies, is a sign of God. And everything in our souls, our psyches, every state of consciousness, in all their unfathomable power and depth and complexity, is also a sign of God. It is very difficult, however, for us to realize this. Most of the time we take our experience of ourselves and the world for granted. We may believe that everything on the horizons and in our souls is a sign of God, but we rarely see this as actually true in the moment before us. Would we continue to live our lives in heedlessness if we did?

Why do we take everything for granted like this? It is because we

274

have forgotten that God is present in this moment. We do not live in the present experience of everything, ourselves included, as totally dependent upon God. Therefore we are always searching for another cause for the things that happen to us and the objects we see around us. And, because we are not consciously standing in the Light of the heavens and the earth, this search is mostly unconsciousness. It is "natural"—for the heedless—to see the universe as our creator. After all, it is both bigger than us and older than us. As we ourselves emerged physically from our mother, so the human race as a whole emerged from the earth, which itself emerged from the universe. This is the unconscious origin of materialism.

On the other hand, we can act. Most of us can turn our thoughts into articulate speech and move our bodies at will. We can look forward in time and begin to "take charge of our destiny." We can make plans, then carry them out. So it is equally "natural"— if we are heedless of God—to unconsciously believe that we are self-created, or at least to act as if we were.

To believe that we create ourselves because we can move and speak and imagine is to pay attention to ourselves at the expense of our surroundings. We take our cues from our own thoughts and desires and impulses, not from the world around us—much less from God. And so the world becomes obscure to us. It becomes an object outside us—as if we were not a part of it, through matter; as if it were not a part of us, through consciousness. So the world too begins to seem like an "existent being" with its own thoughts and desires and impulses. So those who worship themselves instead of God will also tend to worship nature instead of God. They believe in their own self-will; they also believe in the mysterious "will of the situation" that is always inciting yet always thwarting that self-will.

If we find ourselves in this condition of belief (which is actually very common) we need to remember that God shows his signs both on the horizons and in ourselves. God is the Real, and Reality transcends both ourselves and the world—which is why an act of God can sometimes be perceived as a "wave" which passes equally, and simultaneously, through the psyche and through the world, from a Reality which is beyond both of them. World and psyche are partners, equal partners, in any event. The materialist may believe that the psyche merely reacts to events; the "psychic" may believe that the psyche senses events which are to take place in the future, or actually creates these events. But the truth is, only God is the Author of what happens, and the signs He shows appear both on the horizons and in our souls. He witnesses both as one in His eternal present; he does not see or act upon one by means of the other. And if prophet or saint knows the future, it is not because he is seeing ahead in time, but because God has taken him, for a moment at least, into His Own eternal present.

As subjective psyches, as separate individual souls, we cannot stand outside the polarity of psyche and world. It is enough for us to know that God can, and does—and is. Only God can know things as they really are, beyond subject/object polarity. And even if a prophet or saint seems to possess some of this ability, he does not do so in his separate individuality. We cannot know Reality; God can and does know Reality through us—and without us. (Upton)

The Clear Path

The same clear Path has He established for you
as that which He enjoined on Noah,
that which We have sent by inspiration to you,
and that which We designated for Abraham, Moses, and Jesus:
that you should steadfastly uphold the Faith
and make no divisions within it.
To those who worship other things than God,
the way to which you call them may appear difficult.
God draws to Himself those who are willing
and guides to Himself everyone who turns to Him.

[*Sūrah ash-Shūrā* 42:13]

The same clear Path has He established for you as that which He enjoined on Noah . . . Abraham, Moses, and Jesus. As the sequence shows, the term *dīn* cannot apply in this context to "religion" in its widest connotation, including religious *laws*—which, by their very nature, have been different in each successive dispensation—it obviously denotes here only the ethical and spiritual *contents* of religion, i.e., "faith" in its most general sense. With this verse, the discourse returns to the theme sounded at the beginning of this *sūrah*, namely, the unchanging sameness of the spiritual and moral principles underlying all revealed religions.

Make no divisions within it (do not break up your unity therein) reminds us of 3:19: *The only religion in the sight of God is self-surrender to Him*, and 3:85: *If one goes in search of a religion other than self-surrender to God, it will never be accepted from him.* Parallel with this principle, enunciated by all of

277

God's apostles, is the categorical statement in 21:92 and 23:52: *Truly, [O you who believe in Me], this community of yours is one single community, since I am the Sustainer of you all.* Most of the great commentators (e.g., Zamakh-sharī, Rāzī, Ibn Kathīr) understand this as an unequivocal reference to the ecumenical unity of all religions based on belief in the One God, not-withstanding all the differences with regard to "the [specific] statutes and practices enjoined for the benefit of the various communities in accor-dance with their [time-bound] conditions" (as expressed by Zamakhsharī in his comments on this verse). (Asad, pp. 405, 741)

Be Steadfast without Arguments

And so, call out to them
and stand steadfast as you have been commanded,
and do not follow their likes and dislikes, but say:
"I have faith in the Book which God has bestowed from on high;
and I am asked to judge justly between you.
God is our Sustainer and your Sustainer.
To us belongs the responsibility for our deeds, and to you, for your deeds.
Let there be no argument between us and you.
God will bring us all together, and with Him is all journeys' end."

[*Sūrah ash-Shūrā* 42:15]

How beautifully the mission of Islam is commended in this verse! (1) The more sectarianism and division there is in the world, the more need is there for the Gospel of Unity. (2) It must steadfastly pursue its way. (3) It must not be deflected by worldly or political motives. (4) Its faith must be directly in God and in God's revelation. (5) It must judge justly between warring factions, as the Religion of Peace and Unity. (6) The God whom it preaches is not an exclusive God: He is the Lord of the Worlds; to any given person, of whatever faith, "He is your God as well as mine." (7) Our Faith is not a question of words: it is deeds which decide; each one of us has personal responsibility for his own conduct. (8) There is no cause of contention whatever, when we preach Unity, Truth, and Hereafter. (9) If you have doubts, the final arbiter is God, and His Throne is our Goal. (A. Yusuf Ali, p. 1309)

Love Your Fellow Human Beings

In that life to come, you will see the evil-doers full of fear
at what they have earned:
for it is bound to fall back upon them.
And in the flowering meadows of the gardens
you will see those who have attained to faith and done righteous deeds:
all that they might desire shall they have with their Sustainer:
this, this is the great bounty—which God foretold
to those of His servants who attain to faith and do righteous deeds.
Say [O Prophet]: "No reward do I ask of you for this message
other than that you should love your fellow-men."
For if anyone gains a good deed,
We shall grant him through it an increase of good:
and, truly, God is much-forgiving, ever responsive to gratitude.

[*Sūrah ash-Shūrā* 42:22-23]

No reward do I ask of you for this message other than that you should love your fellow-men: literally, *love for those who are near (al-qurbā)*. Some commentators take this to mean "those who are near to *me*," i.e., Muḥammad's kinsfolk: but quite apart from the objection that such a "personal" demand would conflict with the assurance, *No reward do I ask of you*, the deliberate omission of any possessive pronoun in respect of the term *al-qurbā* indicates that it is not limited to any personal relationship but, rather, alludes to a relationship common to *all* human beings: namely, the fellowship of man—a concept which implies the fundamental ethical postulate to care for one another's material and spiritual welfare. (Asad, p. 744)

280

Due Measure

Truly, He has full knowledge of what is inside of hearts;
and it is He Who accepts repentance from His servants,
and pardons bad deeds, and knows all that you do,
and responds to all who attain to faith and do righteous deeds;
and God will give them, out of His bounty,
far more than they will have deserved,
whereas for the deniers of the truth
there is severe suffering in store.
For if God were to grant
abundant sustenance to His servants,
they would behave on earth with wanton insolence:
but as it is,
He bestows from on high in due measure, as He wills:
for, truly, He is fully aware of of His creatures,
and sees them all.

[*Sūrah ash-Shūrā* 42:24-27]

This passage connects with, and elucidates, the statement in the preceding verse that God *responds to all who attain to faith and do righteous deeds*—a statement which, at first glance, seems to be contrary to the fact that whereas many wrongdoers prosper and are happy, many righteous people suffer hurt and deprivation. In reply to this objection, this verse points elliptically to man's innate *greed for more and more* [102:1], which often causes him to become *grossly overweening whenever he believes himself to be self-sufficient* [96:6-7]. To counteract this tendency, the Qur'ān stresses

281

again and again that God's "response" to the righteous—as well as to wrongdoers—will become fully evident only in the life to come, and not necessarily in this world, which, after all, is only the first, short stage of man's existence. (Asad, p. 744)

With God Is the Enduring Good

Whatever you are given here is for the convenience of this life:
but that which is with God is better and more enduring—
for those who have faith and put their trust in their Sustainer;
those who avoid the greater crimes and shameful deeds
and when they are angry, even then forgive;
those who heed their Nurturer[8] and are constant in prayer;
who conduct their affairs by mutual consultation;
and who give out of the sustenance We bestow on them.

[*Sūrah ash-Shūrā* 42:36-38]

Any good (or ill) which is our lot is only a temporary phase to serve the convenience of this life. But there is a higher good, which comes from God's own Presence. Such good is both superior in quality, and more permanent. In the same way, any ills that we may suffer in this life have reference only to the conditions of this our life of probation. The ills that we "earn" in our spiritual life—such as deprivation of God's Grace—are far more momentous and permanent.

But that which is with God is better and more enduring: the higher and more permanent gifts which come from God's Presence are for those who truly worship and serve God. Those who wish to serve God are described by nine of their characteristics: namely, (1) they have faith, and it follows that (2) they trust in God, instead of running after false standards or values. (3) They eschew the more serious offenses against God's Law,

---

[8] *Rabb:* Lord, Sustainer, Educator.

283

and of course keep clear of any offenses against sex (*shameful deeds*). In *those who avoid the greater crimes and shameful deeds* we are speaking of the ordinary man or woman who tries to follow God's Law: he or she is not perfect, but at least eschews the major breaches of conduct. For those higher in spiritual degree, there is of course a stricter standard. But all are entitled to the blessing of Islam, whatever their degree. (4) While knowing that they are not themselves perfect, they are ready to forgive others, even though they are sorely tried with anger and provocation. (5) They are ready at all times to hearken to God's Signs, or to listen to the admonitions of men of God, and to follow the true Path, as they understand it. (6) They keep personal contact with God, by habits of Prayer and Praise. (7) Their conduct in life is open and determined by mutual consultation between those who are entitled to a voice, e.g., in private domestic affairs, as between husband and wife, or other responsible members of the household; in affairs of business, as between partners or parties interested; and in State affairs, as between rulers and ruled, or as between different departments of administration, to preserve the unity of administration (see below). (8) They do not forget charity, or the help due to their weaker brethren, out of the wealth or gifts or talents or opportunities which God has provided for them. And (9) when other people use them despitefully, they are not cowed down or terrorized into submission and acceptance of evil but stand up for their rights within the limits mentioned in 42:40: *The recompense for an injury is an injury equal thereto: but if a person forgives and makes reconciliation, His reward is due from Allāh: for Allāh does not love those who do wrong.* When you stand up for rights, either on private or public grounds, it may be through processes of law or by way of private defense in so far as the law permits private action. But in all cases you must not seek a compensation greater than the injury suffered.

Who conduct their affairs by mutual consultation: consultation is the key word of this *sūrah*, and suggests the ideal way in which a good man should conduct his affairs, so that, on the one hand, he may not become too egotistical, and, on the other, he may not lightly abandon the responsibilities which devolve on him as a personality whose development counts in the sight of God. This principle was applied to its fullest extent by the holy Prophet in his private and public life, and was fully acted upon by the early rulers of Islam. Modern representative government is an attempt—by no means perfect—to apply this principle in State affairs. (A. Yusuf Ali, pp. 1316–1317)

We Have Made the Qur'ān a Light

And it is not given to mortal man that God should speak to him
other than through sudden inspiration,
or from behind a veil,
or by sending a Messenger to reveal, by His permission,
whatever He wills:
for, truly, He is exalted, wise.
And so We have by Our Command sent inspiration to you:
you did not know what revelation was or what faith was;
but We have made the Qur'ān a Light
with which We guide such of Our servants as We will;
and truly you are guiding to the Straight Way, the Way of God
to Whom belongs whatever is in the heavens and whatever is on earth:
witness how all affairs incline towards God!

[*Sūrah ash-Shūrā* 42:51-53]

Sudden inspiration is the primary meaning of *waḥy*, a term which combines the concepts of suddenness and inner illumination (Rāghib); in the usage of the Qur'ān, it is often, though by no means always, synonymous with "revelation."

Whatever He wills [*to reveal*] mirrors 53:10: *And thus did* [*God*] *reveal to His servant whatever He deemed right to reveal.*

You did not know what revelation was or what faith was: i.e., that the very concept of "faith" implies man's complete self-surrender (*islām*) to God.

Witness how all affairs incline towards God!: literally, *to God do all things* (al-umūr) *pursue their course:* i.e., all things go back to Him as their source,

286

and from His will depends the course which they take (Bayḍāwī). (Asad, p. 748)

Pairs

And He it is Who has created all pairs.

[*Sūrah Zukhruf* 43:12]

The term *azwāj* can be translated as opposites but literally means "all pairs." Some commentators regard this term as synonymous in this context with "kind": i.e., they take the above phrase to mean no more than that God created *all kinds* of things, beings, and phenomena. Others see in it a reference to the *polarity* evident in all creation. Ibn 'Abbās (as quoted by Rāzī) says that it denotes the concept of *opposites* in general, like "sweet and sour, or white and black, or male and female"; to which Rāzī adds that everything in creation has its complement, "like high and low, right and left, front and back, past and future, being and attribute," etc., whereas God—and He alone—is unique, without anything that could be termed "opposite" or "similar" or "complementary." Hence, the above sentence is an echo of the statement that *there is nothing that could be compared with Him* [112:4]. (Asad, p. 750)

288

Lost in the Pursuit of Pleasures

And thus it is: whenever We sent, before your time,
a warner to any community, those of its people
who had lost themselves entirely in the pursuit of pleasures
would always say:
"Behold, we found our forefathers agreed on what to believe—
and, truly, it is but in their footsteps that we follow!"

[*Sūrah Zukhruf* 43:23]

Those of its people who had lost themselves entirely in the pursuit of pleasures. The verb *tarifa* means "he enjoyed a life of ease and plenty," while the participle *mutraf* denotes "one who enjoys a life of ease and plenty" or "indulges in the pleasures of life," i.e., to the exclusion of moral considerations. The form *mutarraf* has an additional significance, namely, "one whom a life of softness and ease has caused to behave insolently," or "one whom the [exclusive] pursuit of the pleasures of life has corrupted" (*Mughnī*).

It is but in their footsteps that we follow: commenting on this passage, Rāzī says: "Had there been in the Qurʾān nothing but these verses, they would have sufficed to show the falsity of the principle postulating blind, unquestioning adoption of religious opinions (*ibṭāl al-qawl bi't-taqlīd*): for God has made it clear that those deniers of the truth had not arrived at their convictions by way of reason, and neither on the clear authority of a revealed text, but solely by blindly adopting the opinions of their forebears and predecessors; and all this God has mentioned in terms of blame and sharp disparagement." (Asad, pp. 334, 752)

The Way

And we gave them the stimulus of clear signs:
and it was only after all this knowledge had been given to them
that they began, out of mutual jealousy, to hold divergent views:
but, truly, your Sustainer will judge between them on Resurrection Day
regarding everything about which they differed.
And finally, [O Muḥammad,]
We have set you on a dynamic, purposeful Way;
so follow this and don't be diverted by the likes and dislikes
of those who do not know.

[*Sūrah al-Jāthiyah* 45:17–18]

This is one of the few passages in the Qur'ān that refers to a *sharīʿah*, which is here translated as "Way." What we have translated as *a dynamic, purposeful Way*, Muḥammad Asad translates quite differently: *We have set you on a way by which the purpose [of faith] may be fulfilled.* A literal translation might be: *a way from the command (amr).* What is difficult to put into English words here is that this way comes from some Force with a sense of Purpose. Over time, *sharīʿah* came to refer to a codification of religious law, but here the meaning suggests a dynamic directedness, a flowing power. Taking into account the totality of teachings in the Qur'ān, the purpose of human life is realized and attained when one can live in constant remembrance of God, performing those actions which lead to reconciliation and well-being for all, remaining true to the mission of being God's representative (*khalīfa*) on earth, without being distracted by the opinions and judgments of those who have no knowledge or experience

290

of the spiritual dimension of life. (Helminski)

We gave them clear indications of the purpose [of faith] (translated above as *the stimulus of clear signs*): this, I believe, is the meaning of the phrase *min al-amr* in the above context, although most of the classical commentators are of the opinion that *amr* signifies here "religion" (*dīn*), and interpret the whole phrase, accordingly, as "of what pertains to religion." Since, however, the common denominator in all the possible meanings of the term *amr*—e.g., "command," "injunction," "ordinance," "matter [of concern]," "event," "action," etc.—is the element of *purpose*, whether implied or explicit, we may safely assume that this is the meaning of the term in the above elliptic phrase, which obviously alludes to the purpose underlying all divine revelation and, consequently, man's faith in it. Now from the totality of the Qurʾanic teachings it becomes apparent that the innermost purpose of all true faith is, firstly, a realization of the existence of God and of every human being's responsibility to Him; secondly, man's attaining to a consciousness of his own dignity as a positive element—a *logically necessary* element—in God's plan of creation and, thus, achieving freedom from all manner of superstitions and irrational fears; and, lastly, making man aware that whatever good or evil he does is but done for the benefit, or to the detriment, of his own self.

It is to be borne in mind that the literal meaning of the term *sharīʿah* is "the way to a watering-place," and since water is indispensable for all organic life, this term has in time come to denote a "system of laws," both moral and practical, which shows man the way towards spiritual fulfillment and social welfare: hence, "religious law" in the widest sense of the term. (Asad, p. 767)

Spend Freely in the Way of God

The life of this world is just a play and a passing delight,
yet if you have faith and are mindful of Him,
He will grant you your recompense
and will not ask you for all your possessions.
If He were to ask you for all of them and press you,
you would grasp them more tightly,
and He would elicit all your ill-feeling.
Witness that you are those invited
to spend freely in the Way of God;
but among you are some who are stingy.
But any who are stingy are so at the expense of their own souls.
But God is free of all wants and it is you who are needy.

[*Sūrah Muḥammad* 47:36-38]

Amusement and play are not bad things in themselves. As preparations for the more serious life, they have their value. But if we concentrate on them, and neglect the business of life, we cannot prosper. We must use our life in this world as a preparation for our spiritual or inner life. This life is but an interlude, a preparation for the real Life, which is in the Hereafter. This world's vanities are therefore to be taken for what they are worth; but they are not to be allowed to deflect our minds from the requirements of the inner life that really matters. (*What is the life of this world but play and a passing delight? The life in the hereafter is by far the better for all who are conscious of God. [6:32]. What is the life of this world but a passing delight and play? Truly the life in the hereafter is life indeed, if they but knew*

292

[29:64].)

He will not ask you for all your possessions. Complete self-sacrifice, if voluntarily offered, has a meaning: it means that the person's devotion is exclusively and completely for the cause. But no law or rule can *demand* it. And a mere offer to kill yourself has no meaning. You should be ready to take risks to your life in fighting for the cause, but you should aim at life, not death. If you live, you should be ready to place your substance and your acquisitions at the disposal of the cause. But it is not reasonable to pauperize yourself and become a hanger-on. Moreover, the inborn tendency to self-preservation in an average man would lead to concealment and niggardliness if *all* were asked for the cause, by law, and there would further be a feeling of bitterness and rebellion.

And let not those who covetously withhold of the gifts which Allāh has given them of His Grace think that it is good for them. Nay, it will be the worse for them: soon shall the things which they covetously withheld be tied to their necks like a twisted collar, on the Day of Judgment [3:180]. The gifts of God are of all kinds: material gifts, such as wealth, property, strength of limbs, etc., or intangible gifts, such as influence, birth in a given set, intellect, skill, insight, etc., or spiritual gifts of the highest kind. The spending on all these things (apart from what is necessary for ourselves) for those who need them is charity, and purifies our own character. The withholding of them (apart from our needs) is similarly greed and selfishness, and is strongly condemned.

Witness that you are those invited to spend freely in the Way of God: here the cases of the special devotee and of the average man with his human foibles are distinguished. Stinginess is not a virtue: it hurts more the finer nature of the individual practicing it than it hurts the cause. God is free of all wants and independent of any need that we can meet. His cause is similarly independent of human aid. But it uses human agency for our own human advancement. The need to be able to serve in the Kingdom of Heaven is ours. We are the needy beggars who should claim the privilege before the Lord of bounties unbounded. If we desert the cause, the cause will not fail. (A. Yusuf Ali, pp. 1387, 1047, 1388, 170)

Tranquility

It is He Who sent down tranquility
into the hearts of the faithful
so that they may add faith to their faith;
for to God belong the forces of the heavens and the earth;
and God is All-Knowing, All-Wise.

[*Sūrah al-Fatḥ* 48:4]

Historically, this refers to the Treaty of Ḥudaybiyyah. By this treaty the Meccan Quraish, after many years of unrelenting conflict with Islam, at length recognized Islam as an equal power with themselves. There were 1400 to 1500 unarmed men who had accompanied the Prophet, intending to perform the ʿumrah or lesser pilgrimage. They turned aside to Ḥudaybiyyah when they were threatened with violence by the excited Quriash leaders of Mecca. The successful negotiation of the treaty was achieved by tranquility, calmness, and cool courage among the Prophet and his followers.

So that they may add faith to their faith: are there degrees in faith? The plain meaning is that believers will see one sign of God after another, and with each their faith is confirmed. During all the long years of persecution and conflict they had faith, but when they see their old enemies actually coming out to negotiate with them, their faith is justified, fulfilled, and confirmed, and they turn in gratitude to God. (A. Yusuf Ali, pp. 1391, 1389)

295

The Pledge

Truly those who pledge their loyalty to you
do no less than pledge their loyalty to God.
The Hand of God is over their hands.
Then anyone who violates their oath
does so to the harm of their own soul
and anyone who remains true to what he or she has pledged to God,
God will grant them a supreme recompense. . . .
Indeed, well-pleased was God with the believers
when they pledged their allegiance to you
[O Muḥammad] under that tree,
for He knew what was in their hearts;
and so He bestowed inner peace upon them from on high,
and rewarded them with a victory soon to come
and many war-gains which they would achieve:
for God is indeed almighty, wise.

[*Sūrah al-Fatḥ* 48:10, 18–19]

The hand of God is over their hands refers, in the first instance, to the pledge of faith and allegiance (*bayʿat ar-riḍwān*) which the Muslims assembled at Ḥudaybiyyah gave to the Prophet. Near the end of the sixth year of the *hijrah*, the Prophet went with 1400–1500 men, dressed in the pilgrim's garb and armed only with sheathed swords, to perform the "lesser pilgrimage" or "pious visit" (*ʿumrah*) to Mecca. This was during one of the four "sacred months" during which, in accordance with time-honored Arabian custom, all warfare was outlawed, and particularly so in and

296

around the Holy City. On learning of the Prophet's approach, the Meccans decided—against all Arabian tradition—to oppose the entry of the pilgrims by force of arms. Since the Prophet was neither inclined nor in a position to give battle, he turned westwards to the plain of Ḥudaybiyyah. The Prophet sent ʿUthmān ibn ʿAffān (who belonged to one of the most influential Meccan clans) as his envoy. Shortly after ʿUthmān's arrival in Mecca, a rumor that he had been murdered reached the Muslim camp at Ḥudaybiyyah. Thereupon the Prophet, expecting a treacherous attack by the Meccans, assembled his followers and, sitting under a wild acacia tree, took, amid scenes of the greatest enthusiasm, a pledge from each one of his followers that they would remain steadfast and fight to death; and after the revelation of verse 48:18 , this "Pledge of the Tree" became known to history as Bayʿat ar-Riḍwān ("the Pledge of [God's] Goodly Acceptance"). When a few days later the rumor of ʿUthmān's death proved false and he himself returned to Ḥudaybiyyah, it became clear that the Meccans were prepared to conclude a truce.

Beyond this historical allusion, however, this phrase implies that as one's faith in God's message-bearer is to all intents and purposes synonymous with a declaration of faith in God Himself, so does one's willingness to obey God necessarily imply a willingness to obey His message-bearer. The phrase *the hand of God is over their hands* does not merely allude to the hand-clasp with which all of the Prophet's followers affirmed their allegiance to him, but is also a metaphor for His being a witness to their pledge.

Another mention of a pledge of allegiance (*bayʿah*) is in 60:12: *O Prophet! Whenever believing women come to you to pledge their allegiance to you, that they would not ascribe divinity, in any way, to aught but God, and would not steal, and would not commit adultery, and would not kill their children, and would not indulge in slander, falsely devising it out of nothingness, and would not disobey you in anything right—then accept their pledge of allegiance, and pray to God to forgive them their sins: for, behold, God is much-forgiving, a dispenser of grace*. It should be noted that this pledge doesn't differ essentially from that of a male convert. (Asad, pp. 784, 786, 858)

The Religion of Truth

It is He Who has sent His Messenger with guidance
and the Religion of Truth,
so that it might manifest itself to all religion;
and God is sufficient as witness.
Muḥammad is the Messenger of God;
and those who are with him stand firm
when facing those who deny the Truth,
and are compassionate with each other.
You can see them bow and prostrate themselves in prayer,
seeking grace from God and His good pleasure.
On their faces are their marks, the imprint of prostration.
This is their parable in the Torah,
and their parable in the Gospel:
like a seed which sends forth its shoot, which grows strong,
so that it becomes thick, and then stands firm on its stem,
delighting those who sow with wonder.
And through them the deniers are confounded.
God has promised those among them who have faith
and do righteous deeds forgiveness and a supreme reward.

[*Sūrah al-Fatḥ* 48:28-29]

The first *āyah* is often translated *so that it might prevail over all religion*, implying that the religion Muḥammad brought would dominate or rule all other religions. Another more nuanced translation is possible that is truer

299

to the root meaning of DH-H-R, which means become clear, apparent, or manifest. Thus we translate this passage as *manifest itself to all religion*, which can be understood to mean that the religion of Truth is evident and clear above all religions for those who are willing to perceive it. This is essentially the same idea that is expressed elsewhere in the Qur'ān that *Truth will stand out from falsehood* [17:81], that the clear, undistorted truth brought by the Qur'ān can help to restore the essential truth brought by earlier prophets. (Helminski)

God is sufficient as witness: the divine disposition of events in the coming of Islam and its promulgation by the holy Prophet are themselves evidence of the truth of Islam and its all-reaching character; for there is nothing which it has not influenced. There is really only one true religion, the Message of God, submission to the Will of God: this is called Islam. It was the religion preached by Moses and Jesus; it was the religion of Abraham, Noah, and all the prophets, by whatever name it may be called.

Those who are with him stand firm when facing those who deny the Truth, and are compassionate with each other: the devotees of God wage unceasing war against evil, for themselves, and for others; but to their own brethren in faith—especially the weaker ones—they are mild and compassionate. They seek out every opportunity to sympathize with them and help them.

You can see them bow and prostrate themselves in prayer, seeking grace from God and His good pleasure: their humility is before God and His Apostle and all who have authority from God, but they yield no power or pomp, nor do they worship worldly show or glitter. Nor is their humility before God a mere show for men.

On their faces are their marks, traced by prostration. The traces of their earnestness and humility are engraved on their faces, i.e., penetrate their inmost being, the face being the outward sign of the inner man. If we take it in its literal sense, the traces might mean the marks left by repeated

300

prostration on their foreheads. Moreover, a good man's face alone shows in him the grace and light of God; he is gentle, kind, and forbearing, ever-helpful, relying on God, and possessing a blessed peace and calmness (*sakīnah*, 48:26) that can come from no other source.

This is their parable in the Torah: in the Book of Moses, now found in a corrupt form in the Pentateuch, the posture of humility in prayer is indicated by prostration: e.g., Moses and Aaron "fell upon their faces," Numbers 16:22.

Their parable in the Gospel: like a seed which sends forth its shoot, which grows strong, so that it becomes thick, and then stands firm on its stem, delighting those who sow with wonder. The similitude in the Gospel is about how the good seed is sown and grows gradually, even beyond the expectation of the sower; "the seed should spring and grow up, he knoweth not how; for the earth bringeth forth fruit of herself: first the blade, then the ear, after that the full corn in the ear" (Mark 4:27-28). Thus Islam was preached by the holy Prophet; the seed seemed to human eyes lost in the ground, but it put forth its shoot and grew, and became strong, until it was able to stand on its own legs, and its worst enemies recognized its existence and its right to live. Note how much more complete the parable is in the Qur'ān. The mentality of the sowers of the seed is expressed in the beautiful terms: its growth and strength filled them *with wonder and delight*. The result of the wonderful growth of Islam in numbers and strength was that its enemies were confounded, and raged furiously within their own minds, a contrast to the satisfaction, wonder, and delight of the Prophet and his Companions. (A. Yusuf Ali, pp. 1400-1401, 1541)

Unity Among People of Faith

The faithful are but a single brotherhood.
So make peace between your two contending siblings,
and remain conscious of God
so that you may be graced with God's Mercy.
O you who have faith!
Do not let some men among you laugh at others;
it may be that the others are better than they.
Nor let some women laugh at others;
it may be that the others are better than they.
Nor speak ill nor with sarcasm towards each other,
nor call each other by taunting names:
a name connoting wickedness
is inappropriate after one has come to faith,
and those who do not stop are doing wrong.
O you who have attained to faith!
As much as you can, avoid suspicion,
for suspicion in some cases is a sin;
and do not spy on each other,
nor speak ill of one another behind each other's backs.
Would any of you like to eat the flesh of his dead brother?
No, you would detest it . . . but remain conscious of God:
for truly, God is ever turning one towards repentance,
Infinitely Merciful.
O humankind! We created you all out of a male and a female,
and made you into nations and tribes

that you might come to know each other.
Truly, the noblest of you in the sight of God
is the one who is most mindful.
And God is All-knowing and is Aware of all things.

[*Sūrah al-Ḥujurāt* 49:10-13]

The implication is that believers, whether men or women, shall never deride one another (Zamakhsharī, Bayḍawī).

Nor speak ill nor with sarcasm towards each other, nor call each other by taunting names: a name connoting wickedness is inappropriate after one has come to faith. This applies no less to the faith of the one who insults than to that of the insulted (Rāzī).

As much as you can, avoid suspicion: i.e., guesswork that may lead to unfounded suspicion of another person's motives.

We have created you all out of a male and a female: i.e., "We have created every one of you out of a father and a mother" (Zamakhsharī, Rāzī, Bayḍawī)—implying that this equality of biological origin is reflected in the equality of the human dignity common to all.

We have made you into nations and tribes so that you might come to know each other: i.e., know that all belong to one human family, without any inherent superiority of one over another (Zamakhsharī). This connects with the exhortation, in the preceding two verses, to respect and safeguard each other's dignity. In other words, men's evolution into *nations and tribes* is meant to foster rather than to diminish their mutual desire to understand and appreciate the essential human oneness underlying their outward differentiations; and, correspondingly, all racial, national, or tribal prejudice (ʿaṣabiyyah) is condemned—implicitly in the Qurʾān and most explicitly by the Prophet: "He is not of us who proclaims the cause of tribal partisanship (ʿaṣabiyyah); and he is not of us who fights in the cause of tribal partisanship; and he is not of us who dies in the cause of tribal partisanship" (Abū Dāʾūd, on the authority of Jubayr ibn Mutʿim). When he was asked to explain the meaning of "tribal partisanship," the Prophet answered "It means helping your own people in an unjust cause" (*ibid.*, on the authority of Wāthilah ibn al-Aqsaʿ).

In addition, speaking of people's boasting of their national or tribal past, the Prophet said: "Behold, God has removed from you the arrogance of pagan ignorance (*jāhiliyyah*) with its boast of ancestral glories. Man is but a God-conscious believer or an unfortunate sinner. All people are children of Adam, and Adam was created out of dust." (Fragment of a *ḥadīth* quoted by Tirmidhī and Abū Dāʾʾūd, on the authority of Abū Hurayrah.) (Asad, pp. 794, 591)

Mutual ridicule ceases to be fun when there is arrogance or selfishness or malice behind it. We may laugh *with* people, to share in the happiness of life; we must never laugh *at* people in contempt or ridicule. In many things they may be better than ourselves!

Defamation may consist in speaking ill of others by the spoken or written word, or in acting in such a way as to suggest a charge against some person whom we are not in a position to judge. A cutting, biting remark or taunt or sarcasm is included in the word *lamaza*. An offensive nickname may amount to defamation, but in any case there is no point in using offensive nicknames, or names that suggest some real or fancied defect. They ill-accord with the serious purpose which Muslims should have in life. For example, even if a man is lame, it is wrong to address him as "O lame one!" It causes him pain, and it is bad manners. So in the case of the rude remark, "the black man."

Most kinds of suspicion are baseless and to be avoided, and some are crimes in themselves: for they do cruel injustice to innocent men and women. Spying, or enquiring too curiously into other people's affairs, means either idle curiosity, and is therefore futile, or suspicion carried a stage further, which almost amounts to sin. Backbiting also is a brood of the same genius. It may be either futile but all the same mischievous or it may be poisoned with malice, in which case it is a sin added to sin.

No one would like even to think of such an abomination as eating the flesh of his brother. But when the brother is dead and the flesh is carrion, abomination is added to abomination. In the same way we are asked to refrain from hurting people's feelings when they are present; how much worse is it when we say things, true or false, when they are absent?

O humankind! We created you all out of a male and a female: this is addressed to all mankind and not only to the Muslim brotherhood, though it is understood that in a perfect world the two would be synonymous. As it is, mankind is descended from one pair of parents. Their tribes, races, and nations are convenient labels by which we may know certain differing characteristics. Before God they are all one, and he gets most honor who is most righteous. (A. Yusuf Ali, pp. 1405-1407)

Nearness

It was We Who created the human being
and We know what his inmost self whispers within him,
*for **We are nearer to him than his jugular vein**.*

[*Sūrah Qāf* 50:16]

God created man, and gave him his limited free will. God knows the innermost desires and motives of man even better than man does himself. He is nearer to man than the man's own jugular vein. The jugular vein is the big trunk vein, one on each side of the neck, which brings the blood back from the head to the heart. The two jugular veins correspond to the two carotid arteries which carry the blood from the heart to the head. As the blood stream is the vehicle of life and consciousness, the phrase *nearer than the jugular vein* implies that God knows more truly the innermost state of our feeling and consciousness than does our own ego. (A. Yusuf Ali, p. 1412)

From our point of view, we can speak of being nearer to God or farther away from Him. The proximity to God varies with each human being, and with the spiritual state of any single individual. But no matter how far away from Him we may be, He is always near to us.

Some may imagine that to say God is nearer to man than his jugular vein has something to do with gross anatomy—that it refers, perhaps, to the spinal column, which is the physical center or pole of the human body. But this is too literalistic. To say that God is nearer to man than his jugular vein is simply a way of saying that He is closer to you than you

306

are to yourself.

But what does this mean? How can something be closer to me than I am to myself?

To answer this, we have to ask ourselves exactly who this "self" is. According to the Qur'ān (*Sūrah al-Ḥadīd,* 57:3) God is both the *Outwardly Manifest* and the *Inwardly Hidden.* The stars and galaxies do not, of course, "add up" to God, nor is He the sum of my inner states, or of all the inner states of all the conscious beings in the universe. But behind the veil of outer reality, and beneath the veil of my subjective experiences, God is there. There is nothing we see that is not *essentially* of Him; He is behind my subjective experience; just as He is behind the mask of outer reality. The universe we experience is not God, because everything we experience is limited by our subjectivity, and God is not limited. Nor is our experience itself God; He is beyond anything that can be experienced or known. Nonetheless, He is the ultimate Witness of our experience, as well as the ultimate Object of it. But if this is true, then what is left of what we usually think of as our "self"? Truly nothing at all is left of it; it is simply a "place" where God witnesses God. On the deepest level, this is what the human being is: the mirror of God.

A mirror has no shape or color of its own; it takes on the shape and color of whatever it faces. If we face toward the world, we assume the shape of dispersion and multiplicity; if we face toward God, we reflect only Unity—and God, in witnessing us, sees all possible forms and events reflected in us, and knows them as Himself. This act of God witnessing God in us is nearer to us than our bodies; it is nearer to us than our souls; its home is the spiritual Heart. The Heart is the place in us where God is nearer to us than we are to ourselves, *nearer than our jugular vein.*

The truths expressed in the verses of the Qur'ān are not only doctrines we are called on to believe or commands and prohibitions we are called on to observe; some are precise methods for contemplating God. Try to imagine a Reality that is closer to you than you are to yourself.

What happens? You may begin to have an intuition of such a Reality. In trying to conceive of God as nearer to us than our jugular vein, we come up against an absolute limit. This limit, however, teaches us something real. As Abū Bakr said, "to know that God is unknowable is to know God." Our knowledge of ourselves is always imperfect, but His knowledge of us does not come up against any kind of limit. So we can say that *His knowledge of us is what we truly are.* In the words of the Prophet Muḥammad Σ, "Pray to God as if you saw Him, because even if you don't see Him, He sees you." (Upton)

A Watcher Ever-Present

Whenever the two demands [of his nature] come face to face,
contending from the right and from the left,
not even a word can he utter
but there is a watcher with him, ever-present.

And the twilight of death brings with it the truth—
that from which you would always look away!—
and the trumpet will be blown:
that will be the Day of a warning fulfilled.
And every human being will come forward
with his inner urges and his conscious mind,
and will be told "Indeed, unmindful have you been of this;
but now We have lifted from you your veil,
and clear is your seeing today!

[*Sūrah Qāf* 50:17-22]

The two fundamental motive forces within man's nature are his primal, instinctive urges and desires, both sensual and non-sensual (all of them comprised in the modern psychological term "libido"), on the one side, and his reason, both intuitive and reflective, on the other. The *sitting* (*qāʿid*) *on the right and on the left* is, to my mind, a metaphor for the conflicting nature of these dual forces which strive for predominance within every human being: hence my rendering of *qāʿid* as "contending." This interpretation is, moreover, strongly supported by the reference in verse 50:21 to man's appearing on Judgment Day with *that which drives* (*sāʾiq*)

309

and that which bears witness (*shahīd*)—a phrase which undoubtedly alludes to man's instinctive urges as well as his conscious reason. While *that which drives* evidently circumscribes man's primal urges—and particularly those which drive him into unrestrained self-indulgence and thus into sin—the term *shahīd* alludes here to the awakening of the deeper layers of man's consciousness, leading to a sudden perception of his own moral reality— the *lifting of the veil* referred to in 50:22—which forces him to "bear witness" against himself. (Asad, p. 798)

Conscious Mind

And paradise will be brought near to the God-conscious,
no longer will it be distant:
"This is what was promised for you—
to everyone who would turn to God
and keep Him always in remembrance—
who stood in awe of the Most Compassionate though unseen
and brought a heart turned in devotion to Him;
Enter here in peace and security; this is the Day of eternal Life!"
There will be for them there all that they may wish
and yet more in Our Presence. . . .
In this, behold, there is indeed
a reminder for everyone
whose heart is wide-awake—that is,
who listens and witnesses. . .
Bear then with patience all that they say
and celebrate the praises of your Sustainer
before the rising of the sun and before its setting
and in the night also celebrate His praises
and at the end of prostration.
And listen for the Day
when the Caller will call out from a place quite near.

[*Sūrah Qāf* 50:31-35, 37, 39-41]

The implication of this general call to repentance is that since *man has been created weak* [4:28], no one is ever free of faults and temptations—so much

311

so that even the Prophet used to say, "Truly, I turn to Him in repentance a hundred times every day" (Ibn Ḥanbal, Bukhārī, and Bayhaqī, all of them on the authority of ʿAbd Allāh ibn ʿUmar).

A reminder for everyone whose heart is wide-awake was the understanding provided by Zamakhsharī; literally, the phrase reads, *who has a heart. Who lends ear with a conscious mind as a witness* is literally, *or lends ear and is withal a witness* (wa-huwa shahīd), which latter phrase Zamakhsharī explains as meaning *is present with his intellect,* i.e., with a conscious mind (the term *shahīd* is used in the same way in 50:21). The whole of this passage stresses God's omnipotence, which can be perceived by anyone whose heart is wide-awake. (Asad, pp. 539, 800)

In this life, the ideals of the spirit, the accomplishment of the things in our hearts and our hopes, seem to be ever so far, seem even to recede as we think we come nearer. Not so in the Hereafter. The fruits of right-eousness will no longer be in the distance. They will be realized. They will seem themselves to approach the righteous.

To everyone who would turn to God and keep Him always in remem-brance—who stood in awe of the Most Compassionate though unseen and brought a heart turned in devotion to Him. The description of the righteous is given in four masterly clauses: (1) those who turned away from evil in sincere repentance; (2) those whose new life was good and righteous; (3) those who in their innermost hearts and in their most secret doings were actu-ated by God-fearing love, the fear that is akin to love in remembering God under His title of "Most Gracious"; and (4) who gave up their whole heart and being to Him.

The Most Compassionate, though unseen: their reverence for God is un-affected by the fact they do not see Him, or that other people do not ob-serve them, because their attitude arises out of a genuine love for God.

Enter here in peace and security. This is the true meaning of Islām: peace, security, salutation, and accord with God's Plan in all eternity.

There will be for them there all that they may wish and yet more in Our

Presence. To get all that our purified wishes and desires comprehend may seem to sum up final bliss, but there is something still wanting, which is supplied by the Presence of God, the Light of His countenance.

Celebrate the praises of your Sustainer before the rising of the sun and before its setting and in the night also celebrate His praises. God should be remembered at all times. But the best time for individual adoration is early in the morning before sunrise, late in the day before sunset, and a portion of the night, when there is stillness in the air, and man's spirit loves to commune with things spiritual. Those who would connect this with the five canonical prayers, introduced at a later stage in Medina, would take the *Fajr* for the prayer before sunrise, the *Zuhr* and the *ʿAṣr* for the afternoon prayers before sunset, and the *Maghrib* and the *ʿIshāʿ* for the night prayers. *And at the end of prostration:* this could also be translated as *after the postures of adoration*. Its general meaning would be the contemplation and remembrance of God after prayers. Those who would connect this passage with the five canonical prayers understand these further prayers "following the *sujud* or postures of adoration" to mean the extra or supernumerary prayers known as *nafl*, also the use of prayer beads in remembering the Names of God.

And listen for the Day: the Day of Resurrection when the call to the souls to arise and come to the judgment seat will be immediately answered, and they will all arise and come forth. (See <u>36:47-58</u>.) *When the Caller will call out from a place quite near:* in the life of this world it seemed all so remote. In the new life at the resurrection it will all be so near; for there will be neither time nor space as we know them here. (A. Yusuf Ali, pp. 1415-1418, 1171)

Signs for Inner Certainty

Witness: the God-conscious will be amid gardens and springs,
taking joy in that which their Sustainer gives them
because before then they had lived a good life:
they would sleep only a little at night
and from the core of their hearts they would pray for forgiveness;
and of all that they possessed would grant a rightful share
to the one who asked and the one who was not able.
On the earth are signs for those with inner certainty,
just as within your own selves: will you not then deeply see?
And in heaven is your sustenance
and all that which you are promised.
Then by the Sustainer of heaven and earth, this is the Truth—
as true as the fact that you are able to speak.

[*Sūrah adh-Dhāriyāt* 51:15-23]

Gardens and springs are the two most frequent symbols for the highest satisfaction and bliss.

They would sleep only a little at night: they were engaged most of the night in worship and in the planning of good deeds. They preferred activity to idleness, the service of God and His creatures to the indulgence of self.

And from the core of their hearts they would pray for forgiveness: this could also be translated *and in the hours of early dawn they were praying for forgiveness"* They were up early, before dawn, ready for their devotions. The praying for forgiveness and mercy does not necessarily imply that they

314

had committed fresh sins. Indeed, they *began* the day with such devotions, showing their great humility before God and their anxious care for others, for whom they prayed as much as for themselves. The use of the plural tense indicates that we associate ourselves with all who seek God, thus strengthening ourselves and strengthening them in a fellowship of faith.

And of all that they possessed would grant a rightful share to the one who asked and the one who was not able. True charity remembers not only those in need who ask, but also those who are prevented by some reason from asking. The man of true charity seeks out the latter. There may be various reasons which prevent a man from asking for help: (1) he may be ashamed to ask, or his sense of honor may prevent him from asking; (2) he may be so engrossed in some great ideal that he may not think of asking; (3) he may even not know that he is in need, especially when we think of wealth and possessions in a spiritual sense, as including spiritual gifts and talents; (4) he may not know that you possess the things that can supply his needs; and (5) he may be a dumb and helpless creature, whether a human being or a dumb animal, or any creature within your ken or power. Charity in the higher sense includes all help, from one better endowed to one less endowed.

On the earth are signs for those with inner certainty, just as within your own selves: the signs and evidences of God are in all nature and within the body and soul of man, if man has but the spiritual eyes to see. *We will show them Our signs on the farthest horizons and within their own selves, until it becomes manifest to them that this is the Truth* [41:53].

And in heaven is your sustenance: "sustenance," here as elsewhere, includes physical sustenance, as well as spiritual sustenance. Similarly heaven or sky has both the physical and the spiritual meaning. The physical sustenance grows from rain from the sky; the spiritual sustenance comes from the divine aid, grace, and mercy, and includes the good news and the warning which come from revelation about the hereafter.

Then by the Sustainer of heaven and earth, this is the Truth—as true as the

315

fact that you are able to speak. Attention having been called to the signs or evidences of God's working on the earth, within ourselves, and in the heavens, an appeal is made to our own inner conscience, in the name of the Lord of heaven and earth, to acknowledge and live up to the truth of revelation, and turn to the spiritual realities. For they are as real as our own conscious and self-intelligent existence, on which is based all our knowledge. (A. Yusuf Ali, pp. 1422-1423, 14)

From the core of their hearts they would pray for forgiveness. The expression *bi'l-ashār* is usually taken to mean "at the times before daybreak," or simply "before daybreak." This is in agreement with the Prophet's recommendation to his followers (forthcoming from several authentic Traditions) to devote the latter part of the night, and particularly the time shortly before dawn, to intensive prayer. But while the word *sahar* (also spelled *sahr* and *suhr*), of which *ashār* is the plural, undoubtedly denotes "the time before daybreak," it also signifies—in the spellings *sahar* and *suhr*—"the core of the heart," "the inner part of the heart," or simply "heart" (compare *Lisān al'Arab;* also Lane IV, 1316). It seems to me that in the context of verse 3:17 as well as 51:18—the rendering *pray for forgiveness from their innermost hearts* is preferable to the conventional one; for although the value of praying before daybreak has undoubtedly been stressed by the Prophet, it is not very plausible that the Qur'ān should have tied the *prayer for forgiveness* to a particular time of day.

On the earth are signs for those with inner certainty, just as within your own selves: will you not then see? The intricate structure of human and animal bodies, and the life-preserving instincts with which all living creatures have been endowed, make it virtually impossible to assume that all this has developed "by accident." And if we assume, as we must, that a creative *purpose* underlies all this development, we must conclude, too, that it has been willed by a conscious Power which creates all natural phenomena *in accordance with an inner truth* [10:5].

And in heaven is your sustenance: i.e., both physical (rain) and spiritual

316

(truth and guidance). (Asad, pp. 68, 803, 765)

Polarities

And it is We Who have built the universe with power,
and, truly, it is We Who are expanding it,
And We have spread out the earth,
and how well have We ordered it.
And in everything have We created polarities,
so that you might be mindful.
*And so, say: "**Flee to God**;*
I am a clear warner from Him."

[*Sūrah adh-Dhāriyāt* 51:47–50]

All things are in twos: sex in plants and animals, by which one individual is complementary to another; in the subtle forces of nature, day and night, positive and negative electricity, forces of attraction and repulsion, and numerous other opposites, each fulfilling its purpose and contributing to the working of God's universe; and in the moral and spiritual world, love and aversion, mercy and justice, striving and rest, and so on, all fulfilling their functions according to the artistry and wonderful purpose of God. Everything has its counterpart, or pair, or complement. God alone is One, with none like Him, or needed to complement Him. These are noble things to contemplate. And they lead us to a true understanding of God's purpose and message. (A. Yusuf Ali, p. 1427)

And in everything have We created polarities is literally, *of every thing have We created pairs.* This mirrors: *Limitless in His glory is He Who has created opposites in whatever the earth produces, and in men's own selves, and in that of*

318

which they have no knowledge [36:36]. This is a reference to the polarity evident in all creation, both animate and inanimate, which expresses itself in the existence of antithetic and yet complementary forces, like the sexuality in human beings, animals and plants, light and darkness, heat and cold, positive and negative magnetism and electricity, the positive and negative charges (protons and electrons) in the structure of the atom, and so forth.

And He it is Who has created all living things in pairs as opposites [43:12]. Some commentators regard the term *azwāj* (pairs) as synonymous in this context with "kinds" (Baghawī, Zamakhsharī, Baydāwī, Ibn Kathīr): i.e., they take the above phrase to mean no more than that God created *all kinds* of things, beings, and phenomena. Others (e.g., Tabarī) see in it a reference to the *polarity* evident in all creation. Ibn ᶜAbbās (as quoted by Rāzī) says that it denotes the concept of *opposites* in general, like "sweet and sour, or white and black, or male and female," to which Rāzī adds that everything in creation has its complement, "like high and low, right and left, front and back, past and future, being and attribute," etc., whereas God—and He alone—is unique, without anything that could be termed "opposite" or "similar" or "complementary." Hence the above sentence is an echo of the statement that *there is nothing that could be compared with Him* [112:4]. (Asad, pp. 676, 750)

The Qurʾān urges us to flee to God because God is the ultimate refuge. Whatever winds may blow, whatever earthquakes may shake the bedrock under our feet, God is stronger than any wind and deeper than any rock. His first determination, the first image or echo of His Reality, is Being itself—and whatever *is* by Its own nature cannot not be. It cannot be menaced by the relative non-being we call evil. And the guarantee of His Being is His Absolute Essence, which is beyond even Being.

The command *flee to God* is addressed to the part of us which is always in flight; it is as if the Qurʾān were saying, "since you are already

319

fleeing, you'd better make the most of it." At every moment—unless that moment is drowned in the remembrance of God—we are always running toward something, or away from something, or both. What is "ordinary life" but the endless attempt to avoid this or grasp that, with every breath we take, from birth until death? Whether the good we seek and the evil we flee are of a material or a spiritual nature, the result is the same. The life of the unbeliever, or the still-unbelieving parts of our soul, is nothing but flight, a flight that turns us into chaff, till we are scattered by the winds of life.

But the winds of life are also the winds of God. The very flight we so often find ourselves unable to avoid, or appease, or put to rest, is—if we only knew it—the darker side of Divine Mercy. Our own inability to *be* in any given moment has the potential to teach us that only God *is*. Our scatteredness itself may be, by God's grace, the very thing which reminds us that all things are gathered, as One, in God, and only in God.

We find it hard to approach God, hard to draw near to that overpowering Majesty, that Reality which is so often hidden from us, seemingly so distant, so opaque, so abstract. In fact, we find it impossible. Who are we to approach the Absolute Itself? We can do so only by the command of Allāh. Dragging ourselves through laborious lives, our vital energies scattered, unable to turn toward the *qiblah* of Unity and Life, we are half paralyzed, our spiritual perceptions darkened. Then comes the command: *Flee!* The full terror of our situation hits us all at once. So we run to God like a soldier to cover under a hail of bullets, like a farmer to higher ground when the dam breaks, like a child to its mother when the thunder comes. And what we find there, God willing, will make us thank those bullets, and that flood, and that thunder. All of them were Mercy—hard Mercy—like the verses of the Qurʾān. (Upton)

Created for Worship

Yet go on reminding: for reminding benefits the faithful.
And I have created the invisible beings and human beings
only that they may worship Me.
No sustenance do I require of them
nor do I require that they should feed Me.
For God is the Giver of All Sustenance,
the Lord of All Power, the Eternally Steadfast.

[*Sūrah adh-Dhāriyāt* 51:55-58]

Creation is not for idle sport or play. *Not for sport did We create the heavens and the earth and all that is between!* [21:16]. God has a serious purpose behind creation which, in our imperfect state, we can only express by saying that each creature is given the chance of development and progress towards the goal, which is God. God is the source and center of all power and all goodness, and our progress depends upon our putting ourselves into accord with His Will. This is His service. It is not of any benefit to Him; it is for our benefit.

No sustenance do I require of them in both the literal and the figurative sense; so also *feed Me* at the end of the verse. God is independent of all needs. It is therefore absurd to suppose that He should require *any* sustenance, and still more absurd to suppose that *we* can feed Him! The gifts, the sustenance, the goodness, all come from His side.

For God is the Giver of all sustenance, the Lord of all power, the eternally steadfast. God commands all power; therefore any power we seek must be from Him. And His power is steadfast, the same today as yesterday, and forever. Therefore His help is always sure. (A. Yusuf Ali, p. 1429)

321

Nothing Goes to Waste

And those who have faith
and whose families follow them in faith,
We shall unite them with their families;
and We shall not let anything of their work go to waste:
each human being will be held in pledge for his (or her) own deeds.

[*Sūrah aṭ-Ṭūr* 52:21]

The word translated as families is *ẕurriyat*, literally progeny, offspring, family. It is applied by extension to mean all near and dear ones whether related or not, ancestors and descendants, friends, a circle, a group, whether contemporaneous in time or not. Love is unselfish, and works not merely, or chiefly, for self, but for others. Provided the others have faith and respond according to their capacities or degrees, they will be joined on to the head of the group, even though on individual merits their rank might be less. This applies specially to a prophet and his *ummah* (or following).

Though the love poured out by prophets, ancestors, descendants, friends, or good men and women, will secure for their loved ones the enjoyment of their society, it is an indispensable condition that the loved ones should also, according to their lights, have shown their faith and their goodness in deeds. Each individual is responsible for his conduct. In the kingdom of heaven there is no boasting of ancestors or friends. But it is part of the satisfaction of the good ones who poured out their love that those who were in any way worthy to receive their love should also be admitted to their society, and the satisfaction shall in no wise be diminished to them. (A. Yusuf Ali, p. 1435)

With Our Sight

But, truly, for those who are bent on doing evil,
there is suffering in store
closer at hand than that [supreme suffering in the hereafter]:
but most of them are not aware of it.
Now await in patience the command of your Sustainer:
for truly you are within Our sight.
And celebrate the praises of your Sustainer
whenever you arise,
and for part of the night also praise Him
and at the retreat of the stars!

[*Sūrah aṭ-Ṭūr* 52:47-49]

For truly you are within Our sight or *you are in Our eyes*: the man of God must strive his utmost to proclaim the message of God; as for results, it is not for him to command them. He must wait patiently, in the knowledge that he is not forgotten by God, but is constantly under God's eyes, under His loving care and protection. And he must glorify God's name, as he is a standard-bearer of God's Truth.

And celebrate the praises of your Sustainer whenever you arise: the translators and commentators nearly all understand *taqūmu* in the sense of rising up from sleep. But the rendering I prefer, *the while you stand forth*, is consistent with Qur'anic usage. In 26:218 we have the same two words *ḥīna taqūmu* meaning *standing forth* (*in prayer*). In 57:25 we have *li-yaqūm an-nāsu bil-qisṭi*, which obviously means *that men may stand forth in justice*, i.e., do all their business in justice. In 78:38 we have *yaqūmu* used for the an-

323

gels standing forth in ranks. On my rendering the meaning will be *celebrate Allāh's praises when you stand forth in prayer, or at all times when you go about your business, but also for part of the night and at early dawn when worldly life is at a standstill.*

It is not necessary to understand the reference to part of the night for any particular canonical prayers. It is good to spend a part of the night in prayer and praise (*Truly rising at night for prayer is most potent for governing the self and most suitable for the word of prayer and praise* [73:6]). And the dawn is a daily recurring miracle of nature, full of spiritual influence and "testimony," compare 17:78-79: *Be constant in your prayer from the time when the sun has passed its zenith till the darkness of night and its recitation at dawn: for, behold, the recitation at dawn is indeed witnessed [by all that is holy]. And rise from your sleep and pray Tahajjud during part of the night as a free offering from you, and your Sustainer may well raise you to a station of praise and glory!*

The retreat of the stars, *idbār-un-nujūm,* is the glorious hour of early dawn. In 113:1, we seek God's protection as *Lord of the dawn.* (A. Yusuf Ali, p. 1441)

The Qurʾān stresses here the fact that every evil deed is bound to react in some way or other, even in this world, against him who commits it—either by depriving him of the affection of those who surround him and, thus, deepening his inner loneliness, or, more directly, by creating circumstances which make the achievement of real happiness and satisfaction increasingly impossible. (Asad, p. 811)

His Eye Did Not Waver

This fellow-man of yours has not gone astray, nor is he deluded,
and neither does he speak out of his own desire:
this is nothing less than inspiration
with which he is being inspired—
something that a very mighty one has imparted to him:
[an angel] endowed with surpassing power,
who in time manifested himself in his true shape and nature,
appearing in the horizon's loftiest part,
and then drew near and came close,
until he was but two bow-lengths away, or even nearer.
And thus did God reveal to His servant
whatever He deemed right to reveal.
The heart did not deny what he saw:
will you, then contend with him as to what he saw?
And, indeed, he saw him a second time
by the lote-tree of the farthest limit,
near to the garden of promise,
with the lote-tree veiled in a veil of nameless splendor.
And the eye did not waver, nor did it stray:
truly did he see some of the most profound of his Sustainer's symbols.

[*Sūrah an-Najm* 53:2-18]

Because he enunciated a message that differed radically from anything to
which the Meccans had been accustomed, the Prophet was considered

325

mad by many of his unbelieving contemporaries. The stress on his being *their fellow-man* is meant to emphasize the fact that he is human, and thus to counteract any possible tendency on the part of his followers to invest him with superhuman qualities.

A very mighty one: i.e., the Angel of Revelation, Gabriel. According to the Qurʾān and the testimony of authentic Traditions, the Prophet had no more than twice in his lifetime a vision of this angelic force *manifested in its true shape and nature* (which, as pointed out by Zamakhsharī, is the meaning of the expression *istawā* in this context): once after the period called *fatrat al-waḥy* and another time in the course of his mystic vision known as the "Ascension," alluded to in verses 13–18.

Until he was but two bow-lengths away or even nearer: the graphic description of the angel's approach, based on an ancient Arabian figure of speech, is meant to convey the idea that the Angel of Revelation became a clearly perceptible, almost tangible, presence.

Thus did God reveal to His servant whatever He deemed right to reveal: an allusion to the exceptional manifestation of the angel *in his true shape and nature* as well as to the contents of divine revelation as such. In its deeper sense this phrase implies that even to His chosen prophets God does not *entirely* unveil the ultimate mysteries of existence, of life and death, of the purpose for which He has created the universe, or of the nature of the universe itself.

Will you then contend with him as to what he saw? Thus the Qurʾān makes it clear that the Prophet's vision of the angel was not a delusion but a true spiritual experience: but precisely because it was purely spiritual in nature, it could be conveyed to others only by means of symbols and allegories, which skeptics all too readily dismiss as fancies, *contending with him as to what he saw.*

He saw him a second time, that is, he saw the angel manifested in his true shape and nature, *by the lote-tree of the farthest limit:* i.e., on the occasion of his mystic experience of the "Ascension" (*miʿrāj*). Explaining the vision conveyed in the expression *sidrat al-muntahā,* Rāghib suggests that owing to the abundance of its leafy shade, the *sidr* or *sidrah* (the Arabian lote-tree) appears in the Qur'ān as well as in the Traditions relating to the Ascension as a symbol of the "shade"—i.e., the spiritual peace and fulfillment—of paradise. One may assume that the qualifying term *al-muntahā* (*of the utmost* [or *farthest*] *limit*) is indicative of the fact that God has set a definite limit to all knowledge accessible to created beings, as pointed out in the *Nihāyah*: implying, in particular, that human knowledge, though potentially vast and penetrating, can never—not even in paradise (the *garden of promise* mentioned in the next verse)—attain to an understanding of the ultimate reality, which the Creator has reserved for Himself.

Truly did he see some of the most profound of his Sustainer's symbols (āyāt). The same term was used in 17:1 in reference to the same mystic experience, namely, the Ascension. *Limitless in His glory is He Who transported His servant by night from the Inviolable House of Worship [at Mecca] to the Remote House of Worship [at Jerusalem]—the environs of which We had blessed—so that We might show him some of Our symbols: for, truly, He alone is all-hearing, all-seeing.* Although the term *āyah* is most frequently used in the Qur'ān in the sense of "[divine] message," we must remember that, primarily, it denotes "a sign [or "token"] by which a thing is known" (*Qāmūs*). As defined by Rāghib, it signifies any perceivable phenomenon (irrespective of whether it is apparent to the senses or only to the intellect) connected with a thing that is not, by itself, similarly perceivable: in brief, a "symbol." In both these Qur'anic allusions, the Prophet is said to have been *made to see* (i.e., given to understand) some, but not all, of the ultimate truths. (Asad, pp. 232, 812-813, 417)

327

Vast in Forgiveness

*And so turn away from those who turn from all remembrance of Us
desiring nothing but the life of this world.
That is as much as they know.
Truly, your Sustainer knows best who strays from His path
and He knows best who follows His guidance.
For to God belongs all that is in the heavens and on earth;
so that He rewards those who do evil according to their deeds,
and He rewards those who do good with what is best.*
**As for those who avoid the grave sins and shameful deeds,
though occasionally they may stumble—
truly, your Sustainer is vast in forgiveness.**
*He knows you well when He brings you out of the earth
and when you are hidden in your mother's wombs;
so do not claim purity for yourselves—
He knows best who is conscious of Him.*

[*Sūrah an-Najm* 53:29-32]

Turn away from those who turn from Our Message desiring nothing but the life of this world; this is as much as they know. Literally, *that is their sum-total* [or goal] *of knowledge.*

He rewards those who do evil according to their deeds, and He rewards those who do good with what is best: i.e., whereas good deeds will be rewarded with far more than their merits may warrant, evil will be recompensed with no more than its equivalent, and either will be decided by the Almighty without the need of "mediation" or "intercession." *Whoever shall*

328

come [*before God*] *with a good deed will gain ten times the like thereof; but who-*
ever shall come with an evil deed will be requited with no more than the like
thereof; and none shall be wronged [6:160].

Though occasionally they may stumble: literally, *save for a touch* [*thereof*], a
phrase which may be taken to mean *an occasional stumbling into sin*—i.e.,
not deliberately—followed by sincere repentance (Baghawī, Rāzī, Ibn
Kathīr).

He brings you out of the earth: the frequent Qur'anic references to
man's being "created out of clay" or "out of dust" point to the fact that
his body is composed of various organic and inorganic substances existing
on or in the earth, as well as to the continuous transmutation of those
substances, through the intake of earth-grown food, into reproductive
cells (Rāzī)—thus stressing man's humble origin and hence the debt of
gratitude which he owed to God for having endowed him with a conscious soul. *So do not claim purity for yourselves:* i.e., *never boast about your
own purity,* but remain humble and remember that *it is God Who causes
whomever He wills to grow in purity* [4:49]. (Asad, pp. 815, 520)

*And so turn away from those who turn from Our Message, desiring nothing
but the life of this world. Truly, your Sustainer knows best who strays from His
path and He knows best who follows His guidance.* Men with a materialist turn
of mind, whose desires are bounded by sex and material things, will not
go beyond those things. Their knowledge will be limited to the narrow
circle in which their thoughts move. The spiritual world is beyond their
ken. While persons with a spiritual outlook, even though they may fall
again and again in attaining their full ideals, are on the right Path. They
are willing to receive guidance and Allāh's Grace will find them out and
help them.

*For to God belongs all that is in the heavens and on earth; so that He re-
wards those who do evil according to their deeds, and He rewards those who do
good with what is best.* All deeds have their consequences, good or ill. But

this is not an iron law, as the Determinists in philosophy, or the preachers of bare Karma, would have us believe. Allāh does not sit apart. He governs the world. And Mercy as well as Justice are His attributes. In His Justice every deed or word or thought of evil has its consequence for the doer or speaker or thinker. But there is always in this life room for repentance and amendment. As soon as this is forthcoming, Allāh's Mercy comes into action. It can blot out our evil, and the *reward* which it gives is nearly always greater than our merits.

He knows you well when He brings you out of the earth and when you are hidden in your mother's wombs; so do not claim purity for yourselves—He knows best who is conscious of Him. Allāh's attributes of Mercy and Forgiveness are unlimited. They come into action without our asking, but on our bringing our wills as offerings to Him. Our asking or prayer helps us to bring our minds and wills as offering to Him. That is necessary to frame our own psychological preparedness. It informs Allāh of nothing, for He knows all. As Allāh knows our inmost being, it is absurd for us to justify ourselves either by pretending that we are better than we are or by finding excuses for our conduct. We must offer ourselves unreservedly such as we are: it is His Mercy and Grace that will cleanse us. If we try, out of love for Him, to guard against evil, our striving is all that He asks for. (A. Yusuf Ali, pp. 1447-1448)

We Have Nothing Unless We Strive

Is he not acquainted with what is in the books of Moses
and of Abraham who was true to his trust?
Namely that no bearer of burdens can bear the burden of another;
that the human being can have nothing
but that for which he strives;
that in time his striving will become apparent;
and then he will be recompensed
with the most complete recompense;
that to your Sustainer is the final Goal;
that it is He alone Who causes your laughter and your tears;
that it is He Who grants death and life;
that He created in pairs, male and female,
from a drop of sperm as it is poured forth;
and that with Him rests another coming to life;
that it is He Who gives wealth and contentment;
and that it is He alone Who sustains the brightest star.[9]
And it is He Who destroyed the ancient tribes of ʿĀd and Thamūd,
leaving no trace of them, as well as the people of Noah before them—
truly, they all had been most willful in their evil-doing and overweening.

[*Sūrah an-Najm* 53:36-52]

---

[9] Sirius, of the constellation Canis Major, is the brightest star in the heavens. This phrase might also be understood as, *it is God alone who sustains the brightest of the saints, those who shine with His Light.*

That the human being can have nothing but that for which he strives relates to the basic, extremely well-authenticated saying of the Prophet: "Actions will be [judged] only according to the conscious intentions [which prompted them]; and to everyone will be accounted only what he consciously intended," i.e., while doing whatever he did. This Tradition is quoted by Bukhārī in seven places—the first one as a kind of introduction to his *Ṣaḥīḥ*—as well as by Muslim, Tirmidhī, Abū Dā'ūd, Nasā'ī (in four places), Ibn Mājah, Ibn Ḥanbal, and several other compilations. In this connection it is to be noted that in the ethics of the Qur'ān, the term "action" (*ʿamal*) comprises also a deliberate *omission* of actions, whether good or bad, as well as a deliberate voicing of beliefs, both righteous and sinful: in short, everything that man consciously aims at and expresses by word and deed. Since the expression *that for which he strives* implies consciousness of endeavor, it thus excludes *involuntary actions* (in the widest sense of the latter term, comprising everything that is manifested in word or actual deed), as well as *involuntary omissions*, irrespective of whether the relevant action or omission is morally good or bad. (Asad, pp. 816, 471)

The books of Moses and of Abraham: the books of Moses are apparently not the Pentateuch or Torah but some other book or books now lost. The present Pentateuch has no clear message at all of a Life to come. No original book of Abraham is now extant. But a book called "The Testament of Abraham" has come down to us, which seems to be a Greek translation of a Hebrew original.

Abraham who was true to his trust: one of the titles of Abraham is *Ḥanīf*, "the true in faith." This title is also used in 16:120 (*Abraham was indeed a model, devoutly obedient to Allāh, true in faith, and he joined not gods with Allāh*) and 16:123 (*So We have taught you the inspired message, "Follow the ways of Abraham, the true in faith, and he joined not gods with Allāh"*).

Starting with *no bearer of burdens can bear the burden of another* there are a series of eleven aphorisms of ancient wisdom apparently incorporated in current Semitic folklore. The first is that a man's spiritual burden—the

332

responsibility for his sin—must be borne by himself and not by another, compare 6:164 (*Whatever wrong any human being commits rests upon himself alone; and no bearer of burdens shall be made to bear another's burden.*)

That a human being can have nothing but that for which he strives; that in time his striving becomes apparent, and then he will be recompensed with the most complete recompense. The second and third aphorisms are that man must strive, or he will gain nothing; and that if he strives, the result must soon appear in sight and he will find his reward in full measure.

That to your Sustainer is the final Goal; that it is He alone Who causes your laughter and your tears; that it is He Who grants death and life. The fourth, fifth, and sixth aphorisms are that all things return to God; that all our hopes should be in Him and we should fear none but Him; and that He alone can give Life and Death.

That he created in pairs, male and female, from a drop of sperm as it is poured forth: the seventh aphorism relates to the mystery of sex; all things are created in pairs; each sex performs its proper function, and yet its wonderful working is part of the creative process of God: the living seed fructifies but contains within itself all the factors disclosed in its later development and life.

And that with Him rests another coming to life. No less wonderful is the promise He has made about the raising of the dead, and a new life in the Hereafter, and this is the subject of the eighth aphorism.

That it is He Who gives wealth and contentment. Wealth and material gain are sought by most men, in the hope that they will be a source of enjoyment and satisfaction. But this hope is not always fulfilled. There is a psychical and spiritual side to it. But both the material and spiritual sides depend upon the working of God's Plan. This is referred to in the ninth aphorism.

That it is He alone Who sustains the brightest star. The tenth aphorism refers to a mighty phenomenon of nature, the magnificent star Sirius, which is such a prominent object in the skies in the early part of the solar year, say from January to April. It is the brightest star in the firmament and its bluish light causes wonder and terror in pagan minds. The pagan Arabs worshipped it as a divinity. But God is the Lord, Creator, and Cherisher of the most magnificent part of Creation, and worship is due to Him alone.

And it is He Who destroyed the ancient tribes of ʿĀd and Thamūd, leaving no trace of them, as well as the people of Noah before them—truly, they all had been most willful in their evildoing and most overweening. The eleventh and last aphorism refers to the punishment of the most powerful ancient peoples for their sins They were strong and they were talented, but their strength and their talents did not save them from being destroyed for their sins. The same may be said about the earlier generation of Noah, who were destroyed in the flood. They *rejected Our signs; they were indeed a blind people* [7:64]. (A. Yusuf Ali, pp. 1449-1450)

The Moon is Split

*The last hour draws near, and **the moon is split asunder!***
But if they were to see a sign,
they would turn aside and say, "An ever-recurring delusion!"—
for they are intent on denying it,
being always conditioned to follow their own desires.
Yet everything reveals its truth in the end.

[*Sūrah al-Qamar* 54:1-3]

Most of the commentators see in this verse a reference to a phenomenon said to have been witnessed by several of the Prophet's contemporaries. As described in a number of reports going back to some Companions, the moon appeared one night as if split into two distinct parts. While there is no reason to doubt the *subjective* veracity of these reports, it is possible that what actually happened was an unusual kind of partial lunar eclipse, which produced an equally unusual optical illusion. But whatever the nature of that phenomenon, it is practically certain that the above Qurʾān verse does not refer to it but, rather, to a *future* event: namely, to what will happen when the Last Hour approaches. (The Qurʾān frequently employs the past tense to denote the future, and particularly so in passages which speak of the coming of the Last Hour and of Resurrection Day; this use of the past tense is meant to stress the certainty of the happening to which the verb relates.) Thus, Rāghib regards it as fully justifiable to interpret the phrase *inshaqqa 'l-qamar* (*the moon is split asunder*) as bearing on the cosmic cataclysm—the end of the world as we know it—that will

occur before the coming of Resurrection Day. As mentioned by
Zamakhsharī, this interpretation has the support of some of the earlier
commentators; and it is, to my mind, particularly convincing in view of
the juxtaposition, in the above Qur'ān verse, of the moon's *splitting asun-*
der and the approach of the Last hour. (In this connection we must bear
in mind the fact that none of the Qur'anic allusions to the "nearness" of
the Last Hour and the Day of Resurrection is based on the *human* concept
of "time.")

   Yet everything reveals its truth in the end: literally, *everything is settled in*
its [own] being. That is, everything has an intrinsic reality (*ḥaqīqah*) of its
own, and is bound to reveal that reality either in this world or in the next
(Baghawī, on the authority of Al-Kalbī); hence, everything must have a
purpose or "goal" of its own (Zamakhsharī). These two—mutually complementary—interpretations reflect the repeated Qur'anic statement that
everything that exists or happens has a meaning and a purpose (see 10:5
and 3:191). In the present context, the phrase relates both to the truth
referred to in the preceding verses and to its rejection by those who are
wont to follow [but] their own desires. (Asad, pp. 818-819)

The Easy Remembrance

And We have indeed made the Qur^cān easy
to understand and remember:
who then is willing to take it to heart?

[*Sūrah al-Qamar* 54:17]

The noun *dhikr* primarily denotes "remembrance" or—as defined by Rāghib—the "presence [of something] in the mind." Conceptually, and as used in the above context as well as in verses 54:22, 54:32, and 54:40 (where it is repeated), this term comprises the twin notions of understanding *and* remembering, i.e., bearing something in mind. (Asad, p. 820)

While the Qur'ān sums up the highest philosophy of the inner life, its simple directions for conduct are plain and easy to understand and act upon. Is this not in itself a part of the Grace of God? And what excuse is there for anyone to fail in receiving admonition? (*Who then is willing to take it to heart?* can be translated *Then is there any that will receive admonition?*) (A. Yusuf Ali, p. 1456)

Articulate Thought and Speech

The Most Gracious has imparted this Qurʾān.
He has created the human being:
He has imparted to him articulate thought and speech.
The sun and moon run their appointed courses;
before Him prostrate themselves the stars and the trees.
And the skies has He raised high,
and has devised for all things a measure,
so that you might never transgress the measure:
weigh, therefore, your deeds with equity,
and cut not the measure short!
And the earth has He spread out for all living beings,
with fruit thereon, and palm trees with sheathed clusters of dates,
and grain growing tall on its stalks, and sweet-smelling plants.
Which, then, of your Sustainer's blessings will you deny?

[*Sūrah ar-Raḥmān* 55:1-13]

He has imparted to him articulate thought and speech. The term *al-bayān*—denoting "the means whereby a thing is [intellectually] circumscribed and made clear" (Rāghib)—applies to both thought and speech inasmuch as it comprises the faculty of making a thing or an idea apparent to the mind and conceptually distinct from other things or ideas, as well as the power to express this cognition clearly in spoken or written language (*Tāj al-ʿArūs*): hence, in the above context, *articulate thought and speech*, recalling the *knowledge of all the names* (i.e., the faculty of conceptual thinking) with which man is endowed [2:31].

338

He has devised [for all things] a measure, so that you might never transgress the measure [of what is right]: weigh, therefore, [your deeds] with equity, and cut not the measure short. The noun *mīzān*, usually denoting a "balance," has here the more general connotation of "measure" or "measuring" by any means whatsoever (Zamakhsharī), in both the concrete and abstract senses of the word.

Which, then, of your Sustainer's blessings will you deny? The majority of the classical commentators interpret the dual form of address appearing in this phrase—*rabbikumā* (*the Sustainer of you two*) and *tukadhdhibān* (*do you* [*or can you*] *two disavow*)—as relating to the worlds of men and of the invisible beings (*jinn*); but the most obvious explanation (mentioned, among others, by Rāzī) is that it refers to the two categories of *human* beings, men and women, to both of whom the Qurʾān is addressed. The plural noun *ālāʾ* can be translated as *powers* and signifies literally *blessings* or *bounties.* As this refrain, repeated many times in this *sūrah*, bears not only on the bounties which God bestows on His creation but, more generally, on *all* manifestations of His creativeness and might, some of the earliest commentators—e.g., Ibn Zayd, as quoted by Ṭabarī—regard the term *ālāʾ*, in this context, as synonymous with *qudrah* ("power" or "powers"). (Asad, pp. 824–825)

The revelation comes from God Most Gracious, and it is one of the greatest signs of His grace and favor. He is the source of all Light, and His Light is diffused through the universe.

He has taught him articulate thought and speech: the word *bayān* means intelligent speech, the power of expression and the capacity to understand clearly the relations of things and to explain them. God has given this to man, and besides this revelation in man's own heart, has aided him with revelation in nature and revelation through prophets and apostles.

The sun and moon follow courses exactly computed: in the great astronomical universe there are exact mathematical laws, which bear witness to

339

God's Wisdom and also to His favors to His creatures, for we all profit by the heat and light, the seasons, and the numerous changes in the tides and the atmosphere, on which the constitution of our globe and the maintenance of life depend.

And the stars and trees both prostrate themselves: the word *najm* may mean stars collectively, or herbs collectively; perhaps both meanings are implied. Their prostration means all nature adores God. *Do you not see that to Allāh bow down in worship all things that are in the heavens and on earth, the sun, the moon, the stars, the hills, the trees, the animals, and a great number among mankind?* [22:18]. All created things, animate and inanimate, depend on God for their existence, and this dependence can be construed as their *sajeda* or bowing down in worship. Their very existence proclaims their dependence.

And the skies has He raised high, and has set up a measure: this *measure* or *balance* [*of justice*] is connected with the *balance* in the next two verses, that men may act justly to each other and observe due balance in all their actions, following the golden mean and not transgressing due bounds in anything. But the balance is also connected figuratively with the heavens above in three symbols: (1) Justice is a heavenly virtue; (2) the heavens themselves are sustained by mathematical balance; and (3) the constellation Libra, the Balance, is entered by the sun at the middle of the zodiacal year.

So establish weight with justice [translated above as: *weigh, therefore,* [*your deeds*] *with equity*]. This is to be taken both literally and figuratively. A man should be honest and straight in every daily matter, such as weighing out things which he is selling: and he should be straight, just, and honest in all the highest dealings not only with other people, but with himself and his obedience to God's Law. Not many do either the one or the other when they have an opportunity of deceit. Justice is the central virtue, and the avoidance of both excess and defect in conduct keeps the human world balanced just as the heavenly world is kept balanced by mathematical order.

And the earth has He spread out for all living beings. How can God's favors be counted? Look at the earth alone. Life and the conditions here are mutually balanced for God's creatures. The vegetable world produces fruit of various kinds and corn or grain of various kinds for human food. The grain harvest yields with it fodder for animals in the shape of leaves and straw, as well as food for men in the shape of grain. The plants not only supply food but sweet-smelling herbs and flowers. *Raiḥān* is the sweet basil, but is here used in the generic sense, for agreeable produce in the vegetable world, to match the useful produce already mentioned.

Which, then, of your Sustainer's blessings will you deny? Both the pronoun *your* and the verb *will you deny* in this refrain are in the Arabic in the dual number. All creation is in pairs: *and of everything We have created pairs* [51:49] and *Glory to Allāh Who created in pairs all things that the earth produces, as well as their own kind and things of which they have no knowledge* [36:36]. The whole of *Sūrah Rahman* is a symphony of duality, which leads up to unity. This refrain is interspersed 31 times among the 78 verses. The rhyme in most cases is in the dual grammatical form, and the argument implies that though things are created in pairs, there is an underlying unity, through the creator, in the favors which He bestows and in the goal to which they are marching. Justice is the conciliation of two opposites to unity, the settlement of the unending feud between Right and Wrong. The things and concepts mentioned in this *Sūrah* are in pairs, man and outer nature, sun and moon, stars and trees, heaven and earth, fruit and grain, human food and fodder for cattle, things nourishing and things sweet-smelling, and so on throughout the *Sūrah*.

Will you deny? That is, fail to acknowledge either in word or thought or in your conduct. If you misuse God's gifts or ignore them, that is equivalent to ingratitude or denial or refusal to profit by God's infinite Grace. (Yusuf Ali, pp. 1472, 855, 1473, 1471)

Everything is Perishing except His Face

All that is on earth will perish;
but forever will abide the Face of your Sustainer,
full of Majesty and Abundant Honor.
Then which of your Sustainer's blessings will you deny?
Every creature in the heavens and on earth depends on Him:
every day He manifests in wondrous new ways!
Then which of your Sustainer's blessings will you deny?

[*Sūrah ar-Raḥmān* 55:26-30]

The "face" or "countenance" is a term used metonymically in classical Arabic to denote the "self" or "whole being" of a person—in this case, the essential Being, or Reality, of God. *Everything is bound to perish, save His face* or *eternal Self* [28:88]. (Asad, p. 825)

But forever will abide the Face of your Sustainer. The most magnificent works of man—such as they are—are but fleeting. Ships, empires, the wonders of science and art, the splendors of human glory or intellect, will all pass away. The most magnificent objects in outer nature—the mountains and valleys, the sun and moon, the constellation Orion and the star Sirius—will also pass away in their appointed time. But the only One that will endure forever is the "Face" of God.

"Face" expresses personality, glory and majesty, inner being, essence, self, all the noble qualities which we associate with the Beautiful Names of God. *Wajh* means (1) literally "face," but it may imply (2) countenance or favor, as in *But those most devoted to Allāh shall be removed far from the Fire, those who spend their wealth for increase in self-purification, and have in*

342

their minds no favor from anyone for which a reward is expected in return, but only the desire to seek for the countenance of their Lord Most High, and soon will they attain satisfaction [92:17-21]; (3) honor, glory, Presence as applied to God, as in 2:115 *To God belong the East and the West. Wherever you turn, there is the Presence of God. Indeed, God is infinite, all-knowing;* (4) cause, sake ("for the sake of") as in 76:9 *We feed you for the sake of Allāh alone: no reward do we desire from you, nor thanks;* (5) the first part, the beginning, as in 3:72: *A section of the people of the Book say: "Believe in the morning what is revealed to the believers but reject it at the end of the day; perchance they [themselves] may turn back";* (6) nature, inner being, essence, self, as in 5:111 [5:108 in Asad] (*That they may give the evidence in its true nature and shape*) and 28:88 (*And do not call on another god besides God. There is no god but He. Everything is perishing except His Face. To Him belongs the Command, and to Him will you all return.*).

Full of Majesty and Abundant Honor. Abundant Honor could also be translated *Bounty and Honor.* Two ideas are prominent in the word *ikrām:* (1) the idea of generosity as proceeding from the person whose attribute it is, and (2) the idea of honor, as given by others to the person whose attribute it is. Both these ideas are summed up in "nobility." To make the meaning quite clear, the two words "bounty" and "honor" can be used for the single word *ikrām.* The same attributes recur in the last verse of this *Surāh.* In the fact of God's eternity is the hope of our future.

Every creature in the heavens and on earth depends on Him. Every single creature depends on God for its needs: the Cherisher and Sustainer of all of them is God.

Every day He manifests in wondrous new ways! This could be rendered as *every day in splendor does He shine. Shān* can be translated as state, splendor, aim, work, business, momentous affair. God is still the directing hand in all affairs: He does not sit apart, careless of mankind or of any of His creatures. But His working shows new splendor every day, every hour, every moment. (A. Yusuf Ali, pp. 1475, 48, 1476)

Have You Ever Considered?

Do you see the seed that you sow in the ground?
Is it you that causes it to grow or are We the cause?
Were it Our Will we could crumble it to dry powder
and you would be left in awe,
lamenting: "We are ruined; we've been deprived."
Have you ever considered the water which you drink?
Do you bring it down from the clouds or do We?
Were it Our will We could make it salty and bitter:
why, then, aren't you grateful?
Have you ever considered the fire which you kindle?
Is it you who have brought into being the tree
which feeds the fire, or is it We Who cause it to grow?
It is We Who have made it a reminder
and a comfort for those who wander in the wilderness.
Then celebrate the limitless glory
of the Name of your Sustainer, the Most High.

[*Sūrah al-Wāqiʿah* 56:63-74]

God appeals to the external nature around us, which should be evidence to us (1) of His loving care for us, and (2) of its being due to causes other than those which we produce and control. Three examples are given: (1) the seed which we sow in the soil: it is God's processes in nature which makes it grow; (2) the water which we drink: it is God's processes in nature that send it down from the clouds as rain and distribute it through springs and rivers; (3) the fire which we strike: it is again a proof of God's

Plan and Wisdom in nature.

The cultivator contracts debts for seed and gives labor for plowing, sowing, watering, and weeding, in the hope of reaping a harvest. Should he not give thanks to God when his harvest is in?

Have you ever considered the water which you drink? Do you bring it down from the clouds or do We? Were it Our will We could make it salty and bitter. The mystery of the two streams of water, one sweet and the other salt, constantly mingling, and yet always separate, is referred to more than once. The never-ending circuit is established by streams and rivers mingling with the ocean, the ocean sending forth mists and steam through a process of evaporation which forms clouds, and the clouds by condensation pouring forth rain to feed the streams and rivers again. In the world taken as a whole, there are two bodies of water, namely, (1) the great salt ocean and (2) the bodies of sweet water fed by rain, whether they are rivers, lakes, or underground springs: their source in rain makes them one, and their drainage, whether above ground or underground, eventually to the ocean, also makes them one. They are free to mingle, and in a sense they do mingle, for there is a regular water cycle, and the rivers flow constantly to the sea, and tidal rivers get sea-water for several miles up their estuaries at high tide. Yet in spite of all this, the laws of gravitation are like a barrier or partition set up by God, by which the two bodies of water as a whole are always kept apart and distinct.

Have you ever considered the fire which you kindle? Is it you who have brought into being the tree which feeds the fire, or is it We Who cause it to grow? The relation of fire to trees is intimate. In nearly all the fire that we burn, the fuel is derived from the wood of trees. Even mineral coal is nothing but the wood of prehistoric forests petrified under the earth through geological ages. *It is We Who have made it a reminder:* fire is a fit memorial of God's handiwork in nature. It is also an emblem of man's earliest civilization. It can stand as a symbol of physical comfort and convenience to man, of the source of spiritual light, and also of the warning to Evil about its destruction. In the same way the sower's seed has a symbolic meaning in the preaching of the message and the rain and the streams of water have a symbolic meaning. Seeing all these signs in nature and their symbolic meaning in the spiritual world, man must turn to God and do His Will. (A. Yusuf Ali, pp. 1491-1492, 939)

From Darkness into Light

It is God Who sends to His servants clear signs
that He may lead you out of the depths of darkness
into the Light.
And truly, God is to you most Kind and Merciful.

[*Sūrah al-Ḥadīd* 57:9]

This short selection has vast implications if only we could take it to heart. It describes our essential relationship to God: we are being guided out of darkness and into the light. It is our responsibility to strive, for we have nothing but what we have striven for, and, at the same time, it is up to God to guide us in our striving. Of this we can be sure: if we turn to Him, His guidance will not fail us. We will be shown clear signs and we will not be left in the darkness. In this life we have difficulties and we have problems. They are not the same. Difficulties are obstacles and challenges to be faced. Through them our souls develop new qualities and strengths. Problems, however, are those situations where we do not necessarily know what the right answer is, what we are to do. Our task, then, is to remember to ask both for His guidance, and then for the strength to follow it. (Helminski)

347

Selfless Action

Who will loan to God a beautiful loan?
For God will increase it many times to His credit
and he or she will have a generous recompense.
One Day you will see the faithful men and the faithful women,
how their Light runs forward before them and to their right:
"Good news for you today: gardens beneath which running waters flow,
where you may live—this, this is the highest achievement!"

[*Sūrah al-Ḥadīd* 57:11-12]

Who will loan to God a beautiful loan? i.e., by sacrificing one's life in, or devoting it to, His cause. In this instance, the meaning applies to *all* that man may do selflessly, for the sake of God alone.

In many instances, the metaphor of "the right hand" or "right side" is used in the Qurʾān to denote "righteousness" and, therefore, "blessedness," symbolized in the present context by the *light spreading rapidly before and on the right side* of the believers as a result of their "cognition of God, and their high morality, and their freedom from ignorance and blameworthy traits" (Rāzī). (Asad, pp. 54, 837-838)

Spending in the cause of God is called metaphorically *a beautiful loan.* It is excellent in many ways: (1) it shows a beautiful spirit of self-denial; (2) in other loans there may be a doubt as to the safety of your capital or any return thereon: here you give to the Lord of all in whose hands are the keys of want or plenty; giving, you may have manifold blessings, and withholding you may even lose what you have. If we remember that our goal is God, can we turn away from His cause?

How their Light runs forward before them: in the darkness of the Day of Judgment there will be a Light to guide the righteous to their destination. This will be the Light of their Faith and their good works. Perhaps the Light in the right hand mentioned here is the light of their good works: for the blessed will receive their record in their right hand (69:19-24).

This is the highest achievement: the highest achievement, the highest felicity, the attainment of salvation, the fulfillment of all desires: the negative avoidance of all the consequences of evil, and the positive attainment of all—and more than all—that our hearts could possibly desire. For God's Bounty outstrips anything that our eyes have seen, or our ears have heard of, or our imagination can conceive. (A. Yusuf Ali, pp. 97, 1500, 1353)

Humble Remembrance

Hasn't the time come for the faithful
that their hearts in all humility
should engage in the remembrance of God
and of the truth which has been revealed,
and that they should not become like those
to whom revelation was given but whose hearts have hardened
with the passing of time
so that many among them now rebel
against that which is right?
Know that God gives life to the earth after it has been lifeless!
We have indeed made Our signs clear to you
that you might learn wisdom.

[*Sūrah al-Ḥadīd* 57:16-17]

Humility and the remembrance of God and His Message are never more necessary than in the hour of victory and prosperity.

And that they should not become like those to whom revelation was given but whose hearts have hardened with the passing of time: the men immediately referred to are the contemporary Jews and Christians. To each of these communities (*ummahs*) was given God's revelation, but as time passed, they corrupted it, became arrogant and hard-hearted, and subverted justice, truth, and the purity of Life. But the general lesson is far wider. No one is favored of God except on the score of righteousness. Except on that score, there is no chosen individual or race. There is no blind good fortune or ill fortune. All happens according to the just laws and will of

350

God. But at no time is humility or righteousness more necessary than in the hour of victory or triumph.

Know that God gives life to the earth after it has been lifeless! As the dead earth is revived after the refreshing showers of rain, so is it with the spirit of man, whether as an individual or a race or *ummah*. There is no cause for despair. God's Truth will revive the spiritual faculties if it is accepted with humility and zeal. (A. Yusuf Ali, pp. 1501-1502)

Should not the remembrance of God and His revelation make them humble rather than proud? This is an emphatic warning against all smugness, self-righteousness, and false pride at having "attained to faith"—a failing which only too often attains to such as consider themselves "pious."

Those *whose hearts have hardened with the passing of time so that many among them now rebel against that which is right*: i.e., so that now they act contrary to the ethical precepts of their religion: implying that the purpose of all true faith is make man humble and God-conscious rather than self-satisfied, and that a loss of that spiritual humility invariably results in moral degeneration.

Know that God gives life to the earth after it has been lifeless. According to most of the commentators—and particularly Zamakhsharī, Rāzī, and Ibn Kathīr—this is a parabolic allusion to the effect of a re-awakening of God-consciousness in hearts that had become deadened by self-satisfaction and false pride. (Asad, p. 839)

Conscious Equanimity

Don't despair over things that pass you by
nor exult over blessings that come to you.
For God does not love those who are conceited and boastful,
those who are grasping and encourage others to be greedy.
And as for the one who turns his back—
truly, God alone is Self-Sufficient,
the One to Whom All Praise Is Due.
We have sent our messengers with clear signs,
and through them We bestowed revelation and a balance
so that people might behave with justic;
and We sent down iron in which is awesome power
as well as many benefits for humankind,
that God might test who it is that will help unseen
Him and His messengers;
for truly, God is the Lord of All Power, Almighty.

[*Sūrah al-Ḥadīd* 57:23-25]

Don't despair over things that pass you by nor exult over blessings that come to you. Thus, the knowledge that whatever has happened *had* to happen— and could not have *not* happened—because, obviously, it had been willed by God in accordance with His unfathomable plan, ought to enable a true believer to react with conscious equanimity to whatever good or ill comes to him. *God does not love those who are conceited and boastful, those who are grasping and encourage others to be greedy,* i.e., attributing their good for- tune to their own merit or "luck." *The one who turns his back* means one

352

who does not want to admit that whatever has happened must have been willed by God.

Side by side with enabling man to discriminate between right and wrong (which is the innermost purpose of all divine revelation), God has endowed him with the ability to convert to his use the natural resources of his earthly environment. An outstanding symbol of this ability is man's skill, unique among all animated beings, in making *tools*; and the primary material for all tool-making—and, indeed, for all human technology—is iron: the one metal which is found abundantly on earth, and which can be utilized for beneficial as well as destructive ends. The *awesome power* (*ba's shadīd*) inherent in iron manifests itself not merely in the manufacture of weapons of war but also, more subtly, in man's ever-growing tendency to foster the development of an increasingly complicated technology which places the *machine* in the foreground of all human existence and which, by its inherent—almost irresistible—dynamism, gradually estranges man from all inner connection with nature. This process of growing mechanization, so evident in our modern life, jeopardizes the very structure of human society and, thus, contributes to a gradual dissolution of all moral and spiritual perceptions epitomized in the concept of "divine guidance." It is to warn man of this danger that the Qur'ān stresses—symbolically and metonymically—the potential evil (*ba's*) of "iron" if it is put to wrong use: in other words, the danger of man's allowing his technological ingenuity to run wild and thus to overwhelm his spiritual consciousness and, ultimately, to destroy all possibility of individual and social happiness. (Asad, pp. 840-841)

In the external world, what people may consider misfortune or good fortune may both turn out to be illusory—in Kipling's words, "both impostors just the same." The man of God does not grumble if someone else has possessions nor exult if he has them. He does not covet and he does not boast. If he has any advantages, he shares them with other people, as he considers them not due to his own merits, but as gifts of God.

Neither the covetous nor the boasters have any place in the good pleasure of God. The covetous are particularly insidious, as their avarice and niggardliness not only keep back the gifts of God from men, but their pernicious example dries up the streams of charity in others. It is charity in God's Way that is specially in view here. If people are selfish and with-hold their hand, they only injure themselves. They do not hurt God's Cause, for He is independent of all needs, and He will find other means of assisting His more meagerly endowed servants; He is worthy of all praise in His care for His creatures.

Three things are mentioned as gifts of God. In concrete terms, they are the Book, the Balance, and Iron, which stand as emblems of three things which hold society together, namely, Revelation, which com-mands good and forbids evil; Justice, which gives to each person his due; and the strong arm of the Law, which maintains sanctions for evil-doers.

And We bestowed from on high iron: "bestowed" is literally *sent down, anzala,* in the sense of revealed to man the use of certain things, created in him the capacity of understanding and using them.

Iron is the most useful metal known to man. Out of it is made steel, and from steel and iron are made implements of war, such as swords, spears, guns, etc., as well as instruments of peace, such as plowshares, bricklayers' trowels, architects' and engineers' instruments, etc. Iron stands as the emblem of strength, power, discipline, law's sanctions, etc. Iron and steel industries have also been the foundation of the prosperity and power of modern manufacturing nations.

Even though He is beyond the reach of human perception: bil ghaybi is more literally *unseen* and can also be translated *in their most secret thought.* The sincere man will help the cause, whether he is seen or brought under notice or not. To help God and His Apostles is to help their cause. It is to give man an opportunity of striving and fighting for His cause and prov-ing their true mettle, for thus is their spirit tested. God in Himself is full of strength, exalted in power, and able to enforce His Will, and He has no need of other assistance. (A. Yusuf Ali, pp. 1505–1506)

The Witness of All Intrigues

Don't you see that God knows all
that is in the heavens and on earth?
There is not a secret consultation between three
without His being the fourth among them,
nor between five without His being the sixth,
nor between fewer nor more without His being in their midst
wherever they may be:
in the end He will show them the truth of their actions,
on the Day of Reckoning,
for God has full knowledge of all things.

[*Sūrah al-Mujādalah* 58:7]

The prohibition against secret confabulations arises from the Qurʾanic statement: *No good comes, as a rule, out of secret confabulations—save those which are devoted to enjoining charity, or equitable dealings, or setting things to rights between people* [4:114]. Thus, secret talks aiming at positive, beneficial ends—for instance, peace negotiations between states or communities— are excepted from the disapproval of "secret confabulations" because premature publicity may sometimes be prejudicial to the achievement of those ends or may (especially in cases where charity is involved) hurt the feelings of the people concerned.

Although there is no doubt that, as the classical commentators point out, the "secret consultation" spoken of in this passage relates to intrigues aimed against the Prophet and his followers by some of their unbelieving contemporaries, there is no doubt, either, that the passage has a general

356

import, and is, therefore, valid for all times. (Asad, pp. 127, 845)

Secrecy is a relative and limited term among ourselves. There is nothing hidden or unknown to God. Usually secrecy implies fear or distrust, plotting or wrongdoing. But all is open before God's sight. (A. Yusuf Ali, p. 1512)

Make Room for One Another

Make room for one another in your collective life; do make room:
God makes room for you.
And whenever you are told, "Rise up," do rise up;
God exalts by degrees
those of you who have attained to faith
and those who have been granted knowledge:
for God is fully aware of all that you do.

[*Sūrah al-Mujādalah* 58:11]

Make room for one another in your collective life: literally, *in the assemblies* (al-majālis). Although it is frequently assumed that this refers to the assemblies held by the Prophet, when his followers would throng around him in their eagerness the better to hear what he had to say, or—more generally—to congregations in mosques, etc., in later times, I am (with Rāzī) of the opinion that the plural noun *majālis* is used here in a tropical or metaphorical sense, denoting the totality of men's social life. Taken in this sense, the *making room for one another* implies the mutual providing of opportunities for a decent life to all—and especially to the needy or handicapped—members of the community.

Do make room: [and in return] God will make room for you [in His grace]. Commenting on this passage, Rāzī says: "This verse indicates that if one widens the means (abwāb) of happiness and well-being of God's creatures (ᶜibad), God will widen for him all that is good in this life and in the hereafter. Hence no reasonable person (al-ᶜāqil) could ever restrict [the purport of] this verse to merely making room for one another in an [actual] as-

358

sembly."

The interpretation implied in the words *and do good* interpolated by me above is analogous to that offered by most of the classical commentators, and most explicitly by Ṭabarī; in the words of Qatādah: "Whenever you are called upon to do a good deed, respond to this call."

God will exalt by [many] degrees those of you who have attained to faith and, [above all,] such as have been vouchsafed [true] knowledge. Compare the saying of the Prophet: "The superiority of a learned man (ᶜālim) over a [mere] worshipper (ᶜābid) is like the superiority of the moon on the night when it is full over all other stars" (Ibn Ḥanbal, Abū Dāᵓūd, Tirmidhī, Nasāᵓī, Ibn Mājah, and Dārimī). (Asad, p. 846)

God's People

[Those who believe in God and the Last Day,]
it is they in whose hearts He has inscribed faith,
and whom He has strengthened with inspiration from Himself,
and whom He will admit into gardens
through which running waters flow, therein to abide.
Well-pleased is God with them,
and well-pleased are they with Him.
They are God's people:
oh, truly, it is they, the people of God,
who shall attain to a happy state!"

[*Sūrah al-Mujādalah* 58:22]

Faith in God is indelibly written on the tablets of their hears, and they can never be false to God.

Whom He has strengthened with inspiration from Himself. Compare 2:87 and 2:253, where it is said that God *gave Jesus the son of Mary clear signs and strengthened him with the holy spirit.* Here we learn that all good and righteous men are strengthened by God with the holy spirit. If anything, the phrase used here is stronger, *a spirit from Himself.* Whenever anyone offers his heart in faith and purity to God, God accepts it, engraves that faith on the seeker's heart, and further fortifies him with the divine spirit, which we can no more define adequately than we can define in human language the nature and attributes of God.

Well-pleased is God with them, and well-pleased are they with Him. Again we have the mystic doctrine of God's good pleasure as the highest goal of

360

man, the spiritual heaven which he achieves by a life of purity and faith. He not only attains God's good pleasure as the crown of his felicity, but his own nature is so far transformed to the pattern of God's original creation that his own good pleasure is nothing but in God's good pleasure. The mutual good pleasure shows the heights to which man can attain. (A. Yusuf Ali, p. 1518)

Helpers and Refugees

And those who had homes and had embraced faith,
those who love all that come to them in search of refuge,
and who harbor in their hearts no grudge
for whatever the others may have been given,
but rather give them preference over themselves,
even though poverty be their own lot:
those saved from the covetousness of their own souls,
they are the ones who achieve prosperity.

[*Sūrah al-Ḥashr* 59:9]

This relates, in the first instance, to the historical *anṣār* ("helpers") of Medina, who had embraced Islam before the Prophet's and his Meccan followers' coming to them, and who received the refugees with utmost generosity, sharing with them like brethren their own dwellings and all their possessions. In a wider sense, the above refers also to all true believers, at all times, who live in freedom and security within the realm of Islam, and are prepared to receive with open arms anyone who is compelled to leave his homeland in order to be able to live in accordance with the dictates of his faith. *Those saved from the covetousness of their own souls, they are the ones who achieve prosperity:* thus, greed, niggardliness, and covetousness are pointed out here as the main obstacles to man's attaining to a happy state in this world and in the hereafter. [See *Sūrah* 102.] (Asad, pp. 851-852)

362

To Forget Our Own Souls

O you who have attained to faith!
Remain conscious of God,
and let every soul look to what he or she has prepared
for the day to come.
And remain conscious of God:
for God is well-aware of all that you do.
And do not be like those who forget God,
whom He then causes to forget their own souls! . . .
Had We sent down this Qurᶜ ān on a mountain,
truly, you would have seen it humble itself and break apart
out of awe of God—
such are the parables which We offer to human beings
that they might reflect.

[*Sūrah al-Ḥashr* 59:18-19, 21]

Those . . . whom He causes to forget their own souls: i.e., by having made a deliberately wrong use of the faculty of reason with which God has endowed man, and—by remaining oblivious of Him—having wasted their own spiritual potential.

Had We sent down this Qurᶜ ān on a mountain, truly, you would have seen it humble itself and break apart out of awe of God: this is in contrast with those who, by remaining oblivious of God and all moral imperatives, are spiritually more dead than an inert mountain. (Asad, pp. 853-854)

And remain conscious of God: The "fear of God" is akin to love, for it

363

means the fear of offending Him or doing anything wrong that will forfeit His good pleasure. This is *taqwā*, which implies self-restraint, guarding ourselves from all sin, wrong, and injustice, and the positive doing of good. The positive side of *taqwā* is emphasized here. It is not merely a feeling or an emotion: it is an act, a doing of things which become a preparation and provision for the Hereafter, the next life, which may be described as "the morrow" in relation to the present life, which is "today." The repetition [translated as *remain conscious of God* here] emphasizes both sides of *taqwā*: let your soul fear to do wrong, and let it do every act of righteousness, for God observes both your inner motives and your acts, and in His scheme of things everything will have its due consequences.

To forget God is to forget the only Reality. As we are only reflected realities, how can we understand or do justice to or remember ourselves, when we forget the very source of our being? (A. Yusuf Ali, pp. 1526-1527)

There are two ideas associated in men's minds with a mountain: one is its height, and the other that it is rocky, stony, hard. Now comes the metaphor. The revelation of God is so sublime that even the highest mountains humble themselves before it. The revelation is so powerful and convincing that even the hard rock splits asunder under it. Will man then be so arrogant as to consider himself superior to it, or so hard-hearted as not to be affected by its powerful Message? The answer is "No" for unspoilt man; "Yes" for man when degraded by sin to be the vilest of creatures.

Compare 7:143 where, in the story of Moses, the mount became as dust when the Lord manifested His Glory: *When Moses came to the place appointed by Us, and his Lord addressed him, he said: "O my Lord! Show Yourself to me, that I may look upon You." Allāh said, "By no means can you see Me directly; but look upon the mountain; if it abide in its place then shall you see Me." When his Lord manifested His glory on the mountain, He made it as dust and Moses fell down in a swoon. When he recovered his senses he said: "Glory be to You! To You I turn in repentance, and I am the first to believe."*

Also compare 33:72: *Truly, We offered the Trust to the heavens, and to the earth, and to the mountains; but they refused to undertake it, as they were afraid of it—but the human being undertook it though he was indeed unjust and foolish.* The mountains are mentioned allegorically as an emblem of stability, but as refusing to accept the trust (*amānat*) because they felt themselves to be too humble to be equal to such a tremendous trust. The trust is something given to a person, over which he has a power of disposition; he is expected to use it as directed or expected, but he has the power to use it otherwise. There is no trust if the trustee has no power, and the trust implies that the giver of the trust believes and expects that the trustee would use it according to the wish of the creator of the trust, and not otherwise. The mountains stand for firmness and stability; they have been created for this quality, and they are always true to that quality. An earthquake or a volcano has to do with movements within the earth's crust; it has nothing to do with the mountain's will. In fact, it has no free will of any kind; there is no question of any trust here. If we take the earth as a whole, as a part of the solar system or a compendium of the terrestrial nature we see around us, it obeys the fixed laws of God, and there is no will or trust. The heavens, the earth, and the mountains refusing to undertake a trust or a responsibility, may be imagined as happy without a choice of good or evil being given through their will. In saying that they refused, we imply a will, but we limit it by the statement that they did not undertake to be given a choice between good and evil. They preferred to submit their will entirely to God's Will.

In the hypothetical sending down of the Qur'ān to the mountain, it is mentioned that such parables are put forth in order to aid men to reflection. (A. Yusuf Ali, pp. 1527, 1129-1130)

The Most Beautiful Names

God is He other than Whom there is no god,
Who knows what is hidden and what is manifest;
Hû,[10] *the Infinitely Compassionate, the Infinitely Merciful.*
God is He other than Whom there is no god,
the Sovereign, the Holy One, the Source of Peace,
the Inspirer of Faith, the Preserver of Security,
the Exalted in Might, the Compelling, the Supreme:
Glory to God!
Who is above the partners they attribute to Him—
He is God, the Creator, the Evolver, the Bestower of Forms.
To Him belong the Most Beautiful Names:
whatever is in the heavens and on earth
declares His Praises and Glory,
and He is the exalted in Might, the All-Wise.

[*Sūrah al-Ḥashr* 59:22-24]

This is a passage of great sublimity, summing up the attributes of God. First, in this verse, we have the general attributes, which give us the fundamental basis on which we can form some idea of God. (1) We start with the proposition that no words are adequate to describe Him, and we can only call Him "He" for there is nothing else like Him. (2) We think of His Unity; all the varying and conflicting forces in Creation are controlled by Him and look to Him, and we can never get a true idea of

---

[10] See footnote 3.

Him unless we understand the mystic meaning of Unity. (3) His knowledge extends to everything seen and unseen, present and future, near and far, in being and not in being; in fact, these contrasts, which apply to our knowledge, do not apply to Him. (4) His Grace and (5) His Mercy are unbounded, and unless we realize these, we can have no true conception of our position in the working of His Will and plan.

How can a translator reproduce the sublimity and comprehensiveness of the magnificent Arabic words, which mean so much in a single symbol? (1) *The Sovereign,* in our human language, implies the one undisputed authority which is entitled to give commands and to receive obedience, and which in fact receives obedience; the power which enforces law and justice. (2) Human authority may be misused, but in the title *the Holy One* we postulate a Being free from all stain of evil and replete with the highest Purity. (3) *"Salām"* has not only the idea of Peace as opposed to conflict, but wholeness as opposed to defects, hence *the Source of Peace and Perfection.* (4) *Mūᶜmin,* one who entertains Faith, who gives Faith to others, who is never false to the faith that others place in Him, hence *Guardian of Faith.* (5) *Preserver of Security:* guarding all from danger, corruption, loss, etc.: the same word is used for the Qurʾān in 5:51 [5:48 in Asad]. These are the attributes of kindness and benevolence. There are also attributes of power. (6) *Exalted in Might:* God is not only good, but He can carry out His Will. (7) *The Compelling:* and if anything resists or opposes Him, His Will prevails. (8) For He is *Supreme,* above all things and creatures. Thus we come back to the Unity with which we began in 59:22.

Who is above the partners they attribute to Him: such being God's attributes of goodness and power, how foolish is it of men to worship anything else but Him? Who can approach His glory and goodness?

He is God, the Creator, the Evolver, the Bestower of Forms: God's attributes of goodness and power having been referred to, we are now told of His creative energy, of which three aspects are here mentioned. *Khalaqa* is the general term for creation, and the Author of all Creation is *Khāliq.*

Barā implies a process of evolving from previously created matter or state: the Author of this process is *Bāri-u*, the Evolver. *Ṣawwara* implies giving definite form or color, so as to make a thing exactly suited to a given end or object: hence the title *Muṣawwir*, Bestower of Forms or Colors: for this shows the completion of the visible stage of creation. The point is emphasized that He does not merely create and leave alone; He goes on fashioning, evolving new forms and colors, and sustaining all the energies and capacities which He has put into His Creation, according to various laws which He has established.

To Hū belong the Most Beautiful Names: as we contemplate God's nature, we can use the most beautiful names we can think of, to express His attributes. There are hundreds of such attributes. In the opening *Sūrah*, we have these indicated in a few comprehensive words such as *Raḥmān* (Most Gracious), *Raḥīm* (Most Merciful), *Rabbu-ul-ᶜālamīn* (Cherisher and Sustainer of the worlds). Our bringing such names to remembrance is part of our prayer and praise. For devotional purposes, a list of 99 Beautiful Names is used from *ḥadīth* literature, the list by Tirmidhī being considered authoritative.

Whatever is in the heavens and on earth declares His Praises and Glory, and He is the Exalted in Might, the All-Wise: thus the *sūrah* is rounded off on the same note as was struck at the beginning: *Whatever is in the heavens and on earth, let it declare the praises and glory of Allāh: for He is the Exalted in Might, the All-Wise* [59:1]. The first verse and the last verse of the *sūrah* are the same, except as regards the tense of the verb *sabbaḥa*. In the first verse, it is the optative form of the preterite *sabbaḥa: let everything declare the Glory of God!* After the illustrations given, the declaratory form of the aorist is appropriate, *yusabbiḥu: everything declares the Glory of God.* (A. Yusuf Ali, pp. 1528-1529, 396, 726)

Who knows what is hidden and what is manifest: the term *ash-shahādah* (literally, *that which is* [or *can be*] *witnessed*) is used in this and similar contexts as the exact antithesis of *al-ghayb* (*that which is beyond the reach of a*

368

created being's perception). Thus, it circumscribes those aspects of reality which can be sensually or conceptually grasped by a created being.

The expression *the Most Beautiful Names* (*al-asmāᶜ al-ḥusnā*) appears in the Qurʾān four times (7:180, 17:110, 20:8, 59:24). The term *ism* [as *asmāᶜ*] is, primarily, a word applied to denote the substance or the intrinsic attributes of an object under consideration, while the term *al-ḥusnā* is the plural form of *al-aḥsan* ("that which is best" or "most goodly"). Thus the combination *al-asmāᶜ al-ḥusnā* may be appropriately rendered as *the attributes of perfection*—a term reserved in the Qurʾān for God alone.

The Name *al-Muhaymin* is derived from the quadriliteral *haymana*, "he watched [over a thing]" or "controlled [it]"; it is used to describe the Qurʾān as the determinant factor in deciding what is genuine and what is false in earlier scriptures. In 5:48: *And to you [O Prophet] have We vouchsafed this divine writ, setting forth the truth, confirming the truth of whatever there still remains of earlier revelations and determining what is true therein.*

The Name *al-Jabbār* is derived from the verb *jabara*; it combines the concepts of "setting right" or "restoring" (e.g., from a state of brokenness, ill-health, or misfortune) and of "compelling" or "subduing [someone or something] to one's will." The term *al-Jabbār*, when applied to God, is best rendered as *the One Who subdues wrong and restores right.*

He is God, the Creator, the Maker Who shapes all forms and appearances! thus Bayḍāwī. The Names *al-Bāriᶜ* (*the Maker*) and *al-Muṣawwir* (*the Shaper,* i.e., of all forms and appearances) evidently constitute here one single unit. (Asad, pp. 854, 231, 153)

Abraham's Prayer

"O our Sustainer, in You we have placed our trust
and to You we turn in repentance:
for with You is all journeys' end.
O our Sustainer! Do not make us a trial
for those who deny the Truth,
but forgive us, O our Sustainer!
For You are the Almighty, the Truly-Wise."

[*Sūrah al-Mumtaḥanah* 60:4-5]

This prayer indicates what our attitude should be. We must trust to God, and not to God's enemies to protect and befriend ourselves, or those near and dear to us.

Do not make us a trial: fitnah has many meanings. (1) The root meaning is trial or temptation, as in 2:102 (*The evil forces, teaching men magic and such things . . . but neither of these taught anyone such things without saying "We are only for trial; so do not blaspheme."* Hārūt and Mārūt were a trial to test the righteous who trusted in God from the unrighteous who resorted to evil and superstition.) and 8:28 (*Know that your possessions and your progeny are but a trial, and that it is Allāh with Whom lies your highest reward*). (2) An analogous meaning is trial or punishment, as in 5:74 [5:71 in Asad] (*They thought there would be no trial [or punishment]; so they became blind and deaf. Yet Allāh [in mercy] turned to them.*). (3) Tumult or oppression, as in 2:193 (*And continue to fight them until there is no more tumult or oppression, and there prevail justice and faith in Allāh*) and 8:25 (*And fear tumult or oppression which affects not in particular only those of you who do wrong*), and 8:39

(*And fight with them until there is no more tumult or oppression. And there prevail justice and faith in Allāh altogether and everywhere.*). (4) In 8:25 the further shade of meaning suggested is discord, sedition, civil war. This warning against internal discord or tumult was very necessary in the Civil Wars of early Islam, and was never more necessary than it is now. For it affects innocent and guilty alike. In 60:5, the prayer to God is that we should be saved from becoming so weak as to tempt the unbelievers to try to attack and destroy us. (A. Yusuf Ali, pp. 1533, 421)

The Declaration of Faith

Whenever women of faith come to you, as emigrants,
question them, although only God is fully aware of their faith;
and if you have thus ascertained that they are of the faithful,
do not send them back to the deniers of the truth.

[*Sūrah al-Mumtaḥanah* 60:10]

When several Meccan women embraced Islam against the will of their husbands and fled to Medina, the Quraish demanded their forcible return to Mecca. This the Prophet refused on the grounds that married women did not fall within the category of "persons under guardianship." However, since there was always the possibility that some of these women had gone over to the Muslims not for reasons of faith but out of purely worldly considerations, the believers were enjoined to make sure of their sincerity; and so the Prophet asked each of them: "Swear before God that you did not leave because of hatred of your husband, or out of a desire to go to another country, or in the hope of attaining to worldly advantages: swear before God that you did not leave for any reason save the love of God and His Apostle" (Ṭabarī). Since God alone knows what is in the heart of a human being, a positive response of the woman concerned was to be regarded as the only humanly attainable—and therefore, legally sufficient—proof of her sincerity. The fact that God alone is really aware of what is in a human being's heart is incorporated in the *sharʿī* principle that any adult person's declaration of faith, in the absence of any evidence to the contrary, makes it mandatory upon the community to accept that person—whether man or woman—as a Muslim on the basis of this declaration alone. (Asad, p. 857)

Vain Talk

O you who have faith!
Why do you say that which you do not do?
It is most displeasing in God's sight
that you say that which you do not do.

[*Sūrah aṣ-Ṣaff* 61:2-3]

In the first instance, this may be an allusion to such of the Prophet's companions as had retreated in disorder from their battle stations at Uḥud despite their previous assertions that they were ready to lay down their lives in the cause of God and His Apostle. In a wider sense, the passage is addressed to all those who claim that they are willing to live up to anything that the divine writ declares to be desirable, and then fall short of this determination. (Asad, p. 860)

At Uḥud there was some disobedience and therefore breach of discipline. People had talked much, but had failed to back up their resolution in words with firmness in action. But on all occasions, when men's deeds are not commensurate with their words, their conduct is odious in the sight of God, and it is only due to God's Mercy if they are saved from disaster. (A. Yusuf Ali, p. 1539)

Jesus, the Messenger

Jesus, the son of Mary, said: "O children of Israel!
Behold, I am a Messenger of God to you,
sent to confirm the truth of the Torah,
and to give the glad tiding of a Messenger who shall come after me,
whose name shall be Aḥmad.

[*Sūrah aṣ-Ṣaff* 61:6]

This prediction is supported by several references in the Gospel of St. John to the *Paráklûtos* (usually rendered as "Comforter") who was to come after Jesus. This designation is almost certainly a corruption of *Períklytos* ("the Much-Praised"), an exact Greek translation of the Aramaic term or name *Mawḥamana*. (It is to be borne in mind that Aramaic was the language used in Palestine at the time of, and for some centuries after, Jesus, and was thus undoubtedly the language in which the original—now lost—texts of the Gospels were composed.) In view of the phonetic closeness of *Períklytos* and *Paráklûtos* it is easy to understand how the translator—or, more probably, a later scribe—confused these two expressions. It is significant that both the Aramaic *Mawḥamana* and the Greek *Períklytos* have the same meaning as the two names of the Last Prophet, *Muḥammad* and *Aḥmad*, both of which are derived from the verb *ḥamida* ("he praised") and the noun *ḥamd* ("praise"). An even more unequivocal prediction of the advent of the Prophet Muḥammad—mentioned by name, in its Arabic form—is said to be forthcoming from the so-called Gospel of St. Barnabas, which, though now regarded as apocryphal, was accepted as authentic and was read in the churches until the year 496 of the Christian era, when it was banned as "heretical" by a decree of Pope Gelasius. However, since the original text of that Gospel is not available (having come down to us only in an Italian translation dating from the late sixteenth century), its authenticity cannot be established with certainty. (Asad, p. 861)

God Will Perfect His Light

They seek to extinguish God's light with their mouths,
but though the unbelievers hate it,
God will perfect His light.
He it is Who sent His Messenger with guidance
and the religion of Truth.

[*Sūrah aṣ-Ṣaff* 61:8-9]

On the most obvious level, this verse has to do with the power of the religion of the Truth, sent by God through the Prophet Muḥammad Σ to triumph over all those who would slander it. The word of the Truth has weight; slander, which seems so powerful, is scattered like chaff in the wind of God's Spirit.

God's Light has power over vicious slander because His Light is objective. When light arrives, everyone can see what that light reveals, and know that they are looking, from their different points-of-view, at the same objects. Slander, however, is subjective. It has to do with opinion—with the kind of opinion that does not want to base itself on objective truth, but shies away from it instead, so that later it can rebel against it. Slander and gossip are an attempt to put opinion on a higher level than truth, as if a mass of subjective beliefs could finally gain power over Reality.

But what, exactly, is a *belief?* It is a firm conviction that this or that is *objectively* true. A belief depends upon objective Reality for any validity it may have. Insofar as it conforms with that Reality it is true, and leads us toward that Reality. Insofar as it departs from that Reality it is false, and leads us away from it. But those who use slander and gossip cannot un-derstand this simple and obvious truth. Because they have been able to reach—temporarily—a false sense of security by telling themselves that this or that is so, and because they have been able to influence the beliefs and actions of others, they start to believe, unconsciously, that they have the power to determine what is real—which is the same thing as saying that they have begun to believe, unconsciously, that they are God.

When God commanded the angels to prostrate themselves before Adam, Iblīs refused. By so doing, he followed his own understanding, based on belief, instead of God's command, based on Reality. He be-lieved he had very good reasons for disobeying God, having foreseen that humanity would wreak havoc on earth, and priding himself on the fact that he was willing to prostrate himself to God alone. In his view, to prostrate himself to Adam would be to ascribe a partner to God, whereas his refusal to do so was nothing but the purest faith in God's Unity. Yet his refusal to obey God's command was itself the act of ascribing a partner to God—Iblīs himself. And to place his own idea of faithfulness to God above God's direct command was certainly not a very good example of faithfulness.

Each of us has an Iblīs in his or her own soul—or one could say that, as long as our soul is not submitted to God's will, as long as we consult its promptings instead of listening to the word of God, our soul *is* Iblīs. This Iblīs-soul of ours can construct an entire religion based on personal belief instead of objective Truth, and even call it "Islam." But if we follow this "Islam" we are really making submission, not to God, but to our own desires and passions.

Slander and gossip, then, are forms of idolatry, in which we worship our own beliefs instead of God's Truth. And slander is related to flattery. If we flatter someone, or give undue praise to any thing or any person which does not deserve it—in order to further our own selfish interests, of course—then we automatically slander someone or something else, usually without even realizing it. Listening to the irreverent comedian, and so blinded by laughter; listening to the vain self-important poet, and so blinded by glamour; watching the seductive actress, and so blinded by lust, we may not notice the fact that the King has just entered the room, that we are still giggling or making catcalls, when everyone else—even the comedian, the actress, the poet—is standing in respectful silence. And to make an idol out of this or that mere human being is also to fail to recognize that virtue, wisdom, and sanctity actually are God's attributes reflected in human beings.

But God will perfect His light. Whatever has been hidden in darkness will ultimately be revealed. Whatever has been hidden in our souls, all our vices and all our virtues, will finally appear in the clear light of day: in this life, at the moment of repentance or retribution; in the world to come, at the moment when the souls are weighed and the paths separate, those to the right being admitted to Paradise, those on the left entering into the Fire. God will perfect His Light; Truth will prevail; the world, including each one of us, will perform its duty as the mirror of God's Attributes and Names. Submitted to Him, we mirror His Mercy; rebelling against Him, we mirror His wrath; in both mirrors, God witnesses only the perfection of His Light.

God's Light within us is sanctity and wisdom. In light of this Light, all our imperfections will appear in bold relief, either to be repented of or to be rationalized or justified, thus extinguishing that Light.

It is these rationalizations and justifications which make up the habitual chatter of our minds, unless we remember God—it is our own automatic, reactive thoughts which seek to *extinguish God's light with their mouths*. But that Light will not be extinguished. It will ultimately penetrate every veil that covers It. It will prevail. In view of the fact that this Light will prevail, one way or another, we had best submit to it. And the way we submit to it, internally, is by *listening* instead of *talking to ourselves*. When our whole being rests in a state of listening, we are ready to obey God's commands because we are ready to *hear* them; in the silence of our own wills and beliefs and imaginations, God's Light can fully appear. But if we are always talking to ourselves, then all the theoretical willingness to obey will count for nothing, because we will never hear the Command. (Upton)

Remember God Often

O faithful ones!
When the call to prayer is proclaimed on Friday,
hasten earnestly to the remembrance of God
and leave aside your business and trade:
that is best for you if only you knew!
And when the prayer is completed,
then you may move about through the land
and seek out God's abundance:
and remember God often
that you may prosper.[11]
But when they catch sight of some bargain or amusement,
they head off towards that and leave you standing.
Say: "That which is from the Presence of God[12] **is better**
than any passing delight or bargain!
For God is the best of providers."

[*Sūrah al-Jumuᶜah* 62:9-11]

When the call to prayer is proclaimed on the day of assembly refers to Friday, when the congregational prayer at noon is obligatory. Nevertheless, as the sequence shows, Friday is not a day of compulsory rest in Islamic Law. *When the prayer is completed, then you may move about through the land and seek out God's abundance,* i.e., you may devote yourselves to worldly pur-

---

[11] True well-being and happiness; from the root FLḤ, as in the call to prayer: *falāḥ.*
[12] Literally, "what God has," ᶜ*indallāhi.*

380

suits. *They . . . leave you standing*" alludes to an historical incident, when most of the congregation, on hearing that a long-expected trade caravan had come from Syria, rushed out of the mosque in the midst of the Prophet's Friday-sermon. In a wider, timeless sense, the above verse contains an allusion to an all-too-human weakness against which even true believers are not always immune: namely, the tendency to overlook religious obligations for the sake of a transitory, worldly advantage. (Asad, pp. 864–865)

Friday, the Muslim "Sabbath," is primarily the day of assembly, the weekly meeting of the congregation, when we show our unity by sharing in common public worship, preceded by a *Khuṭba*, in which the *Imām* (or Leader) reviews the week's spiritual life of the community and offers advice and exhortation on holy living. Notice the gradations of social contact for Muslims if they followed the wise ordinances of their faith. (1) Each individual remembers God for himself or herself five or more times every day, in the home or place of business or local mosque, or open air, as the case may be. (2) On Friday in every week, there is a local meeting in the central mosque of each local center—it may be a village, or town, or ward of a big city. (3) At the two ʿĪds every year, there is a large local area meeting in one center, the ʿĪd-gah. (4) Once at least in a lifetime, where possible, a Muslim shares in the vast international assemblage of the world, in the center of Islam, at the Meccan pilgrimage. A happy combination of decentralization and centralization, of individual liberty and collective meeting, and contact at various stages or grades. The mechanical part of this ordinance is easy to carry out. Are we carrying out the more difficult part—the spirit of unity, brotherhood, mutual consultation, and collective understanding and action?

Hasten earnestly to the remembrance of God and leave aside your business and trade: that is best for you, if only you knew! The idea behind the Muslim weekly day of assembly is different from that behind the Jewish Sabbath

381

(Saturday) or the Christian Sunday. The Jewish Sabbath is primarily a commemoration of God's ending His work and resting on the seventh day (Gen. 2:2, Exod. 20:11). We are taught that *God needs no rest, nor does He feel fatigue* [2:255]. The Jewish command forbids work on that day but says nothing about worship or prayer (Exod. 10); our ordinance lays chief stress on the remembrance of God. Jewish formalism went so far as to kill the spirit of the Sabbath, and call forth the protest of Jesus: "The Sabbath was made for man, and not man for the Sabbath" (Mark 2:27). But the Christian Church, although it has changed the day from Saturday to Sunday, has inherited the Jewish spirit: witness the Scottish Sabbath, except in so far as it has been secularized. Our teaching says: "When the time for *Jumuᶜa* prayer comes, close your business and answer the summons loyally and earnestly, meet earnestly, pray, consult, and learn by social contact: when the meeting is over, scatter and go about your business."

And when the prayer is completed, then you may move about through the land and seek out God's abundance: and remember God often that you may may prosper. Prosperity is not to be measured by wealth or worldly gain. There is a higher prosperity—the health of the mind and the spirit.

That which is from the Presence of God is better than any bargain or passing delight! For God is the best of providers. Do not be distracted by the craze for amusement or gain. If you lead a righteous and sober life, God will provide for you in all senses, better than any provision you can possibly think of. (A. Yusuf Ali, pp. 1547-1548)

Even in those times when we should be spiritually sensitized, such as on Friday at the time of congregational prayer, human beings are prone to distraction, ready to rush off in the direction of some new bargain or entertainment. If this were true in seventh century Arabia, how much more so in today's world, dominated as it is by commercialism, consumerisim, and the entertainment industry.

Islam recognizes the legitimate needs of human life to *seek out God's abundance,* but it also proposes mindful pauses from the activities of the outer world. Such moments of worship, of reconnecting with our Sustainer, provides the true sustenance for our lives. We are offered an insight: *That which is from the presence of God is better than any bargain or passing delight! For God is the best of providers.* Whereas a continual preoccupation with gain and distraction can only weaken the soul, to *remember God often* leads to true well-being and success.

It is important to be able to observe ourselves right at the moment when we are becoming distracted in order to be able to be the master of our own attention. The world (*dunyā*) is a thief of attention, and the practice of Islam is the safeguarding (*taqwā*) of the substance of our own souls, one aspect of which is our attention. Therefore, to remember God often means at the same time to keep our hearts free of unnecessary and inappropriate entanglements and distractions. Even in those times when we are engaged in the activities of making a living, or becoming educated, we can preserve an aspect of remembrance by being aware that it is God's abundance, *fadhlillāh*, that we are seeking. *(Helminski)*

He Has Created with Truth

Whatever is in the heavens and on earth
declares the praises and glory of God:
to Him belongs all sovereignty and to Him belongs all praise,
and He has power over all things.
It is He Who has created you;
and among you there are some who deny the Truth
and some who are faithful;
and God sees well all that you do.
He has created the heavens and the earth
in accordance with Truth
and has shaped you and made your shapes beautiful;
and with Him is your journey's end.
He knows what is in the heavens and on earth;
He knows what you conceal and what you reveal:
yes, God knows well the secrets of hearts.

[*Sūrah at-Taghābun* 64:1-4]

All things by their very existence proclaim the glory and the praises of God. He has dominion over all things, but He uses His domination for just and praiseworthy ends. He has power over all things: therefore He can combine justice with mercy, and His Plan and Purpose cannot be frustrated by the existence of evil along with good in His Kingdom. It is not that He does not see rebellion and evil, nor that He cannot punish them. He created all things pure and good, and if evil crept in by the grant of a limited free-will by Him, it is not unforeseen: it is in His wise

384

and universal plan for giving man a chance of rising higher and ever higher.

He has created the heavens and the earth in accordance with Truth and has shaped you and made your shapes beautiful: in addition to the beauty and grandeur of all God's creation, He has endowed man with special aptitudes, faculties, and capacities, and special excellencies which raise him at his best to the position of God's representative on earth. "Beautiful" also includes the idea of "adapted to the ends for which they were created."

It is We Who created you and gave you shape [7:11]: shape or form must be interpreted not only to refer to the physical form, which changes day by day, but also the various forms or shapes which our ideal and spiritual existence may take from time to time according to our inner experiences. Compare 82:8: *In whatever Form He wills, does He put you together.* The original Form or Idea or Pattern, according to Plato's mystic doctrine as developed in his *Republic* may also be compared with the "names" or nature and quality of things, which God taught Adam (as standing for all mankind) (2:31, 6:94).

And with Him is your journey's end. "The final goal" is not only of mankind but of all things created, whether material or in the realm of ideas and events. All things return to God: as they derive their origin from Him, so is the return or destination of all of them to God.

He knows what you conceal and what you reveal. Not only does He create and develop and sustain all things: but all thoughts, motives, feelings, ideas, and events are known to Him. Therefore we must not imagine that, if some evil seems to go unpunished, it is not known to Him or has escaped His notice. His plan is wise and good in its fullest compass: sometimes we do not see its wisdom and goodness because we see only a broken fragment of it, as our own intelligence is narrow. (A. Yusuf Ali, pp. 1555, 343, 1556)

385

In this verse we can begin to see how dense with meaning the Qur'ān is—how packed with Truth. It is miraculous how so much Truth, of such depth, can be expressed in so few words.

What does it mean that God created the heavens and the earth with nothing but Truth? Was Truth a kind of raw material He discovered, or knew about from all eternity, out of which He made all that we see around us, and ourselves as well? Certainly not; to believe this would be to ascribe a partner to God, Who is One without a second. Then what exactly is this "Truth" out of which He created the heavens and the earth?

"Truth" is one of God's Names, a Name of His Essence. So the Qur'ān would seem to be saying that God created the heavens and the earth out of His Own Substance, since there was nothing else beside Him, or other than Him, which He could lay His hands upon when He came to make the universe. But there is a problem with this interpretation, too, since it implies that the Universe is either somehow actually God, or else that it is a kind of second God created by the "first" one, out of His Own Substance. We know of course that the first implication is untrue because *there is absolutely nothing to which He can be compared* [112:4]; we know that the second implication is also untrue because *He neither begets nor is He begotten* [112:3]. To believe that the Universe is God is the error of pantheism or incarnationism; to believe that God could somehow create a second God is, again, the error of ascribing a partner to God, Who alone is Absolute Truth.

So if the Universe is neither God, nor made out of something different from God, then what is it?

According to the Qur'ān, God has only to say to something "Be!" and it is (2:117, 3:47, 3:59, 16:40, 19:35, 36:82, 40:68). The universe, then, is neither a part of God, nor is it something which exists in its own right, as if it were a second God. It is an act of God. The motion of your hand is not a part of you, nor is it a separate object that can exist apart from you. Any action you perform depends entirely upon you; any action you perform is perfectly at one with you, with no division; any action you perform has no existence in itself apart from you. God is the only One Who is in His own Nature; all other things only are because God Is. Therefore all things, both forms and events, must be acts of God. What else could they be?

This is metaphysical knowledge, the kind of knowledge that the senses and the rational mind alone cannot bring us. But what is the place of such knowledge? What does it mean for our lives, in concrete terms?

If God created the heavens and the earth with nothing but Truth, then everything is significant. Everything, both within us and in the world around us, is like a word spoken by God. There are no meaningless events, no "neutral" moments. Everything that happens, everything that is, is like the flow of God's speech, and God did not create the universe in jest; He means something by it. This divine speech of existence is abstract and not only general; it is also directed, specifically, to each one of us. Every moment of our lives is an expression of God's Will for us, based on His perfect Knowledge of us.

What would life be like if we could really see this? What if we not only believed, but really saw, that everything is an act of God?

On the level of doing, the knowledge that everything that happens is a word or an act of God is the root of *islām*, submission to God's Will—and the fruit of this submission is peace. This is why all Muslims greet each other in the name of peace. But this submission is not fatalistic. It is not a hopeless paralysis in the face of events. If we resign ourselves to God's Will, this is not the same as always accepting the status quo. Our own actions, too, are a response to God's Will (either that, or a flight from it). In the Qur'ān, God has given us a mark to meet, which can only be met through effort, through struggling in the way of God; so our effort, too, is part of God's will. In our submission to God we resign ourselves to events, but we also resign ourselves, so to speak, to our own efforts.

On the level of knowing, our understanding that everything is a word or an act of God lets us learn about Who God is from everything that happens, everything that is. Some of God's acts appear to us as events; others appear as truths, as things which are always so, no matter what happens or doesn't happen. Whatever happens or doesn't happen, God is all-Merciful; whatever happens or doesn't happen, God is all-Powerful; whatever happens or doesn't happen, God is all-Aware. While we are in this world, all our actions happen in time; they begin and end. But God is beyond happening, beyond time; all His actions happen in eternity. The universe we know is only that tiny part of them which overflows into space and time.

We need to know how to live. And to know how to live, we need to see things as they really are. This was the prayer of the Prophet Muḥammad Σ: "O God, show me things as they really are." Beyond the actions the Law requires of us, our knowledge of religion tends to be more or less abstract or theoretical; our practical knowledge comes from our dealings with the world. But if we can truly see how God created the heavens and the earth with nothing but Truth, then there is no theoretical understanding of religion which is not immediately practical, and no practical know-how which does not illustrate some "theoretical" truth of God. We see ourselves performing actions, we watch things happening to us, and every event and every action—if we only knew—is a Name of God Himself.

Work, leisure, sleep, study, driving a car, eating, struggling to change things, accepting things as they are, fasting, prayer, giving alms, breathing air, dying, giving birth: all are signs of eternal realities lying within the mystery of God. (Upton)

Among you there are some who deny the Truth and some who are faithful: since all human beings are endowed with the instinctive ability to perceive the existence of the Creator, one man's denial of this truth and another's belief in it is, in the last resort, an outcome of free choice. Accord-

THE BOOK OF REVELATIONS

ing to the Qur'ān, the ability to perceive the existence of the Supreme Power is inborn in human nature (*fiṭrah*); and it is this instinctive cognition—which may or may not be subsequently blurred by self-indulgence or adverse environmental influences—that makes every sane human being "bear witness about himself" before God (7:172).

He has created the heavens and the earth in accordance with Truth, i.e., to fulfill a definite purpose in consonance with His planning wisdom (Zamakhsharī, Baghawī, Rāzī): implying that everything in the universe—whether existent or potential, concrete or abstract—is meaningful, and nothing is "accidental." (Asad, pp. 869, 230, 289)

A Way of Emergence

For the one who remains conscious of God;
He always prepares a way of emergence
and He provides for him in ways he could never imagine.
And if anyone puts his trust in God, sufficient is God for him.
For God will surely accomplish His purpose:
truly, for all things has God appointed an appropriate measure. . . .
And for everyone who is conscious of God,
He makes it easy to obey His commandments:
all this is God's commandment,
which He has bestowed upon you from on high.
And to everyone who is conscious of God
will He pardon his bad deeds,
and will grant him a vast reward.

[*Sūrah aṭ-Ṭalāq* 65:2-3, 4-5]

In these very delicate and difficult matters [this *sūrah* deals with divorce], the wisdom of jurists provides a less satisfactory solution than a sincere desire to be just and true, which is described as the "fear of God" [remaining conscious of God]. Where such a desire exists, God often provides a solution in the most unexpected ways or from the most unexpected quarters: e.g., the worst enemies may be reconciled, or the cry or the smile of an infant baby may heal seemingly irreparable injuries or unite hearts seemingly alienated forever. And faith is followed at once by a psychological feeling of rest for the troubled spirit.

For God will surely accomplish His purpose: our anger and our impatience have to be curbed. Our friends and our mates or associates may seem to us ever so weak and unreasonable, and the circumstances may be

390

ever so disheartening; yet we must trust in God. How can we measure our own weakness or perhaps blindness? He knows all. His universal purpose is always good. His Will must be accomplished, and we should wish for its accomplishment. His ordering of the universe observes a due, just, and perfect proportion. (A. Yusuf Ali, pp. 1563-1564)

For the one who remains conscious of God, He always prepares a way of emergence. This is one of God's beautiful promises. If we remain mindful of God, if we exercise *taqwā*, God will guide us out of the conditions that imprison or entrap us. All human beings are in need of a way of emergence from the limitations of their own *nafs* or ego, and toward the true spiritual freedom of the soul. And furthermore, God provides *in ways we could not imagine*, or literally, *from a direction one does not expect*. In other words, the Divine Intelligence is sometimes better at problem-solving than our own limited minds.

These verses are found in the *Sūrah* of "Divorce," and may be a comfort to those struggling with the difficulties of relationship. The "way out," however, will not necessarily be divorce, which of all things permitted is the least liked by God. The *way of emergence* may instead be the freeing from our own egoistic viewpoint.

Muḥammad Asad writes: "It is to be noted that the relative pronoun *man* ('whoever' or 'everyone who;)—although grammatically requiring the use of the masculine gender in the verbs or pronouns to which it relates—applies to *persons of either sex*, as is evidenced by innumerable passages in the Qurʾān: hence, the present passage, too, including the sentence that follows, must be understood as relating to the women as well as to the men in question, and the same holds of verses 65:5 and 65:11. (Asad, p. 873)

He makes it easy to obey His commandment suggests that being mindful of God helps us to submit to the discipline of a spiritual life, as well as to the sacrifices life demands, to whatever God wills for us. (Helminski)

391

No Undue Burden

Let the person of means spend according to his means:
and the one whose resources are restricted,
let him spend according to that which God has given.
God puts no burden on any soul beyond what He bestows.
Surely, after hardship God will bring ease.

[*Sūrah aṭ-Ṭalāq* 65:7]

We must not be frightened by difficulties. God will give us relief and provide a solution if we act with honest integrity.

Whatever difficulties or troubles are encountered by men, God always provides a solution, a way out, relief, a way to lead to ease and happiness, if we only follow His Path and show our faith by patience and well-doing. The solution or relief does not merely come *after* the difficulty: it is provided *with* it. (A. Yusuf Ali, pp. 1565, 1755)

We Breathed Our Spirit into Mary

And God sets forth as an example to those who have faith
the wife of Pharaoh:
witness, she said: "O my Sustainer!
Build for me in nearness to You a mansion in the Garden
and save me from Pharaoh and his actions
and save me from those who do wrong";
and also Mary, the daughter of 'Imran,
who guarded her chastity,
and We breathed into her of Our spirit,
and she witnessed to the truth of the words of her Sustainer
and of His revelations and was one of those devoted.

[*Sūrah at-Taḥrīm* 66:11-12]

Traditionally the wife of Pharoah is known as ʿĀsiya, one of the four perfect women, the other three being Mary the mother of Jesus, Khadīja the wife of the holy Prophet, and Fāṭima his daughter. Pharoah is the archetype of arrogance, godlessness, and wickedness. For his wife to have preserved her faith, her humility, and her righteousness was indeed a great spiritual triumph. She was probably the same who saved the life of the infant Moses.

Build for me in nearness to You a mansion in the Garden: her spiritual vision was directed to God, rather than to the worldly grandeur of Pharoah's court.

Mary, the daughter of ʿImrān: ʿImrān was traditionally the name of the father of Mary, the mother of Jesus. She was herself one of the purest of

393

women, though the Jews accused her falsely of unchastity.

And We breathed into her of Our spirit: as a virgin she gave birth to Jesus [19:16-29]. In 32:9 it is said of Adam's progeny, man, that God *fashioned him in due proportion and breathed into him something of His spirit.* In 15:29 similar words are used with reference to Adam. The virgin birth should not therefore be supposed to imply that God was the father of Jesus in the sense in which Greek mythology makes Zeus the father of Apollo by Latona or Minos by Europa. And yet that is the doctrine to which the Christian idea of "the only begotten son of God" leads.

Mary had true faith and testified her faith in the Prophet Jesus and in his revelation as well as in the revelation which he came to confirm (and to foreshadow). She was of the company of the devout of all ages. The fact that *qānitīn* (devout) is not here in the feminine gender implies that the highest spiritual dignity is independent of sex. And so we close the lesson of this *sūrah,* that while sex is a fact of our physical existence, the sexes should act in harmony and cooperation, for in the highest spiritual matters we are all one. *We made her and her son a sign for all peoples. Truly this brotherhood of yours is a single brotherhood, and I am your Lord and Cherisher therefore serve Me and no other* [21:91-92]. (A. Yusuf Ali, pp. 1573-1574)

A Flawless Universe

Blessed be the One in Whose hands is sovereignty:
and He has power over all things—
He Who created death and life
that He may test which of you is best in deeds.
And He is the Almighty, the One Who is Ever Ready to Forgive,
He Who created the seven heavens in harmony;
no lack of proportion will you see
in that which the Most Compassionate has created—
just look again: can you see any flaw?

[*Sūrah al-Mulk* 67:1-3]

Since what is termed "death" is stated here to have been *created*, it cannot be identical with "non-existence," but obviously must have a positive reality of its own. To my mind, it connotes, firstly, the inanimate state of existence preceding the emergence of life in plants or animated beings; and, secondly, the state of transition from life as we know it in this world to the—as yet to us unimaginable—condition of existence referred to in the Qurʾān as "the hereafter" or "the life to come" (*al-ākhirah*). (Asad, p. 879)

What do we mean when we bless the name of God, or proclaim that the whole Creation should bless the name of the Lord? We mean that we recognize and proclaim His beneficence to us; for all increase and happiness is through Him, *in His hands,* in the hands of Him Who also holds Dominion or Power. In our human affairs we sometimes see the separation of Dominion or Power from Goodness or Beneficence: in the divine nature we recognize that there is no separation or antithesis.

Mulk [which appears in the first verse and gives this *sūrah* its name] can be translated as Dominion, Lordship, Sovereignty, the Right to carry out His Will or to do all that He will. *Power* (in the clause following) is the capacity to carry out His Will, so that nothing can resist or neutralize it. Here is beneficence completely identified with Lordship and Power: and it is exemplified in the verse following. Note that *Mulk* here has a different shade of meaning from *Malakūt* in 36:83 *So glory to Him in whose hands is the dominion of all things; and to Him will you all be brought back.* Both words are from the same root, and I translate both by the word "Dominion." But *Malakūt* refers to Lordship in the invisible world, while *Mulk* refers to Lordship in the visible world. God is Lord of both.

He Who created death and life. Death is here put before life, and it is created. Death is therefore not merely a negative state. In 2:28 we read: *Seeing that you were without life* (literally, *dead*) *and He gave you life: then will He cause you to die, and will again bring you to life; and again to Him will you return.* In 53:44, again, death is put before life (*That it is He Who grants death and life*). Death, then, is: (1) the state before life began, which may be non-existence or existence in some other form; (2) the state in which Life as we know it ceases, but existence does not cease: a state of *Barzakh* (23:100), or barrier or partition, after our visible death and before Judgment; after that will be the new life, which we conceive of under the term eternity.

That He may test which of you is best in deeds. Creation, therefore, is not mere sport, or without a purpose with reference to man. The state before our present life, or the state after, we can scarcely understand. But our present life is clearly given to enable us to strive by good deeds to reach a nobler state.

He Who created the seven heavens in harmony. Compare 65:12 *Allāh is He Who created seven firmaments.* The literal meaning refers to the seven orbits or firmaments that we see clearly marked in the motions of the

396

heavenly bodies in the space around us. In poetical imagery there are the seven planetary spheres, which form the lower heaven or heavens, with higher spheres culminating in the empyrean or God's Throne of Majesty. The heavens as they appear to our sight seem to be arranged in layers one above another, and ancient astronomy accounted for the motions of the heavenly bodies in an elaborate scheme of spheres. What we are concerned with here is the order and beauty of the vast space and the marvelous bodies that follow regular laws of motion in those enormous spaces in the visible world. From these we are to form some conception of the vastly greater invisible world, for which we want special spiritual vision. The mystical meaning refers to the various grades in the spiritual or heavenly kingdom, the number seven being itself a mystical symbol, comprising many and yet forming an indivisible integer, the highest indivisible integer of one digit.

Just look again: can you see any flaw? Reverting to the symbolism of the external or visible world, we are asked to observe and study it again and again, and as minutely as our powers will allow. However closely we observe it, we shall find no flaw in it. Indeed the region of enquiry is so vast and stretches so far beyond our ken, that our eyes, aided with the most powerful telescope, will confess themselves defeated in trying to penetrate to the ultimate mysteries. We shall find no defect in God's handiwork; it is our own powers that we shall find fail to go beyond a certain compass. (A. Yusuf Ali, pp. 1576, 1567, 1577)

The Sublime Standard of Character

In the Name of God,
the Infinitely Compassionate and Most Merciful.
Nun.[13] By the Pen and by that which they write,
by the grace of your Sustainer, you are not crazy.
And truly, yours is an unceasing recompense:
for surely, you stand upon
a sublime standard of character.
Soon you will see and they will see
which of you it is who is without reason.

[*Sūrah al-Qalam* 68:1-6]

We have several well-authenticated Traditions according to which Muḥammad's widow ʿĀʾishah, speaking of the Prophet many years after his death, repeatedly stressed that "his character (*khuluq*) was the Qurʾān" (Muslim, Ṭabarī, and Ḥākim, on the authority of Saʿīd ibn Hishām; Ibn Ḥanbal, Abū Dāʾūd, and Nasāʾī, on the authority of Al-Ḥasan al-Baṣrī; Tabarī, on the authority of Qatādah and Jubayr ibn Nufayl; and several other compilations). (Helminski)

Nūn is an abbreviated letter. It may mean fish, or an ink-holder, or it may be just the Arabic letter of the alphabet, N. In the last case, it may refer to either or both of the other meanings. Note also that the Arabic rhyme in this *Sūrah* ends in N. The reference to ink would be an appropriate link with the mystic pen in verse 1. The reference to the fish would

---

[13] See footnote 1.

be appropriate with reference to the story of Jonah in verses 68:48–50. Jonah's title is "the companion of the fish" as he was, in the story, swallowed by the fish. The letter N could also symbolically represent Jonah in the Arabic form Yunus, where the characteristic "firm letter" is N.

By the Pen and by that which they write: the mystic pen and the mystic record are the symbolical foundations of the revelation to man. The adjuration by the pen disposes of the flippant charge that God's Messenger was mad or possessed. For he spoke words of power, not incoherent, but full of meaning, and through the record of the pen, that meaning unfolds itself, in innumerable aspects to countless generations. Muḥammad was the living Grace and Mercy of God, and his very nature exalted him above abuse and persecution.

By the grace of your Sustainer, you are not crazy: people usually call anyone mad whose standards are different from their own. And madness is believed by superstitious people to be due to demonical possession, an idea distinctly in the minds of the New Testament writers; for Luke speaks of a man of whom the "devils" were cast out, as being then "clothed, and in his right mind" (Luke 8:35).

And truly, yours is an unceasing recompense: instead of being out of his right mind, the man of God had been raised to a great spiritual dignity, a reward that was not like an earthly reward that passes away, but one that was in the very core of his being, and would never fail him in any circumstances. He was really granted a nature and character far above the shafts of grief or suffering, slander or persecution.

Soon you will see and they will see which of you it is who is without reason. Though Muṣṭafā's nature raised him above the petty spite of his contemporaries, an appeal is made to their reason and to the logic of events. Was it not his accusers that were really mad? What happened to Walīd ibn Mughaira, or Abū Jahl, or Abū Lahab? And to God's Apostle and those who followed his guidance? The world's history gives the answer. And the appeal is not only to his contemporaries, but for all time. (A. Yusuf

Ali, pp. 1585–1586)

Gardens of Bliss

For behold it is the God-conscious
for whom gardens of bliss await with their Sustainer:
or should we treat those who surrender themselves to us
as those who remain lost in sin?

[*Sūrah al-Qalam* 68:34-35]

Should we treat those who surrender themselves to us (muslimūn) *as those who remain lost in sin?* This is the earliest occurrence of the term *muslimūn* (sing. *muslim*) in the history of Qur'anic revelation. *Muslim,* in accordance with its original connotation, is "one who surrenders [or "has surrendered"] himself to God" and *islām* is "man's self-surrender to God." It should be borne in mind that the "institutionalized" use of the terms *Muslim and Islām*—that is, their exclusive application to the followers of the Prophet Muḥammad—represents a definitely post-Qur'anic development. (Asad, p. 886)

How can we best clothe our idea of Heaven in human language? Our Heaven is independent of time, or place, or fleeting circumstance. No one can know precisely now the spiritual delights hidden in reserve for him (32:17). But we must necessarily use terms that imply all these three conditions. Therefore they can only be expressed by allegory or imagery. If we understand what the essence of the allegory or imagery is, we shall profit by it. If we branch out into fantastic applications that leave us in the material world, we shall never be able to get a glimpse of the spiritual world into which such allegory or imagery is intended to open a window for our spiritual eyes. Such allegory or imagery is supplied in abundance in the Qur'ān.

The simplest and yet the most far-reaching allegory that we can employ is that of the Garden—the Garden of Bliss (*Jannat* or *Jannat-un Na'īm*, 5:68 [5:65 in Asad]). In all Muslim languages, that word *Jannat* (Garden) is now specialized for Heaven. Let us analyze a few of the ideas which we can legitimately associate in this connection with the concrete word "Garden" and the abstract term "Bliss."

In this life, most of our sensations depend upon sense-perceptions, and we can reduce the highest and noblest of them to terms connected with the Garden. To each of our five senses, in their most refined form, does the Garden minister. For the eye there is the general green, with all the most delicate tints of green in the foliage, and the wonderful colors and shapes in flowers; the arrangement of paths and parterres; the various gradations of light and shade; the soft and melting beauty of clouds and mists; and the landscape views with cool rivers flowing underneath, or perhaps murmuring brooks. For the ear is the music of birds, the music of waterfalls, and the appropriate moonlight music of the human voice with or without the accompaniment of an instrument like a guitar. For the smell there is not only the perfume of flowers but the more subtle scents of foliage, moisture or morning dew, or even garden soil. For taste and touch the exquisite fruits and for touch the soft rose petals and the carpet-like lawns, besides the gentle kiss of breezes, all minister to the highest bliss and fulfillment that we can imagine through our senses.

We picture not only a Garden, but a Garden with rivers or springs flowing beneath. This further enlarges our horizon. We can picture a landscape with banks, terraces, and sloping lawns, high ground, and valleys. What is the spiritual analogy for this? We must not imagine a dull place where all are engaged in perpetual psalm-singing. There will be differences in ranks, dignities, and tastes, according to each individual's growth and individuality: for that is the meaning of the persistence of personality. And yet they will form one equal brotherhood of peace, one society of concord. There will be the four-fold classification according to the varying spiritual experiences gained in this life: (1) the Prophets who taught and led mankind; (2) the sincere devotees of truth, who supported the cause in their person and with all their resources; (3) the martyrs and witnesses who suffered and served; and (4) the righteous people generally, those who led ordinary lives, but always with righteous aims. All these are united in one beautiful fellowship (see 4:69). Or take that other classification indicated in 56:27 and 56:11: the righteous generally, the companions of the right hand (distinguished from the companions of the left hand, who will not have reached Heaven), and those nearest to God in rank and dignity. The latter will have no interposing veils of light to obscure the pure light of God from them (24:35); for, in Sufi language, they will have had the ineffable bliss of seeking the "Divine Eyes." Possibly the companions of the garden and those on the heights (7:46) refer to the same two categories of souls. Whatever the precise interpretation of these mystic passages may be, there is no doubt that the retention of individual personality in the hereafter will mean bliss of different kinds of each category.

How can we understand a psychological term like bliss in general symbolical terms? If it is to convert the idea of satisfaction in any but abstract terms, we must have the symbolism of ordinary life, yet lifted up to ideas of refinement, delicacy, and satisfaction. The acts of eating and drinking are spiritualized and socialized. The choicest of meats, fruits, and drinks, which minister to the most sensitive taste, will be provided. Dress of most artistic taste will add dignity to social intercourse and there will be thrones and symbols of honor. There will be companionship, individual companionship, companionship of equal age, as well as general companionship. And those whom we loved in this life—mothers, wives, sisters, relatives, children, friends—will all add to our joy by their company in a transformed Love as superior to earthly love as is the Garden of Heaven to an earthly garden. The condition of faith and good life is of course attached: for no disharmony can enter to mar the dignity of Heaven. (See 13:23 and 43:70-72.) Perfected Love will not be content with self, but like a note of music will find its melody in communion with others.

All symbols of delight, expressed in terms of sense, are spiritualized by their being referred to the presence of God. The Garden is a joy, but the joy of this spiritual Garden is the sense of nearness to God.

Or should we treat those who surrender themselves to us as those who remain lost in sin? The spiritual arrogance which rejects faith in God is perhaps the worst sin, because it makes itself impervious to the Mercy of God, as a bed of clay is impervious to the absorption of water. It sets up its own standards and its own will, but how can it measure or bind the Will of God? It sets up its own fetishes—idols, priests, gods, or godlings. The fetishes may be even God-given gifts or faculties, intellect or science, if pushed up to the position of idols. If they are made rivals to God, question them: will they solve God's mysteries, or even the mysteries of life and soul? It is clearly against both logic and justice that men of righteousness should have the same end as men of sin. Even in this life, man cannot command whatever he chooses, though he is allowed a limited freedom of choice. How can he expect such a thing under a reign of perfect Justice and Truth? (A. Yusuf Ali, pp. 1466-1467, 1591)

Laying–Bare the Truth

Oh, the laying-bare of the truth!
How awesome that laying-bare of the truth!
And what could make you conceive
what that laying-bare of the truth will be?

[*Sūrah al-Ḥāqqah* 69:1-3]

The *laying-bare of the truth* refers to the Day of Resurrection and Judgment, on which man will become fully aware of the quality of his past life and, freed from all self-deception, will see himself as he really was, with the innermost meaning of all his past doings—and thus of his destiny in the hereafter—blindingly revealed. This sudden perception of the ultimate reality will be beyond anything that man can anticipate or imagine: hence, no answer is given to the rhetorical question in 69:3. [See 50:16-22.] (Asad, p. 888)

Truly the Word of an Honored Messenger

And so I call to witness all that you can see
and what you do not see,
that this is truly the word of an honored Messenger.
It is not the word of a poet; how little faith you have!
Nor is it the word of a soothsayer;
what little counsel you take to heart.
It is a revelation from the Sustainer of all the Worlds.
And if he were to invent any sayings in Our name
We should certainly seize him by his right hand
and We should certainly then cut off the life-blood of his heart,
nor could any of you save him.
But truly, this is a reminder for those who are mindful of God.
And We certainly know that there are among you
those who deny Our signs;
but truly revelation is a source of remorse for the deniers.
And surely it is the certain truth.
So glorify the name of your Sustainer, the Most High.

[*Sūrah al-Ḥāqqah* 69:38-52]

The phrase *all that you can see* comprises all the observable phenomena of nature—including man himself and the organic conditions of his own existence—as well as the configuration of human society and the perceptible rules of its growth and decay in the historical sense; whereas *that which you cannot see* relates to the intangible spiritual verities accessible to man's intuition and instinct, including the voice of his own conscience.

406

All of these "bear witness," as it were, to the fact that the light which the divine writ (spoken of in the sequence) casts on the innermost realities and interrelations of all that exists objectively—or, as the case may be, manifests itself subjectively in man's own psyche—*must* be an outcome of genuine revelation, inasmuch as it goes far beyond anything that unaided human intellect could ever achieve. (Asad, p. 890)

And so I call to witness: this is an adjuration in the same form as that which occurs in 56:75, 70:40, 90:1, and elsewhere. God's Word is the quintessence of Truth. But what if someone doubts whether a particular Message is God's Word communicated through His Apostle, or merely an imaginary tale presented by a poet, or a soothsayer's vain prophecy? Then we have to examine it in the light of our highest spiritual faculties. The witness to that Word is what we know in the visible world, in which falsehood in the long run gives place to truth, and what we know in the invisible world, through our highest spiritual faculties. We are asked to examine and test it in both these ways.

This is truly the word of an honored Messenger: one that is worthy of honor on account of the purity of his life, and may be relied upon not to invent things but to give the true inner experiences of his soul in revelation.

It is not the word of a poet: a poet draws upon his imagination, and the subjective factor is so strong that though we may learn much from him, we cannot believe as facts the wonderful tales he has to tell. And the poet who is not a seer is merely a vulgar votary of exaggeration and falsehood.

Nor is it the word of a soothsayer: a soothsayer merely pretends to foretell future events of no profound spiritual consequence. Most of his prophecies are frauds and none of them is meant to teach lessons of real admonition. Such admonition is the work of an honored apostle.

We should certainly seize him by his right hand: the right hand is the hand of power and action. Anyone who is seized by his right hand is prevented from acting as he wishes or carrying out his purpose. The argument is that if an imposter were to rise, he would soon be found out. He could not carry out his fraud indefinitely. But the men of God, however much they are persecuted, gain more and more power every day, as did the holy Prophet, whose truth, earnestness, sincerity, and love for all were recognized as his life unfolded itself.

And We should certainly then cut off the life-blood of his heart: this would effectually stop the functioning of his life. *Nor could any of you save him:* the protection which the men of God enjoy in circumstances of danger and difficulty would not be available for impostors.

But truly revelation is a source of remorse for the deniers. The Message of God is glad tidings for those who believe in Him and follow His Law, for it is a message of Mercy and Forgiveness through repentance and amendment. But in the case of the wicked it is a cause of sorrow, for it denounces sin and proclaims the punishment of those who do not turn from evil.

And surely it is the certain truth. All Truth is in itself certain. But as received by men, and understood with reference to men's psychology, certainty may have certain degrees. There is the probability or certainty resulting from the application of man's power of judgment and his appraisement of evidence. This is *ʿilm-ul-yaqīn,* certainty by reasoning or inference. *Nay, were you to know with certainty of mind, [you would beware!]* [102:5]. We hear from someone, or we infer from something we know: this refers to our own state of mind. If we instruct our minds in this way, we should value the deeper things of life better, and not waste all our time in ephemeral things. But if we do not use our reasoning faculties now, we shall yet see with our own eyes the penalty for our sins. This refers to the next kind of certainty of knowledge, certainty of sight. This is the certainty of seeing something with our own eyes. "Seeing is believing." This is *ʿayn-ul-yaqīn,* certainty by personal inspection. *Again, you shall see it with certainty of sight!* [102:7]. Then here in 69:51, *surely it is the certain truth,* there is the absolute Truth, with no possibility of error of judgment or error of the eye (which stands for any instrument of sense-perception and any ancillary aids, such as microscopes, etc.). This absolute Truth is the *ḥaqq-ul-yaqīn* spoken of here.

So glorify the name of your Sustainer, the Most High. As God has given us this absolute Truth through His revelation, it behooves us to understand it and be grateful to Him. We must celebrate His praises in thought, word, and deed. (A. Yusuf Ali, pp. 1602–1603, 1780)

Created Restless

Truly the human being was born restless—
filled with self-pity when difficulty touches him
and selfish when good fortune comes to him—
but not those who consciously turn towards God in prayer—
those who continually persist in their prayer,
and in whose wealth is a recognized right
for those who ask and for the one who cannot ask,
and who grasp the truth of the Day of Reckoning.

[*Sūrah al-Maʿārij* 70:19-26]

Literally, *man has been created restless* (*halūʿan*)—that is, endowed with an inner restlessness which may equally well drive him to fruitful achievement or to chronic discontent and frustration. In other words, it is the manner in which man utilizes this God-willed endowment that determines whether it shall have a positive or a negative character. The next two verses, 20-21, allude to the latter, while verses 22-25 show that only true spiritual and moral consciousness can mold that inborn restlessness into a positive force, and thus bring about inner stability and abiding contentment.

Filled with self-pity when difficulty touches him: the participle *jazūʿ*—derived from the verb *jaziʿa*—combines the concepts of "lacking patience" and "lamenting over one's misfortune" and is therefore the contrary of *ṣabr* (Jawharī).

Those who consciously turn towards God in prayer: this, I believe, is the meaning of the expression *al-muṣallīn* (literally, "the praying ones"),

410

which evidently does not relate here to the mere *ritual* of prayer but, rather, as the next verse shows, to the attitude of mind and the spiritual need underlying it. In this sense it connects with verse 19 that *man is born with a restless disposition* which, when rightly used, leads him towards conscious spiritual growth, as well as to freedom from all self-pity and selfishness. (Asad, p. 893)

Truly the human being was born restless: man, according to the Plan of God, was to be in the best of moulds [95:4]. But in order to fulfill his high destiny he was given free-will to a limited extent. The wrong use of this free-will makes his nature weak [4:28], or hasty [17:11], or impatient, as here. That becomes his nature, by his own act, but is spoken as so created because of the capacities given to him in his creation.

Filled with self-pity when difficulty touches him and selfish when good fortune comes to him. In adversity he complains and gets into despair. In prosperity he becomes arrogant and forgets other people's rights and his own shortcomings. Compare 43:49-50, where Pharoah and his Chiefs said: "O *Sorcerer! Invoke your Lord for us according to His covenant with you; for we shall truly accept guidance.*" *But when We removed the penalty from them, behold, they broke their word.* In spite of their unbelief, they had fear in their minds, and in order to stop the plagues, one after another, they promised to obey God. When the particular plague was removed, they again became obdurate.

But not those who consciously turn towards God in prayer: the description of those devoted to prayer is given in a number of clauses that follow. Devoted to prayer is here but another aspect of what is described elsewhere as faithful and the righteous. Devotion to prayer does not mean merely a certain number of formal rites or prostrations. It means a complete surrender of one's being to God. This means an earnest approach to and realization of God's Presence (*continually persist in their prayer*); acts of practical and real charity; an attempt to read this life in terms of the here-

411

after; the seeking of the Peace of God and avoidance of His displeasure; chastity; probity; true and firm witness; and guarding the sacredness of the Presence (*those who guard [the sacredness of] their worship* [70:34]).

And in whose wealth is a recognized right for those who ask and for the one who cannot ask. True charity consists in finding out those in real need, whether they ask or not. Most frequently those who ask are idle men who insolently wish to live upon others. But all cases of those who ask should be duly investigated, in case a little timely help may set the erring on the way. But the man with wealth or talent or opportunity has the further responsibility of searching out those in need of his assistance, in order to show that he holds all gifts in trust for the service of his fellow-creatures. (A. Yusuf Ali, pp. 1608-1610, 238, 1334)

The One Who Loves to Forgive

So I've called to them openly,
and I've spoken to them publicly and also in private,
saying: "Seek the forgiveness of your Sustainer,
for He is the One Who Loves to Forgive;
He will shower you with abundant blessings,
and will strengthen you with wealth and children,
and give you gardens and rivers of flowing water.
What's wrong with you that you don't place your hope
in God's Beneficence,
seeing that it is He Who has created you in successive stages?
Don't you see how God has created the seven heavens in harmony
and made the moon a light in their midst
and made the sun a glorious lamp?
And how God has caused you to grow gradually from the earth,
and in the end He will return you to it
and then raise you forth anew?
And God has unfolded wide the earth for you
that you might move about there on spacious paths."

[*Sūrah Nūḥ* 71:8-20]

This is part of *Sūrah Nūḥ* or Noah. Noah used all the resources of the earnest preacher: he drummed the Message of God into their ears, he spoke in public places, and he took individuals into his confidence and appealed privately to them, but all in vain.

He will shower you with abundant blessings, and will strengthen you with wealth and children, and give you gardens and rivers of flowing water. Each of these blessings—rain and crops, wealth and man-power, flourishing gardens and perennial streams—are indications of prosperity, and have not only a material but also a spiritual meaning. Note the last point: *rivers of flowing water.* The perennial springs make the prosperity as it were permanent: they indicate a settled population, honest and contented, and enjoying their blessings here on earth as the foretaste of the eternal joys of heaven.

Seeing that it is He Who has created you in successive stages. Compare this to 22:5: *If you are in doubt as to the resurrection, remember that truly We have created every one of you out of dust, then out of a drop of sperm, then out of a germ cell, then out of an embryonic lump complete in itself and yet incomplete, so that We might make your origin clear to you. And whatever We will to be born We cause to rest in the wombs for a term set by Us and then We bring you forth as infants and allow you to live so that some of you might attain to maturity: for among you are such as are caused to die in childhood, just as many a one of you is reduced in old age to a most abject state, ceasing to know anything of what he once knew so well. You can see the earth dry and lifeless and when We send down waters upon it, it stirs and swells and puts forth every kind of beauty in pairs.* If they really have doubts in their minds about the life after death, they have to turn their attention either to their own nature or the nature around. How wonderful is their own physical growth, from lifeless matter, to seed, fertilized ovum, fetus, child, youth, age, and death! How can they doubt that the Author of all these wonderful stages in their life here can also give them another kind of life after the end of this life? Or, if they look at external nature, they see the earth dead and barren, and God's fertilizing showers bring it to life, growth, and beauty in various forms. The Creator of this pageant of beauty can surely create yet another and a newer world.

Man in his various states exhibits various wonderful qualities or capacities, mental and spiritual, that may be compared with the wonderful workings of nature on the earth and in the heavens. Will he not then be grateful for these Mercies and turn to God, Who created all these marvels?

Don't you see how God has created the seven heavens in harmony and made the moon a light in their midst and made the sun a glorious lamp? See 67:3, *He Who created the seven heavens in harmony; no lack of proportion will you see in that which the Most Compassionate has created—just look again: can you see any flaw?* In 25:61, the sun is also referred to as the glorious Lamp of the heaven: *Blessed is He Who made the constellations in the skies and placed therein a lamp and a moon giving light.*

And how God has caused you to grow gradually from the earth, and in the end He will return you to it and then raise you forth anew? Compare this to 3:37, where the growth of the child Mary, the mother of Jesus, is described by the same word, *nabāt*, ordinarily denoting the growth of plants and trees. *Right graciously did her Lord accept her: He made her grow in purity and beauty.* The simile is that of a seed sown, that germinates, grows, and dies, and goes back to the earth. In man, there is the further process of the resurrection. *From the earth did We create you, and into it shall We return you, and from it shall We bring you out once again* [20:55].

And God has unfolded wide the earth for you that you might move about there on spacious paths. Compare this to 20:53: *He Who has made for you the earth like a carpet spread out; has enabled you to go about therein by roads; and has sent down water from the sky.* *Fijāj*, translated here as *spacious paths*, implies valley-roads or passes between mountains. Though there are mountain chains on the earth, God's artistry has provided, even in such regions, valleys and channels by which men may go about. Mountain roads usually follow the valleys. (A. Yusuf Ali, pp. 1614-1615, 851, 1616)

Rising by Night

O you who are covered!
Stand in prayer by night but not all the night—
half of it or a little less,
or a little more; and recite the Qur°ān, slowly and distinctly.
We shall soon send down to you a weighty word.
Truly, the rising by night
is the strongest means of governing the soul
and the most appropriate for words of prayer.
Truly, by day there is a long chain of duties for you;
but keep in remembrance the name of your Sustainer
and devote yourself to Him wholeheartedly.
Sustainer of the East and the West, there is no god but Him
take Him therefore as the guardian of your affairs.

[*Sūrah al-Muzzammil* 73:1-9]

The expression *muzzammil* has a meaning similar to that of *muddaththir*, which occurs at the beginning of the next *sūrah*: namely, "one who is covered [with anything]," "enwrapped," or "enfolded [in anything]." Like that other expression, it may be understood in a concrete, literal sense—i.e., "wrapped up in a cloak" or "blanket"—as well as metaphorically, i.e., "wrapped up in sleep" or even "wrapped up in oneself." Hence, the commentators differ widely in their interpretations of the above apostrophe, some of them preferring the literal connotation, others the metaphorical; but there is no doubt that irrespective of the linguistic sense in which the address *O you enwrapped one* is understood, it implies a

416

call to heightened consciousness and deeper spiritual awareness on the part of the Prophet.

Recite the Qurᶜān calmly and distinctly, with your mind attuned to its meaning: this, I believe, is the closest possible rendering of the phrase *rattil al-qurᶜāna tartīlan.* The term *tartīl* primarily denotes "the putting [of something] together distinctly, in a well-arranged manner, and without any haste" (Jawharī, Bayḍawī; also *Lisān al-ᶜArab, Qāmūs*). When applied to the recitation of a text, it signifies a calm, measured utterance with thoughtful consideration of the *meaning* to be brought out.

Truly, the hours of night impress the mind most strongly and speak with the clearest voice: literally, *are strongest of tread and most upright of speech.* (Asad, p. 903)

O you who are covered: muzzammil. Some commentators understand by this, "properly dressed for prayer" or "folded in a sheet, as one renouncing the vanities of this world." *Muzzammil* is one of the titles of our holy Prophet. But there is a deeper mystic meaning in this and the address *You wrapped up* of the next *sūrah.* Human nature requires warm garments and wrappings to protect the body from cold or heat or rain. But in the spiritual world those wrappings are useless: the soul must stand bare and open before God, in the silence of the night, but not too austerely, as the following verses show.

Stand in prayer by night but not all the night—half of it or a little less or a little more. The Prophet was prone to austerities in the cave of Ḥirāʾ, both before and after he received his mission, spending days and nights in prayer and contemplation. Midnight and after midnight contemplation and prayers have technically received the name of *Tahajjud. And pray in the small watches of the morning: an additional prayer for you. Soon will your Lord raise you to a station of praise and glory!* [17:79].

And recite the Qurᶜān, slowly and distinctly. At the time this *sūrah* was revealed, there were only *sūrahs* 96, 68, and possibly 74, and the opening

417

sūrah (*Al-Ḥamd*); but the heart of the Apostle had received enlightenment, and that Light was gradually finding expression in the verses of the Qurʾān. For us, now, with the whole of the Qurʾān before us, the injunction is specially necessary. The words of the Qurʾān must not be read hastily, merely to get through so much reading. They must be studied, and their deep meaning pondered over. They are themselves so beautiful that they must be lovingly pronounced in tones of rhythmic music.

Truly, the rising by night is the strongest means of governing the soul and the most appropriate for Words of prayer. For contemplation, prayer, and praise, what time can be so suitable as the night, when calm and silence prevail, the voices of the market-place are still, and the silent stars pour forth their eloquence to the discerning soul?

Truly, by day there is a long chain of duties for you; but keep in remembrance the name of your Sustainer and devote yourself to Him wholeheartedly. A man of God, as a man, a member of a family, or a citizen, has many ordinary duties to perform; and his work may be made difficult and irksome, especially in so far as he has responsibilities in protecting those under his guidance who may be persecuted by the world. But while discharging all his ordinary duties, he should work as in the presence of God, and in all matters and at all times retain the sense of God's nearness. His work may be on earth, but his heart is in Heaven.

Sustainer of the East and the West, there is no god but Hū: take Hū therefore as the guardian of your affairs. God is all-in-all. He is not in one place, but in all; and He is Lord of all places. He rules the world. Therefore be not discouraged by the plots or enmity of wicked men. Leave all things to God. Trust Him: He is just and will do justice. Only turn away from the unjust, but in a worthy and noble way; i.e., to show them clearly that you do not fear them, but that you leave all affairs in God's hands. If we divide the world into hemispheres from north to south, *East and West* will cover all directions. (A. Yusuf Ali, pp. 1633-1634)

Lend to God a Beautiful Loan

So recite then as much of the Qur^cān as may be easy;
and be constant in prayer and spend in charity;
and loan to God a beautiful loan.
And whatever good you send forth for your souls,
you shall find it in God's Presence richer and better in reward.
And always seek God's grace:
for God is Ever Ready to Forgive, Most Merciful.

[*Sūrah al-Muzzammil* 73:20]

This is the earliest reference in the Qur'ān to spending in charity, *zakāh*.

See <u>57:11</u> for another reference to loaning a beautiful loan to God. The *beautiful loan* should be that of our own souls. We should expect no returns in kind, for that is not possible. But the reward we shall find with God will be infinitely greater and nobler. Compare the biblical phrase, "Lay up for yourselves treasure in heaven" (Matt. 6:20). Any good that we do raises our own spiritual status and dignity. We must not think that when we speak of God's service or God's cause, we are doing anything for His benefit: He is independent of all needs whatsoever.

And always seek God's grace: this emphasizes the need of God's Grace. Whatever good we do, our own merits are comparatively small. God's Grace must lift us up and blot out our shortcomings. Even in piety there may be an arrogance which may become a sin. We should always seek God's Mercy in all humility. (A. Yusuf Ali, p. 1638)

Purify Your Heart

O you who are enfolded!
Arise and give guidance!
And glorify the greatness of your Sustainer!
And purify your inmost heart!
And turn away from all that is unclean!
And do not expect in giving any increase for yourself!
But for your Sustainer's sake be patient and steadfast!

[*Sūrah al-Muddaththir* 74:1-7]

The expression *muddaththir* (an abbreviated form of *mutadaththir*) signifies "one who is covered [with something]" or "enfolded [in something]"; and all philologists point out that the verb *dathara*, from which the above participial noun is derived, may equally well have a concrete or abstract connotation. Most of the commentators understand the phrase *O you enfolded one* in its literal, concrete sense, and assume that it refers to the Prophet's habit of covering himself with a cloak or blanket when he felt that a revelation was about to begin. Rāzī, however, notes that this apostrophe may well have been used metaphorically, as an allusion to Muḥammad's intense desire for solitude before the beginning of his prophetic mission. This, according to Rāzī, would explain his being thus addressed in connection with the subsequent call *Arise and warn*—i.e., "Give now up your solitude, and stand up before all the world as a preacher and warner."

Purify your inmost heart is literally *your garments* (*thiyāb*) *purify;* but almost all the classical commentators point out that the noun *thawb* and its plural *thiyāb* are often metonymically applied to that which a garment encloses, i.e., a person's "body" or, in a wider sense, his "self" or his "heart," or even his "spiritual state" or "conduct" (*Tāj al-'Arūs*). Thus, commenting on this verse, Zamakhsharī draws the reader's attention to the well-known idiomatic phrases *ṭāhir ath-thiyāb* (literally, "one who is clean in his garments") and *danis ath-thiyāb* ("one who is filthy in his garments"), and stresses their tropical significance of "free from faults and vices" and "vicious and perfidious," respectively. Rāzī states with approval that "according to most of the [earlier] commentators, the meaning [of this verse] is *purify your heart of all that is blameworthy.*"

Do not through giving seek yourself to gain: literally, *and do not bestow favors to obtain increase.* (Asad, pp. 906-907)

As usual in these wonderful early mystic verses, there is a triple thread of thought: (1) a particular occasion or person is referred to; (2) a general spiritual lesson is taught, and (3) a more profound mystical reverie is suggested. As to (1) the Prophet was now just past the stage of personal contemplation, lying down or sitting in his mantle; he was now to go forth boldly to deliver his Message and publicly proclaim the Lord. His heart had always been purified, but now all his outward doings must be dedicated to God, and conventional respect for ancestral customs or worship must be thrown aside. The work of his Apostleship was the most generous gift that could flow from his personality, but no reward or appreciation was to be expected from his people, but quite the contrary: there would be much call on his patience, but his contentment would arise from the good pleasure of God. As to (2), similar stages arise in a minor degree in the life of every good man, for which the Prophet's life is to be a universal pattern. As to (3), the Sufis understand, by the mantle and outward wrappings, the circumstances of our phenomenal existence, which are necessary to our physical comfort to a certain stage. But we soon outgrow them, and our inner nature should then boldly proclaim

421

itself; not that it brings any credit or reward with men—the very hope or expectation of such would be inconsistent with our higher nature, which should bear all checks and rejoice in the favor of God.

And turn away from all that is unclean: rujz or *rijz,* abomination, usually understood to refer to idolatry. It is even possible that there was an idol called Rujz. But it has a wider significance, as including a mental state opposed to true worship, a state of doubt or indecision.

And do not expect in giving any increase for yourself. The legal and commercial formula is that you give in order to receive. And usually you expect to receive what is worth *to you* a little more than you give. The spiritual consideration is that you give, but expect nothing from the receiver. You serve God and God's creatures.

But for your Sustainer's sake be patient and steadfast! Our zeal for God's cause itself requires that we should not be impatient, and that we should show constancy in our efforts for His cause. For we have faith, and we know that He is All-Good, All-Wise, and All-Powerful, and everything will ultimately be right. (A. Yusuf Ali, pp. 1640-1641)

Muhammad's Frown

He frowned and turned away
because the blind man came to him.
But how were you to know whether he might grow in purity,
or whether he might have received counsel
and been helped by this reminder?
And the one who regards himself as self-sufficient,
to him you pay attention;
though if he does not grow in purity you are not to blame.
But as for the one who came eagerly to you
and with an inner awe,
him you disregarded.
By no means should it be so!
For this is indeed a reminder
for anyone who will remember.

[*Sūrah ʿAbasa* 80:1-12]

One day, as recorded in many well-authenticated Traditions, the Prophet was engrossed in a conversation with some of the most influential chieftains of pagan Mecca, hoping to convince them—and, through them, the Meccan community at large—of the truth of his message. At that point, he was approached by one of his followers, the blind ʿAbd Allāh ibn Shurayḥ—known after his grandmother's name as Ibn Umm Maktūm—with the request for a repetition or elucidation of certain earlier passages of the Qurʾān. Annoyed by this interruption of what he momentarily regarded as a more important endeavor, Muhammad *frowned and turned away*

423

from the blind man—and was immediately, there and then, reproved by the revelation of the first ten verses of this *sūrah*. In later years, he often greeted Ibn Umm Maktūm with these words of humility: "Welcome to him on whose account my Sustainer has rebuked me (*ᶜātabanī*)!" Indirectly, the sharp Qurʾanic rebuke (stressed, in particular, by the use of the third-person form in verses 1-2) implies, firstly, that what would have been a minor act of discourtesy on the part of an ordinary human being, assumed the aspect of a major sin, deserving a divine rebuke, when committed by a prophet; and, secondly, it illustrates the objective nature of the Qurʾanic revelation: for, obviously, in conveying God's reproof of him to the world at large, the Prophet *does not speak out of his own desire* (compare 53:3).

The one who regards himself as self-sufficient, i.e., who does not feel the need of divine guidance: a reference to the arrogant pagan chieftains with whom the Prophet was conversing. *If he does not grow in purity you are not to blame*: it is not upon you (*ᶜalayka*) that he does not attain to purity.

For this is indeed a reminder for anyone who will remember: remember, that is, the existence and omnipotence of God. The Qurʾān is described here, as in many other places, as a "reminder" because it is meant to bring man's instinctive—though sometimes hazy or unconscious—realization of God's existence into the full light of consciousness. (Asad, pp. 930-931)

This is connected with an incident which reflects the highest honor on the Prophet's sincerity in the revelations that were vouchsafed to him, even if they seemed to reprove him for some natural and human zeal that led him to a false step in his mission according to his own high standard. He was once deeply and earnestly engaged in trying to explain the holy Qurʾān to pagan Quraish leaders, when he was interrupted by a blind man, ᶜAbdullah ibn Ummi-i-Maktūm, one who was also poor, so that no one took any notice of him. He wanted to learn the Qurʾān. The holy Prophet naturally disliked the interruption and showed impatience. Perhaps the poor man's feelings were hurt. But he whose gentle heart ever sympathized with the poor and the afflicted, got new Light from above and without the least hesitation published this revelation, which forms part of the sacred scripture of Islam. And the Prophet always afterwards held the man in high honor.

The lesson is that neither spiritual worth nor the prospect of effective spiritual guidance is to be measured by a man's position in life. The poor, or the blind, the halt, or the maimed, may be more susceptible to the teaching of God's Word than men who are apparently gifted, but who suffer from arrogance and self-sufficiency.

But how were you to know whether he might grow in purity, or whether he might have received counsel and been helped by this reminder? It may be that the poor blind man might, on account of his will to learn, be more likely to grow in his own spiritual development or to profit by any lessons taught to him even in reproof than a self-sufficient leader. In fact it was so. For the blind man became a true and sincere Muslim and lived to become a governor of Medina.

And the one who regards himself as self-sufficient: such a one would be a pagan Quraish leader, whom the Holy Prophet was anxious to get into his fold, in order that the work of preaching God's Message might be facilitated. But such a Message works first among the simple and lowly, the poor and despised folk, and the mighty ones of the earth only come in when the stream rushes in with irresistible force.

Though if he does not grow in purity you are not to blame: God's Message is for all, but if the great ones arrogantly keep back from it, it is no fault of the preacher, so long as he has proclaimed the Message. He should attend to all, and specially to the humble and lowly.

But as for the one who came eagerly to you and with an inner awe, him you disregarded. The fear in the blind man's heart may have been twofold: (1) he was humble and God-fearing, not arrogant and self-sufficient; (2) being poor and blind, he feared to intrude: yet his earnest desire to learn the Qur'ān made him bold, and he came, perhaps unseasonably, but was yet worthy of encouragement, because of the purity of his heart.

For this is indeed a reminder for anyone who will remember. God's Message is a universal Message, from which no one is to be excluded—rich or poor, older, young, great or lowly, learned or ignorant. If anyone had the spiritual craving that needed satisfaction, he was to be given precedence if there was to be any question of precedence at all.

At the time this *sūrah* was revealed, there were perhaps only about 42 or 45 *sūrahs* in the hands of the Muslims. But it was a sufficient body of revelation of high spiritual value, to which the description given could apply: *It [a reminder for anyone who will remember] is in books held greatly in honor, exalted, keep pure and holy, by the hands of scribes honorable, pious and just* [80:13-16]. It was held in the highest honor; its place in the hearts of Muslims was more exalted than that of anything else. As God's Word, it was pure and sacred, and those who transcribed it were men who were honorable, just, and pious. The legend that the early *sūrahs* were not carefully written down and preserved in books is a pure invention. The recensions made later in the time of the first and third Khalīfas were merely to preserve the purity and safeguard the arrangement of the text at a time when the expansion of Islam among non-Arabic-speaking peoples made such precautions necessary. (A. Yusuf Ali, pp. 1686-1688)

Give Full Measure

Woe to those who commerce in fraud,
those who when they are to receive from other people
exact full measure,
but when they must measure out give less than is due.
Do they think they won't be called to account—
on an awesome day,
a day when all humankind will stand
before the Sustainer of all Worlds?

[*Sūrah al-Muṭaffifīn* 83:1-6]

Fraud must here be taken in a widely general sense. It covers giving short measure or short weight, but it covers much more than that. These verses make it clear that it is the spirit of injustice that is condemned—giving too little and asking too much. This may be shown in commercial dealings, where a man expects a higher standard of justice for himself than he is willing to concede to others. In domestic or social matters, an individual or group may ask for honor, or respect, or services which he or they are not willing to give on their side in similar circumstances. It is worse than one-sided selfishness: for it is double injustice. But it is worst of all in religion or spiritual life: with what face can a man ask for Mercy or Love from God when he is unwilling to give it to his fellow men? In one aspect this is a statement of the Golden Rule, "Do unto others as you would have them do unto you." But it is more completely expressed. You must give in full what is due from you, whether you expect or wish to receive full consideration from the other side or not.

Do they think they won't be called to account? Legal and social sanctions against fraud depend for their efficacy on whether there is a chance of being found out. Moral and religious sanctions are of a different kind. "Do you wish to degrade your own nature? Do you not consider that there is a Day of Account before a Judge Who knows all, and Who safe-guards all interests, for He is the Lord and Cherisher of the Worlds? Whether other people know anything about your wrong or not, you are guilty before God." (A. Yusuf Ali, p. 1703)

The Rust of the Heart

Nay, but their hearts are corroded
by all that they were wont to do!

[*Sūrah al-Muṭaffifīn* 83:14]

Literally, *that which they were earning has covered their hearts with rust:* implying that their persistence in wrongdoing has gradually deprived them of all consciousness of moral responsibility and, hence, of the ability to visualize the fact of God's ultimate judgment. (Asad, p. 938)

Hope within Painful Toil

When the sky is split apart
in obedience to its Sustainer—and it must—
and when the earth is leveled,
and casts forth what is within it, and becomes utterly empty,
in obedience to its Sustainer—and it must—
O human being! Truly, you are laboring towards your Sustainer,
painfully struggling, but then you shall meet Him.

[*Sūrah al-Inshiqāq* 84:1-6]

The passing away of this world of sense to make way for a new world of reality is here indicated by two facts which are themselves symbols for a complete revolution in our whole knowledge and experience. At the beginning of *Sūrahs* 82 and 81, other symbols were used, to lead up to the arguments there advanced. Here the two symbols are (1) the sky being rent asunder and giving up its secrets and (2) the earth being flattened out from the globe it is and giving up its secrets. We may think that the heavens we see above—high and sacred, seemingly vast and limitless, eternal and timeless—are not created matter. But they are. And they remain just so long as God wills it so, and not a moment longer. As soon as His Command issues for their dissolution, they will obey and vanish, and all their mystery will be emptied out. But it must necessarily be so: their very nature as created beings requires that they must hearken to the voice of their Creator even to the extent of their own extinction.

When the earth is leveled and casts forth what is within it and becomes utterly empty: the earth is a globe, enclosing within it many secrets and mys-

430

teries—gold and diamonds in its mines, heat and magnetic forces in its entrails, and the bodies of countless generations of men buried within its soil. At its dissolution all these contents will be disgorged; it will lose its shape as a globe and cease to exist. A more mystic meaning lies behind the ordinary meaning of the vanishing of the heavens and the earth as we see them. Our ideas of them—their subjective contents with reference to ourselves—will also shape and form and vanish before the eternal verities. We think the earth so solid and real. All our perishable things dissolve into the earth. But the earth itself will dissolve into a truer Reality.

O human being! Truly, you are laboring towards your Sustainer, painfully struggling. This life is ever full of toil and misery, if looked at as empty of the eternal hope which revelation gives us. Hence the literature of pessimism in poetry and philosophy, which thinking minds have poured forth in all ages, when that hope was obscured to them. "Our sweetest songs are those that tell of saddest thought." "To each his suffering; all are men condemned alike to groan." It is the noblest men that have to "scorn delights and live laborious days" in this life. The good suffer on account of their very goodness; the evil on account of their evil. But the balance will be set right in the end. Those that wept shall be made to rejoice, and those that went about thoughtlessly rejoicing shall be made to weep for their folly. They will all go to their account with God and meet Him before His Throne of Judgment. (A. Yusuf Ali, pp. 1709-1710)

An allusion to the fact that in man's earthly life—irrespective of whether one is consciously aware of it or not—sorrow, pain, drudgery, and worry by far outweigh the rare moments of true happiness and satisfaction. Thus, the human condition is described as *painful toiling towards the Sustainer*—i.e., towards the moment when one meets Him on resurrection. (Asad, p. 940)

Gradual Unfoldment

So I call to witness the rosy glow of sunset,
the night and its progression,
and the moon as it grows in fullness;
surely, you shall travel from stage to stage.
What then is the matter with them that they do not have faith,
and when the Qurʾān is read to them,
they do not fall down in prostration?

[*Sūrah al-Inshiqāq* 84:16-21]

Thus God *calls to witness* the fact that nothing in His creation is ever at a standstill, since everything moves unceasingly from one state of being into another, at every moment changing its aspect and its condition: a phenomenon aptly described by the Greek philosopher Heraclitus by the phrase *panta rhei* ("everything is in flux"). *Surely you shall travel from stage to stage* or *from one state to another state* (Zamakhsharī): i.e., in an unceasing progression—conception, birth, growth, decline, death, and finally, resurrection. *What then is the matter with them that they do not have faith?* Since the inexorable movement of all that exists from stage to stage or from one condition into another corresponds to a fundamental law evident in all creation, it is unreasonable to assume that man alone should be an exception, and that *his* onward movement should cease at the moment of his bodily death, not to be followed by a change-over into another state of being.

The phrase *call to witness* is also used in 81:15-21: *I call to witness the revolving stars, the planets that run their course and set, and the night as it darkly*

432

falls, and the morn as it softly breathes: behold, this [divine writ] is indeed the [inspired] word of a noble Apostle, with strength endowed, secure with Him who in almightiness is enthroned, [the word] of one to be heeded, and worthy of trust! By "calling to witness" certain natural phenomena which are familiar to man because of their permanent recurrence, attention is drawn to the fact that what we call "laws of nature" are but the observable elements of God's plan of creation—a plan in which His revelations play a decisive role: and so, by implication, the divine writ granted to Muḥammad is as intrinsically "natural" as any other phenomenon, concrete or abstract, in the realm of God's creation. (Asad, pp. 941, 934)

I call to witness is the same form of adjuration used in 69:38-39 (*So I call to witness what you see and what you do not see*). The substantive statement is in verse 19: *surely you shall travel from stage to stage.* Nothing in this life is fixed or will last. Three things are mentioned which on the one hand have remained from age to age for as far back as the memory of man can go, and yet each of them is but a short phase, gone as it were in the twinkling of an eye. So our life here is but a fleeting show. Its completion is to be looked for elsewhere.

The rosy glow of sunset: (1) the sun seems such a great reality that people worshipped it as a divinity. The beautiful glow it leaves when it sets is but momentary; it changes every moment and vanishes with the twilight.

The night and its progression: (2) the night is a phenomenon you see during almost half of every twenty-four hours in ordinary latitudes. At nightfall, all the wandering flocks and herds come home. The men scattered abroad for their livelihood return home to rest and sleep. The night collects them in the homes, and yet this phase of homing lasts but a little while. Presently all is silent and still. So will it be with our souls when this life is ended with our death. We shall be collected in a newer and larger homing.

The moon as it grows in fullness: (3) the astronomical full moon does

433

not last a moment. The moment the moon is full, it begins to decline, and the moment it is in its "inter-lunar swoon," it begins its career anew as a growing new moon. So is man's life here below. It is not fixed or permanent, either in its physical phases, or, even more strikingly, in its finer phases, intellectual, emotional, or spiritual.

Surely, you shall travel from stage to stage: man travels and ascends stage by stage. In 67:3 the same word in the form *ṭibāqan* was used of the heavens, as if they were in layers one above another (*He Who created the seven heavens one above another*). Man's spiritual life may similarly be compared to an ascent from one heaven to another.

What then is the matter with them that they do not have faith? Considering man's high destiny, and the fact that this life is but a stage or a sojourn for him, it might be expected that he would eagerly embrace every opportunity of welcoming God's revelation and ascending by faith to heights of spiritual wisdom. There is something wrong with his will if he does not do so. Notice the transition from the second person in verse 19, *you shall travel from stage to stage* where there is a direct appeal to God's votaries, to the third person in verses 20-21, *What then is the matter with them that they do not have faith, and when the Qurᶜān is read to them, that they do not fall down in prostration?* Here men who are rebels against God's Kingdom are spoken of as if they were aliens. The reason they would fall in prostration is out of respect and humble gratitude to God. (A. Yusuf Ali, pp. 1711-1712)

Guardian of the Soul

Consider the sky and the night-visitor.
And what will explain to you what the night-visitor is?
It is the star of piercing brightness.
There is no soul that does not have a protector over it.

[*Sūrah aṭ-Ṭāriq* 86:1-4]

Some commentators assume that what is described here as *aṭ-ṭāriq* (*that which comes in the night*) is the morning-star, because it appears towards the end of the night. Others, like Zamakhsharī or Rāghib, understand by it "*the* star" in its generic sense. Now if we analyze the origin of this noun, we find that it is derived from the verb *ṭaraqa*, which primarily means "he beat [something]" or "knocked [at something]"; hence, *ṭaraqa 'l-bāb*, "he knocked at the door." Figuratively, the noun signifies "anything [or "anyone"] that comes in the night," because a person who comes to a house by night is expected to knock at the door (*Tāj al-ʿArūs*). In the Qurʾanic mode of expression, *aṭ-ṭāriq* is evidently a metaphor for the heavenly solace which sometimes comes to a human being lost in the deepest darkness of affliction and distress; or for the sudden, intuitive enlightenment which disperses the darkness of uncertainty; or, finally, for divine revelation, which knocks, as it were, at the doors of man's heart, and thus fulfills the functions of both solace and enlightenment.

There is no soul that does not have a protector over it: literally, *there is no human being without a guardian* [or *without a watch being kept*] *over it.* This is resonant of 82:10-12: *There are ever-watchful forces over you, noble, recording, aware of whatever you do!* The classical commentators are of the opinion

435

that those verses refer to the guardian angels who record, allegorically, all of men's deeds. However, another explanation is that the "watchful force" (*ḥāfiẓ*) set over every human being is *his own conscience*, which "records" all his motives and actions in his subconscious mind. Since it is the most precious element in man's psyche, it is described as "noble." (Asad, p. 944, 936)

The appeal here is to a single mystic symbol, namely the sky with its night-visitor, and the substantive proposition is in verse 4: *There is no soul that does not have a protector over it.* In the darkest sky shines out most brilliantly the light of the most brilliant star. So in the night of spiritual darkness—whether through ignorance or distress—shines the glorious star of God's revelation. By the same token the man of faith and truth has nothing to fear. God will protect His own. If man has a true spiritual understanding, he has nothing to be afraid of. He is protected by God in so many ways that he does not even know. He may be an insignificant creature as a mere animal, but his soul raises him to a dignity above other creation. And all sorts of divine forces guard and protect him. (A. Yusuf Ali, p. 1719)

Glorify the Name of Your Sustainer

Glorify the name of your Sustainer Most High
Who has created and further given order and proportion;
Who has determined the order, and gives guidance;
and Who brings forth the fertile pasture
and then reduces it to darkened stubble.

We shall teach you to remember
so that you shall not forget, except as God wills:
for truly, He knows what is manifest and all that is hidden.
And We will make easy for you the path towards true ease.
So remind in case the reminder may benefit the hearer.
It will be kept in mind by those who stand in awe of God.

[*Sūrah al-Aʿlā* 87:1-10]

The word "Lord" [*Sustainer*] by itself is an inadequate rendering for *rabb*, for it implies cherishing, guarding from harm, sustaining, granting all the means and opportunities of development, and bringing to maturity.

Glorify the name of your Sustainer Most High Who has created and further given order and proportion. The story of creation is wonderful and continuous. There are several processes which we contemplate in glorifying God's name. First, He brings us into being. Secondly, He endows us with forms and faculties exactly suited to what is expected of us, and to the environments in which our life will be cast, giving to everything due order and proportion.

Who has determined the order, and gives guidance. Thirdly, He has or-

437

dained laws and decrees, by which we can develop ourselves and fit our-selves into His whole scheme of evolution for all His Creation. He has measured exactly the need of all, and given us instincts and physical and psychical predispositions which fit into His decrees. Fourthly, He gives us guidance, so that we are not the sport of mechanical laws. Our reason and our will are exercised, that we may reach the higher destiny of man.

And Who brings forth the fertile pasture and then reduces it to darkened stubble. Fifthly, after maturity comes decay. But even in that decay, as when green pasture turns to stubble, we serve other ends. In so far as we are animals, we share these processes with other forms of material crea-tion, animal, vegetable, and even mineral, which all have their appointed laws of growth and decay. But man's higher destiny is referred to in the subsequent verses.

We shall teach you to remember so that you shall not forget, except as God wills. The soul, as it reaches the Light of God, makes gradual progress, like a man going from darkness into light. So the Qur'ān was revealed by stages. So all revelations from God comes by stages. *By degrees shall We teach you to declare, so you shall not forget.* As usual, there are two parallel meanings: (1) that connected with the occasion of direct inspiration to the holy Prophet, and (2) the more general message to mankind for all time. Everyone who understands the message must declare it, in words, and still more in his conduct.

The particular occasion was an assurance to the Prophet, that though he was unlettered, the message given to him would be preserved in his heart and in the hearts of men. The more general sense is that mankind, having once seized great spiritual truths, will hold fast to them, *except as God wills, for truly, He knows what is manifest and all that is hidden.*

There can be no question of this having any reference to the abro-gating of any verse of the Qur'ān. For this *sūrah* is one of the earliest re-vealed, being placed about eighth according to the most accepted chrono-logical order. While the basic principles of God's Law remain the same, its form, expression, and application have varied from time to time, e.g., from Moses to Jesus, and from Jesus to Muḥammad. It is one of the beneficent mercies of God that we should forget some things of the past, lest our minds become confused and our development is retarded. Besides, God knows what is manifest and what is hidden, and His Will and Plan work with supreme wisdom and goodness.

And We will make easy for you the path towards true ease. The path of Islam is simple and easy. It depends on no abstruse mysteries or self-mortifications, but on straight and manly conduct in accordance with the laws of man's nature as implanted in him by God (30:30: *Turn your face toward the primordial religion, according to the innate nature with which He has made humankind; do not allow what God has made to be corrupted.*) On the other hand, spiritual perfection may be most difficult, for it involves complete surrender on our part to God in all our affairs, thoughts, and desires: but after that surrender God's Grace will make our path easy.

So remind in case the reminder may benefit the hearer. It will be kept in mind by those who stand in awe of God. God's message should be proclaimed to all, but particular and personal admonitions are also due to those who attend and in whose hearts is the fear of God. (A. Yusuf Ali, pp. 1723-1724)

Who has created and further given order and proportion: God endows everything with inner coherence and with qualities consistent with the functions which it is meant to perform, and thus adapts it *a priori* to the exigencies of its existence. *Who has determined the order, and gives guidance:* i.e., in accordance with the function assigned by Him to each individual thing or phenomenon. (*For it is He Who creates every thing and determines its nature in accordance with [His own] design [25:2].*)

You shall not forget, except as God wills. The classical commentators assume that these words are addressed specifically to the Prophet, and that, therefore, they relate to his being *taught the Qurᶜān* and being promised that he would not forget anything thereof, *save what God may will.* This last clause has ever since given much trouble to the commentators, inasmuch as it is not very plausible that He Who has revealed the Qurʾān to the Prophet should cause him to forget *anything* of it. Hence, many unconvincing explanations have been advanced from very early times down to our own days, the least convincing being that last refuge of every perplexed Qurʾān-commentator, the "doctrine of abrogation." However, the supposed difficulty of interpretation disappears as soon as we allow ourselves to realize that the above passage, though ostensibly addressed to the Prophet, is directed at *man in general*, and that it is closely related to an earlier Qurʾanic revelation—namely, the first five verses of *sūrah* 96 ("The Germ Cell") and in particular verses 3-5, which speak of God's having *taught man what he did not know*. This alludes to mankind's cumulative acquisition of empirical and rational knowledge, handed down from generation to generation and from one civilization to another: and it is to this very phenomenon that the present passage, too, refers. We are told here that God, Who has formed man in accordance with what he is meant to be and has promised to guide him, will enable him to acquire (and thus, as it were, "impart" to him) elements of knowledge which mankind will accumulate, record, and collectively "remember"—except what God may cause man to "forget" (in another word, to abandon) as having become redundant by virtue of his new experiences and his acquisition of wider, more differentiated elements of knowledge, empirical as well as deductive or speculative, including more advanced, empirically-acquired skills. However, the very next sentence makes it clear that all knowledge arrived at through our observation of the external world and through speculation, though necessary and most valuable, is definitely limited in scope and does not, therefore, in itself suffice to give us an insight into ultimate truths.

He knows what is manifest and all that is hidden, i.e., all that is intrinsically beyond the reach of human perception (*al-ghayb*). The implication is that, since human knowledge must forever remain imperfect, man cannot really find his way through life without the aid of divine revelation.

And We will make easy for you the path towards true ease, i.e., towards an ease of the mind and peace of the spirit. (Asad, pp. 946-947, 549)

Tests

Now as for man, when his Sustainer tests him,
honoring him with gifts, he boasts: "My Lord has honored me,"
but when He tests him with scarcity,
then he moans, "My Sustainer has disgraced me!"

But no! You don't honor the orphans!
Nor do you encourage one another to feed the poor!
And you greedily devour inheritance.
And you love wealth with undue love!

No! When the earth is crushed to dust,
and your Sustainer comes and His angels rank upon rank,
and the Fire that Day is brought face to face,
on that Day the human being will remember,
but what use will it be then?
He will say:
"Oh! How I wish that I had prepared better for this Life."

[*Sūrah al-Fajr* 89:15-24]

Contrast man's selfishness and pettiness with Allāh's justice and watchful care. Allāh tries us both by prosperity and adversity: in the one we should show humility and kindness; and in the other patience and faith. On the contrary, we get puffed up in prosperity and depressed in adversity, putting false values on this world's goods.

But when He tests him with scarcity, then he moans, "My Sustainer has disgraced me! Man is tried by God restricting his subsistence, in both the

442

literal and figurative sense. Allāh provides for all, but people complain if the provision is measured and restricted to their needs, circumstances, and antecedents, and does not come up to their desires or expectations, or is different from that given to people in quite different circumstances.

But no! You don't honor the orphans! Even at our own valuation, if we are favored with superfluities, do we think of the fatherless children, or the struggling poor? On the contrary, too many men are but ready to embezzle the helpless orphan's inheritance, and to waste their own substance in worthless riot instead of supplying the people's real needs.

Nor do you encourage one another to feed the poor! Kindness and generosity set up standards which even worldly men feel bound to follow out of social considerations even if they are not moved by higher motives. But the wicked find plausible excuses for their own hard-heartedness, and by their evil example choke up the springs of charity and kindness in others.

And you greedily devour inheritance. Inheritance is abused in two ways. (1) Guardians and trustees for the inheritance of minors or women or persons unable to look after their own interests should fulfill their trusts with even more care than they devote to their own interests. Instead of that they selfishly "devour" the property. (2) Persons who inherit property in their own rights should remember that in that case, too, it is a sacred trust. They must use it for the purposes, objects, and duties which they also inherit. It gives them no license to live in idleness or waste their days in riotous show.

When the earth is crushed to dust: our attention is now called to the Day of Reckoning. Whether we failed to respect the rights of the helpless here or actually suppressed those rights in our mad love for the good things of this life, we shall have to answer in the realm of Reality. This solid earth, which we imagine to be so real, will crumble to powder like dust before the real Presence, manifested in glory.

On that Day the human being will remember, but what use will it be then? The retribution will at last come, and we shall realize it in our inmost being, all the illusions of this fleeing world having been swept away. Then we shall remember, and wish, too late, that we had repented. Why not repent now? Why not bring forth the fruits of repentance now, as a preparation for the Hereafter? (A. Yusuf Ali, pp. 1733-1734)

O Tranquil Soul

"O soul in complete rest and satisfaction!
Return to your Sustainer well-pleased and well-pleasing!
Enter then among my devoted ones!
Yes, enter my Garden!"

[*Sūrah al-Fajr* 89:27-30]

The righteous enter into their inheritance and receive their welcome with a title (*O soul in complete rest and satisfaction*) that suggests freedom from all pain, sorrow, doubt, struggle, disappointment, passion, and even further desire; at rest, in peace; in a state of complete satisfaction. In Muslim theology, this stage of the soul is the final stage of bliss.

Our doctors postulate three states or stages of the development of the human soul. The unregenerate human soul that seeks its satisfaction in the lower earthly desires is the *nafsi ammāra* (12:53: "Man's *inner self does incite to evil,* and saved are only they upon whom My Sustainer bestows His Mercy, but surely My Sustainer is Oft-Forgiving, Most Merciful"). The *nafsi ammāra* is prone to evil and, if not checked and controlled, will lead to perdition. *Ammāra* means prone, impelling, headstrong, passionate The self-reproaching soul that feels conscious of sin and resists it is the *nafsi lawwama* (75:2: *I call to witness the self-reproaching spirit of man's own conscience*). It asks for Allāh's grace and pardon after repentance and tries to amend; it hopes to reach salvation. It may be compared to conscience, except that in English usage conscience is a faculty and not a stage in spiritual development. *Nafsi mutmainna*, mentioned in this passage (*the righteous soul . . . in complete rest and satisfaction*), is the highest stage of all, where the human soul achieves full rest and satisfaction.

Return to your Sustainer well-pleased and well-pleasing! Evil finds itself isolated and cries out in lonely agony (89:24: *Ah, would that I had sent forth good deeds for this my future life*), while good receives a warm welcome from the Lord of Goodness Himself. It is the soul which enters heaven, and not the gross body which perishes.

Enter then among my devoted ones! Yes, enter My Garden (My Heaven)! This is the climax of the whole. Men may have imagined all kinds of heaven before, and many types are used in the sacred Word itself. But nothing can express the reality itself better than *My Heaven*—Allāh's own Heaven! May we reach it through Allāh's Grace! (A. Yusuf Ali, pp. 1735, 571, 1649)

Consider the Soul

Consider the sun and its radiant brightness,
and the moon as it reflects it.
Consider the day as it reveals the world,
and the night as it veils it darkly!
Consider the sky and its wondrous make,
and the earth and all its expanse!
Consider the human soul and the order and proportion given to it,
and how it is imbued with moral failings
as well as with consciousness of God!
Truly, the one who purifies it shall reach a happy state
and the one who corrupts it shall truly be lost!

[*Sūrah ash-Shams* 91:1-10]

Six types are taken in three pairs, from Allāh's mighty works in nature, as tokens or evidence of Allāh's providence and the contrasts in His sublime creation, which yet conduce to cosmic harmony (verses 1-6). Then, in verses 7-8, the soul of man, with internal order and proportion in its capacities and faculties, as made by Allāh, is appealed to as having been endowed with the power of discriminating between right and wrong. Then the conclusion is stated in verses 9-10, that man's success or failure, prosperity or bankruptcy, would depend upon his keeping that soul pure or his corrupting it.

Consider the sun and its radiant brightness, and the moon as it reflects it. The first pair is the glorious sun, the source of our light and physical life, and the moon which follows or acts as second to the sun for illuminating

447

our world. The moon, when she is in the sky with the sun, is pale and inconspicuous; in the sun's absence she shines with reflected light and may metaphorically be called the sun's viceregent. So with revelation and the great Prophets who brought it; and the minor Teachers who derive their light reflected, or perhaps doubly reflected, from the original source.

Consider the day as it reveals the world, and the night as it veils it darkly! The next contrasted pair consists not of luminaries, but of conditions or periods of time, Day and Night. The Day reveals the sun's glory and the Night conceals it from our sight. So there may be contrasts in our subjective reception of divine light, but it is there, working all the time, and must reappear in its own good time.

Consider the sky and its wondrous make, and the earth and all its expanse! The next contrasted pair is the wonderful firmament on high, and the earth below our feet, stretching away to our wide horizons. The sky gives us rain, and the earth gives us food. Yet both work together; for the rain is moisture sucked up from the earth, and the food cannot grow without the heat and warmth of the sun. There are many other contrasts under this head; yet they all point to unity.

Consider the human soul and the order and proportion given to it, and how it is imbued with moral failings as well as with consciousness of God! Allāh makes the soul, and gives it order, proportion, and relative perfection, in order to adapt it for the particular circumstances in which it has to live its life. Compare 32:9: *But He fashioned man in due proportion and breathed into him something of His spirit. And He gave you hearing and sight and feeling: little thanks do you give!* He breathes into it an understanding of what is sin, impiety, wrong-doing, and what is piety and right conduct, in the special circumstances in which it may be placed. This is the most precious gift of all to man, the faculty of distinguishing between right and wrong. After the six external evidences mentioned in verses 1-6, this internal evidence of Allāh's goodness is mentioned as the greatest of all. By these various tokens man should learn that his success, his prosperity, his salvation depends on himself—on his keeping his soul pure as Allāh made it; and his failure, his decline, his perdition depends on his soiling his soul by choosing evil.

The one who corrupts it shall truly be lost: this is the core of the *sūrah,* and is illustrated by a reference in the following verses to the story of the Thamūd, an arrogant people who oppressed the poor and denied them their rights of watering and pasture for their cattle. (A. Yusuf Ali, pp. 1742-1743)

The moon as it reflects it is literally *as it follows it* (*talāhā*), i.e., the sun. According to the great philologist Al-Farrāʾ, who lived in the second century after the *hijrah,* "the meaning is that the moon derives its light from the sun" (quoted by Rāzī). This is also Rāghib's interpretation of the above phrase.

Consider the day as it reveals the world, literally "it," a pronoun apparently indicating "the world" or "the earth" (Zamakhsharī). It is to be noted that these verses stress the polarity—both physical and spiritual—inherent in all creation and contrasting with the oneness and uniqueness of the Creator.

Consider the sky and its wondrous make, literally, *and that which has built it*—i.e., the wondrous qualities which are responsible for the harmony and coherence of the visible cosmos (which is evidently the meaning of the term *samāʿ* in this context). Similarly, the subsequent reference to the earth, which reads literally, *that which has spread it out,* is apparently an allusion to the qualities responsible for the beauty and variety of its expanse.

Consider the human soul or *self:* as in so many other instances, the term *nafs,* which has a very wide range of meanings, denotes here the human self or personality as a whole: that is, a being composed of a physical body and that inexplicable life-essence loosely described as "soul."

And the order and proportion given to it (the *nafs*) is literally: *and that which has made [or formed] it* (sawwāhā) *in accordance with what it is meant to be.* The reference to man and that which constitutes the "human person-

449

ality," as well as the implied allusion to the extremely complex phenomenon of a life-entity in which bodily needs and urges, emotions, and intellectual activities are so closely intertwined as to be indissoluble, follows organically upon a call to consider the inexplicable grandeur of the universe—so far as it is perceptible and comprehensible to man—as a compelling evidence of God's creative power.

How it (the nafs) *is imbued with moral failings as well as with consciousness of God!* Literally, *and [consider] that which has inspired it with its immoral doings* (fujūrahā) *and its God-consciousness* (taqwāhā)"—i.e., the fact that man is equally liable to rise to great spiritual heights as to fall into utter immorality is an essential characteristic of human nature as such. [See 4:28: *man has been created weak.*] In its deepest sense, man's ability to act wrongly is a concomitant to his ability to act rightly: in other words, it is this inherent polarity of tendencies which gives to every "right" choice a value and, thus, endows man with moral free will. (Asad, p. 954-955)

The Path to Bliss

By the night when it falls.
By the day when it breaks.
By what has made the male and the female,
You strive toward different ends.
So the one who gives and stands in awe of God
and sincerely affirms that which is best,
We will indeed ease for him or her the path to bliss.
But the one who greedily withholds what is given,
considering himself or herself self-sufficient,
and betrays the good,
We will indeed ease for such a person the path to misfortune;
nor will wealth be of use when he or she falls.
In truth, it is up to Us to guide,
and truly, to Us belong the End and the Beginning.

[*Sūrah al-Layl* 92:5-13]

The Night begins with a divine invocation of the night and the day—two signs frequently evoked in Qur'anic oaths—and "what made the male and the female." The male and the female—like day and night or odd and even—are viewed as polarities that act as signs in the world and point back to their creator, who is beyond the polarities they represent. In Islamic thought, the deity is neither male nor female. Here the divine oath speaks of the very creation of gender distinction and places the creator explicitly beyond gender categories.

The Night goes on to offer a summary of the basic choices confronting humankind. The primary virtues are said to be the sharing of wealth, the affirming of the right *(al-husna)* in all, and the virtue rendered as mindfulness *(taqwa)*. The term *taqwa* is notoriously difficult to translate. The root meaning is that of protecting oneself or being vigilant. Islamic commentators describe *taqwa* as a consistent and intense moral vigilance. I have used the terms "mindful" and "mindfulness" here as the closest actively used English approximation. "Righteous" and "Righteousness" have a certain power in the King James tradition, but it is difficult to find such terms being used without archaicism or some form of irony. Indeed, the word righteous in contemporary speech is now frequently used to mean self-righteous—an indication that the word has evolved in usage and no longer can be used as effectively as it was.

The divine voice, the Qur'anic "we," announces that the deity will ease the way of the mindful to the good life and the way of the unmindful to hardship. This concept becomes central in Islamic theological discussion of the issue of divine providence and human free will. In this Sura, the concept of "easing the way" implies a slippery slope. Those who engage in certain forms of behavior find that their way is eased; they find certain short-term gains that reinforce their behavior. The deity here personalizes its activity in "easing the way" to hardship for such people, bringing up an issue that was to engage Islamic psychologists and theologians. Moral psychologists would explore the way certain actions, such as exploitive accumulation of wealth, lead people into a self-validating world of comfort and reward, and deeper into the bonds of habit. Islamic theologians would explore, with brilliant subtlety, the tension between divine providence and human responsibility brought out by the notion that the deity "eases" those engaged in such activity to further entrenchment in their spiritual alienation. (Michael Sells)

The good are distinguished here by three signs: (1) large-hearted sacrifices for Allāh and men; (2) fear of Allāh, which shows itself in righteous conduct, for *taqwā* includes just action as well as a mental state (restraint and guarding one's tongue, hand, and heart from evil); and (3) truth and sin-

452

cerity in recognizing and supporting all that is morally beautiful, for *ḥusn* is the good as well as the beautiful.

We will indeed ease for him or her the path to bliss. So far from there being any hardship in a good life, the righteous will enjoy their life more and more, and Allāh will make their path smoother and smoother until they reach eventual bliss.

But the one who greedily withholds what is given, considering himself or herself self-sufficient, and betrays the good, We will indeed ease for such a person the path to misfortune. The evil are distinguished here by three signs: (1) selfish greed and denial of other people's rights; (2) arrogance and self-sufficiency, *man does transgress all bounds in that he looks upon himself as self-sufficient* [96:6-7]; and (3) knowingly dishonoring Truth out of spite, or seeing ugliness where there is beauty. Such men's downward progress gathers momentum as they go, and their end can be nothing but misery. Where will be their boasted wealth and possessions, or their self-confidence?

Nor will wealth be of use when he or she falls. Wealth amassed in this world will be of no use at the Day of Final Judgment, nor will any material advantages of this life bring profit by themselves in the Hereafter. What will count will be a life of truth and righteousness, and of goodness to all the creatures of Allāh.

In truth, it is up to Us to guide. Allāh in His infinite Mercy has provided full guidance to His creatures. All through His creation there are sign-posts indicating the right way. To man He has given the five senses of perception, with mental and spiritual faculties for coordinating his physical perceptions and leading him higher and higher in thought and feeling. He has besides sent inspired men as prophets for further teaching and guidance.

And truly, to Us belong the End and the Beginning. In the End man will return to Allāh, and even from the beginning of man's life Allāh's mercies and loving care surround him. In the probationary period of man's life, he has a measure of free will, and he is expected to use it in such a way as to bring his whole being into harmony with the universal Will and Law, for he will have to answer for the right use of his talents and opportunities. If man's will has any meaning, he has the choice of accepting Allāh's guidance or rejecting it, and in the latter case he must take the consequences. (A. Yusuf Ali, pp. 1746-1747, 17)

Expansion

Have We not expanded your chest?
And removed from you the burden which weighed down your back?
And increased your remembrance?
So, truly, with every difficulty comes ease;
truly, with every difficulty comes ease.
So when you are free from your task continue to strive,
and to your Sustainer turn with loving attention.

[*Sūrah ash-Sharḥ* 94:1-8, complete]

Have we not expanded your chest? Compare the prayer of Moses in 20:25-26: *O my Lord! Expand my chest, ease my task for me.* The chest or breast is symbolically the seat of knowledge and the highest feelings of love and affection, the treasure-house in which are stored the jewels of that quality of human character which approaches nearest to the divine. The holy Prophet's human nature had been purified, expanded, and elevated, so that he became a mercy to all creation. Such a nature could afford to ignore the lower motives of ordinary humanity which caused shameful attacks to be made on him. Its strength and courage could also bear the burden of the galling work which it had to do in denouncing sin, subduing it, and protecting Allāh's creatures from its oppression. But Allāh sends His grace and aid, and that burden is removed or converted into joy and triumph in the service of the one true God.

So, truly, with every difficulty comes ease; truly, with every difficulty comes ease. This verse is repeated for extra emphasis. Whatever difficulties or troubles are encountered by men, Allāh always provides a solution, a way out, a relief, a way to lead to ease and happiness, if we only follow His path and show our faith by patience and well-doing. The solution of relief does not merely come after the difficulty; it is provided with it.

So when you are free from your task: when you are free, or when you are relieved. These words may be understood as being free or relieved from your immediate task, that of preaching to men, denouncing sin, and encouraging righteousness; or, from the difficulties that confronted you. When that happens, that does not finish the labors of the man of Allāh. It is only one step on the way. He has constantly and insistently to go on. When there is rest from the task of instructing the world, the contact with the spiritual kingdom continues, and indeed it becomes more intimate and concentrated.

And to your Sustainer turn with loving attention. The kingdom of God is everything. Other things are incidental, and really do not matter. Worldly greatness or success may be a means to an end, but it may also be a hindrance to true spiritual greatness. Allāh is the goal of the righteous man's whole attention and desire. (A. Yusuf Ali, pp. 1755-1756)

This surah is very closely connected to the preceding one, and some commentators consider it to be a direct continuation of Surat ad-Duha. In any case, it is also addressed to the Prophet, *salla-llahu 'alayhi wa alihi wa sallam,* and by extension to all who would follow in his footsteps.

1 *Have we not expanded your breast for you?*

*Sharah*a means "to uncover, disclose, to explain, to make clear or apparent," and "to *expand*." *Sharaha* also means "to cut." surgical usage, the word *tashnh* means "the cutting of sections of flesh so that what is inside can easily be seen."

Sadara means "to return, go back, turn away (from water, a country, a place)" and *sadr* is "the bosom, breast or chest." If a person says he want to "get something off his chest," this something is not, of course, a physical object. Rather, it is something which he has taken upon himself, so that he feels constricted or burdened, as though he can no longer breathe freely. By relieving himself of this weight, by "expanding," that which is far is made near and that which is difficult is made easy.

The ultimate *sharh* (exposition, explanation) is the knowledge, the direct witnessing that there is only Allah. This is the final *sharh;* there is nothing beyond it. There is no relief beyond direct witnessing.

This ayah is directed to the Prophet, *salla-llahu 'alayhi waalihiwa sallam,* and therefore to all of us. Allah is saying, "Did We not relieve your breast of the burden of your ignorance?" But as there cannot be one without the other, the burden of ignorance was replaced with the burden of prophethood, but that burden too was relieved by having the secrets of the cosmos revealed to him.

2   *And alleviated your burden for you,*

Wazara the root of *wizr* burden, heavy load), is "to bear or carry [a burden]." From it comes the word *wazir,* usually pronounced vizier in English, meaning "a minister, vice-regent or counselor," that is, someone who helps the ruler and who, by taking on burdens from the king, takes on the burden of the state. This ayah means that we are relieved, and that we have no responsibility other than to be the slaves of our Creator. If we truly take on slavehood, then we are no longer burdened in the same way as before, but rather we only discharge our responsibilities and obligations to Allah, without adding any more weight to ourselves.

3   *Which had so heavily weighed down your back?*

This is again a metaphorical reference. There are those of us who appear to take on heavy burdens, although, in truth, no burdens exist. If we maintain ourselves in a state of *dhikr,* aware that at any moment our breath may stop, and that we will soon return to dust, then we will realize that we can only serve and try to do our best. There is nothing else for us to do. We may not consciously attract trouble in this world, yet the world's trouble will come and find us. If we do nut take on people's concerns *fi sabili'llah* (in the way of Allah), if we .do not help people, serve, and guide them, troubles will come to afflict us.

4   And raised up for you your remembrance?

Allah says, "And raised you high in *dhikr*," referring to the outer *dhikr*, remembrance, esteem) of the Prophet, *salla-llahu 'alayhi wa alihi wa sallam*. We cannot have a higher outer *dhikr* than the Name of Allah. The Prophet's inner *dhikr* was his perpetual, constant, uninterrupted awareness of his Creator, and his *dhikr* of his Creator was the highest because of all Allah's creation he was the closest to Him.

5   For certainly with every difficulty there is ease,

6   Certainly, with every difficulty there is ease.

This means that "With *the* difficulty there is ease," and again, "with *the* difficulty there is ease," indicating that there is only one difficulty. This means that with every difficulty there are two eases or solutions. One solution is that the difficulty will pass: it may not pass by itself, but it will ultimately pass by our slipping away from it through death. The second solution is for the true seeker; it lies in knowledge of how the difficulty originally arose and in seeing the perfection in it.

A person may, for example, make the mistake of visiting a dangerous place and is hit on the head. He may not have known all the factors involved, whether the people there were plotting this or not, but he will experience the blow. Once he sees how it came to pass, how perfect! His head will hurt but that hurt will pass — that is the other ease. With the difficulty of feeling separation, comes the relief of knowing that we are connected.

7   So when you are freed, remain steadfast, expend!

The *shari'ah* meaning of this ayah is that once we have finished dealing with the world and with our responsibilities in it, we will be ready to seek direct knowledge of the Divine Reality. According to the interpretation of this ayah by the people of Ahl al-Bayt, when we have finished our formal prayers, we should go on to the next stage, that of staying up during the night to engage in more prayers, *dhikr* and study. When we have finished our duties towards creation and towards our Creator, then we should do more, and expend ourselves to the utmost. This inner struggle

458

and effort is the literal meaning of the word *jihad* which is usually translated as "holy war."

8   *And make your Lord your exclusive object (of longing)!*

When we put our desire to know into practice, if we desire knowledge, then we will *become* knowledge, and if we put into practice anger, then we will *become* anger. Once we have laid the groundwork necessary to discharge our duties, then we will be authorized to make Allah our sole object. Discharging our duties first is essential, however, for otherwise we will be acting out of the desire to escape. (Haeri)

The Best of Proportions

By the fig and the olive,
and Mount Sinai,
and this city of security,
truly, We have created human beings in the best proportion.
Then We reduce them to the lowest of the low
except those who have faith and act rightly:
for they shall have an unceasing reward.
Then what after this can turn you away from this Way?
Is God not the wisest of judges?

[*Sūrah at-Tīn* 95:1-8, complete]

The fig and the olive symbolize, in this context, the *lands* in which these trees predominate: i.e., the countries bordering on the eastern part of the Mediterranean, especially Palestine and Syria. As it was in these lands that most of the Abrahamic prophets mentioned in the Qurʾān lived and preached, these two species of tree may be taken as metonyms for the *religious teachings* voiced by the long line of those God-inspired men, culminating in the person of the last Judaic prophet, Jesus. *Mount Sinai,* on the other hand, stresses specifically the apostleship of Moses, inasmuch as the religious law valid before, and up to, the advent of Muḥammad—and in its essentials binding on Jesus as well—was revealed to Moses on a mountain of the Sinai Desert. Finally, *this land secure* signifies undoubtedly (as is evident from 2:126) Mecca, where Muḥammad, the Last Prophet, was born and received his divine call. Thus, verses 1-3 draw our attention to the fundamental ethical unity underlying the teachings—the *genuine*

460

teachings—of all the three historic phases of monotheistic religion, metonymically personified by Moses, Jesus, and Muḥammad. The *specific* truth to be considered here is referred to in the next three verses.

We have created human beings in the best proportion, i.e., endowed with all the positive qualities, physical as well as mental, corresponding to the functions which this particular creature is meant to perform. The concept of *the best conformation* is related to the Qurʾanic statement that everything which God creates, including the human being or self (*nafs*), is *formed in accordance with what it is meant to be* [91:7]. In a more general sense, 87:2 says: *Who creates [every thing], and thereupon forms it in accordance with what it is meant to be.* That is to say, He endows it with inner coherence and with qualities consistent with the functions which it is meant to perform, and thus adapts it *a priori* to the exigencies of its existence. The statement *We create man in the best conformation* does not in any way imply that all human beings have the *same* "best conformation" in respect of their bodily or mental endowments; it implies simply that irrespective of his natural advantages or disadvantages, each human being is endowed with the ability to make the, for him, best possible use of his inborn qualities and of the environment to which he is exposed.

We have created human beings in the best proportions is like *your bountiful Sustainer . . . has created you, and formed you in accordance with what you are meant to be, and shaped your nature in just proportions* [82:6-7]. That is, He has "endowed you with all the qualities and abilities relevant to the exigencies of your individual life and your environment" and "made you proportionate": i.e., a being subject to physical needs and emotional urges, and at the same time endowed with intellectual and spiritual perceptions. In other words, a being in whom there is no *inherent* conflict between the demands of "the spirit and the flesh," since both these aspects of the human condition are God-willed and, therefore, morally justified.

Thereafter We reduce him to the lowest of low: this is a consequence of

461

man's betrayal—in another word, corruption—of his original, positive disposition: that is to say, a consequence of man's own doings and omissions. Regarding the attribution, by God, of this "reduction" to His Own doing, 2:7 says: *God has sealed their hearts and their hearing, and over their eyes is a veil; and awesome suffering awaits them.* This is a reference to the natural law instituted by God, whereby a person who persistently adheres to false beliefs and refuses to listen to the voice of truth gradually loses the *ability* to perceive the truth, "so that finally, as it were, a seal is set upon his heart" (Rāghib). Since it is God Who has instituted all laws of nature—which, in their aggregate, are called *sunnat Allāh* ("the way of God")—this "sealing" is attributed to Him: but it is obviously a consequence of man's free choice and not an act of "predestination."

Then what after this can turn you away from this Way? What then could henceforth cause you to give the lie to this moral law? That is to say, what could cause you to give the lie to the validity of the moral law—which, to my mind, is the meaning of the term *dīn* in this context—outlined in the preceding three verses. The above rhetorical question has this implication: Since the moral law referred to here has been stressed in the teachings of all monotheistic religions, its truth ought to be self-evident to any unprejudiced person; its negation, moreover, amounts to a negation of all freedom of moral choice on man's part, and, hence, of justice on the part of God, Who, as the final verse points out, is—by definition—*the most just of judges*. (Asad, pp. 961-962, 935, 946, 4-5)

The substantive proposition of this *sūrah* is in verses 4-8, and it is clinched by an appeal to four sacred symbols, namely the fig, the olive, Mount Sinai, and the sacred city of Mecca. About the precise interpretation of the first two symbols, and especially of the symbol of the fig, there is much difference of opinion. If we take the fig literally to refer to the fruit or the tree, it can stand as a symbol of man's destiny in many ways. Under cultivation it can be one of the finest, most delicious and most wholesome fruits in existence; in its wild state, it is nothing but tiny seeds,

462

and is insipid, and often full of worms and maggots. So man at his best has a noble destiny; at his worst, he is *the lowest of the low*. Christ is said to have cursed a fig tree for having only leaves and not producing fruit (Matt. 21:18-20), enforcing the same lesson. There is also a parable of a fig tree in Matt. 24:32-35. See also the parable of the good and evil figs in Jeremiah 24:1-10.

The sacred symbolism of the olive occurs in two other verses. In 23:20, *a tree springing out of Mount Sinai which produces oil and relish for those who use it for food.* For Arabia, the best olives grow round about Mount Sinai. Olive oil is an ingredient in medicinal ointments. If used for food, the olive has a delicious flavor. In 24:35, the parable of Allāh's Light includes a reference to the olive: *God is the Light of the heavens and the earth. The parable of His light is, as it were, that of a niche containing a lamp; the lamp is enclosed in glass, the glass like a radiant star; lit from a blessed tree—an olive-tree that is neither of the east nor of the west—the oil of which would almost give light even though fire had not touched it: light upon light!* The olive tree is not a very impressive tree in its outward appearance. Its leaves have a dull greenish-brown color, and in size it is inconspicuous. Pure olive oil is beautiful in color, consistency, and illuminating power. The world has tried all kinds of illuminants, and for economic reasons or convenience, one replaces another. But for coolness, comfort to the eyes, and steadiness, vegetable oils are superior to electricity, mineral oils, and animal oils. And among vegetable oils, olive oil takes a high place and deserves its sacred associations. Its purity is almost like light itself: you may suppose it to be almost light before it is lit. It is possible that the olive in 95:2 refers to the Mount of Olives, just outside the walls of the city of Jerusalem, for this is the scene in the Gospel story (Matt. 24:3-4) of Christ's description of the Judgment to come.

Mount Sinai was the mountain on which the Law was given to Moses: *And We called him from the right side of Mount Sinai and made him draw near to Us for mystic converse* [19:52]. The Law was given, and the glory of Allāh was made visible.

This city of security is undoubtedly Mecca. Even in pagan times its sacred character was respected, and no fighting was allowed in its territory. But the same city, with all its sacred associations, persecuted the greatest of the Prophets and gave itself up for a time to idolatry and sin, thus presenting the contrast of the best and the worst.

Having discussed the four symbols in detail, let us consider them together. It is clear that they refer to Allāh's Light or Revelation, which offers man the highest destiny if he will follow the Way. Mecca stands for Islam, Sinai for Israel, and the Mount of Olives for Christ's original and pure Message. Even if we refer the fig and the olive to the symbolism in their fruit, and not to any particular religion, the contrast of best and worst in man's destiny remains, and that is the main thing.

Truly, We have created human beings in the best proportion. Taqwīm: mould, symmetry, form, nature, constitution. There is no fault in Allāh's creation. To man Allāh gave the purest and best nature, and man's duty is to preserve the pattern on which Allāh has made him (30:30). But by making him representative, Allāh exalted him even higher than the angels, for the angels had to make obeisance to him (2:30-34). But man's position as representative also gives him will and discretion, and if he uses them wrongly he falls even lower than the beasts: *Then we reduce them to the lowest of the low, except those who have faith and act rightly, for they shall have an unceasing reward.* If man rebels against Allāh and follows evil, he will be abased to the lowest possible position. For Judgment is sure. Those who use their faculties aright and follow Allāh's Law will reach the high and noble destiny intended for them. That reward will not be temporary but unfailing.

Then what after this can turn you away from this Way? This may refer to the holy Prophet, or to man collectively. *After this* when it is clearly shown to you that Allāh created man true and pure, that He guides him, and that those who rebel and break His law will be punished and brought down in the Hereafter, who can doubt this, or contradict the Prophet when he gives warning?

Is God not the wisest of judges? Allāh is wise and just. Therefore the righteous have nothing to fear, but the evil ones cannot escape punishment. (A. Yusuf Ali, pp. 1758, 908, 877, 1759)

1   *By the fig tree and the olive tree,*

In our traditions, the fig-tree represents the tree of Sayyidna Adam, *'alayhi-s-salam,* and the olive-tree represents the tree of the Prophet Ibrahim, *'alayhi-s-salam.* In the traditions of the people of Allah, the fig-tree also refers to the Mosque of Ilyas in Palestine, and the olive-tree is the mosque of the Prophet Musa, *'alayhi-s-salam.* The *Turi Sinin* is also the mosque of Sayyidna Musa, *'alayhi-s-salam,* and the *balad al-amin* of the following ayah is the mosque of the Ka'bah, the mosque of the Muslims. So the "land made secure" of the third ayah is also the mosque of Nabiy-Allah Ibrahim, *'alayhi-s-salam,*

The *tin* (fig) and *zaytun* (olive) are basically the fruits or products of the Garden, and it is in that sense to which they are referred. They have come from the greater Garden to the outer garden; they are representatives of where these great prophesies have taken place, which is why we say that they come from Paradise. It does not mean that they miraculously appeared from Paradise, but rather, that the areas from which these prophets came and the cultures of their people were based on these trees. If we examine the function of these fruits, including that of dates, we find them to be the thread that links various cultures through time. Although civilizations come and go, these trees remain constant. Their hardiness enables them to live for hundreds of years and continuously bear fruit, though they may be wrinkled and old. They are like an echo of truth, linking era after era. Armies battle and kill each other, but the trees remain.

2   *And by Mount Sinai,*

This is where Sayyidna Musa, *'alayhi-s-salam,* had his recognition of Allah and came face to face with knowledge. It is where his heart opened, where he saw the truth. And it is also where he later took forty of his closest men to experience the truth for themselves.

3   And by this land made secure.

Some people of the Path say that this is the heart of the *'arif bi'llah* (knower or gnostic of Allah). In the language of the Path, they call the heart of such a one, "The city of peace." Outwardly, it means Mecca.

4   Certainly, We created man in the best form.

By the evidence of all of this, man has been created in the best conformation, in the most harmonious and symmetrical form, and with the most potential. This is how the Creator intended man to be.

5   Then We reduce him to the lowest of the low.

From the physical point of view, anything that is green and succulent will eventually become yellow and dry, barren and dark. Anything that is created will be destroyed. As we see man grow up in the best form, in the most erect and perfect symmetry — young, virile, active and healthy — so too will we see him stoop and start once more to bend over, as though he were shrinking back to his childhood. It also means that in the inward sense if he goes to the extreme end of the spectrum of his *nafs* he will become worse than an animal.

6   Except those who believe and do good works, so they will have an unending reward.

Human nature is divine, but man sometimes allows himself to gravitate downwards. For those who trust and believe, man is created here in order to have his breast expanded, in order for that which is already near to be recognized as near. It is not enough to have trust in the abstract sense. We have to act on that trust so that we actualize it. If we do not do this we are left either with theoretical knowledge or with empty ritual. A ritual without a philosophy is merely ignorant folklore and a philosophy without a ritual is just an intellectual exercise; either one alone is meaningless. The two must be combined through man because man is one, and he is the unifier.

The reward for those who believe is unending because their reward is their very state and the state of self-abandonment is unending and boundless.

7   *Then who can give you the lie after this about the judgement?*

After these visible evidences, the gardens, the trees, the outer trees as well as the inner trees of knowledge brought by the repeated message of prophethood – after all of this — how can we deny our debt? How can we deny that we are here only to unburden ourselves of this debt to our Creator, to execute our transactional obligation to Allah in the fullest way? How can we deny this truth?

8   *Is not Allah the most Just of the judges?*

Is the Creator not the most Just, the most Firm in judgement? Does not the whole creation embody absolute justice? If we do not act accordingly and do not recognize the signs, then we will continue to flounder about without guidance, causing ourselves great loss and harm.

(Haeri)

The First Revelation

Read! In the name of your Sustainer Who created,
created the human being out of a clinging substance:
Recite! And your Sustainer is the Most Generous,
the One Who taught by the pen,
taught humankind what it did not know.
No, but humankind goes beyond all bounds
when it considers itself self-sufficient.
In truth, to their Sustainer all will return.

[*Sūrah al-ʿAlaq* 96:1-8]

This is the first revelation received by Muḥammad while he was alone in a cave on Mount Ḥirāʾ. It occurred at a time when, as far as we can tell, he had no expectation of receiving a revelation or of being a prophet. His first experience of the revelation stunned him so much that he was bewildered and sought the comfort of his wife, Khadījah. Having heard of his experience, she said, "A man like you doesn't lose his mind. You are generous, responsible, and sincere. We should talk with my wise cousin Waraqa. Perhaps he has an insight." When Waraqa heard of Muḥammad's experience, he suggested, based on his knowledge of the prophets of Israel, that Muḥammad had received a communication from the Angel Jibrīl, or Gabriel.

The first word that Muḥammad heard was: ʿiqraʿ, which means both "read" and "recite." It is from the same root as the word "Qurʾān," the reading or the recitation. ʿIqraʿ occurs again in the third line and is followed by mention of the Pen (*qalam*) in the fourth line. So these first five lines are held together by a theme of reading, writing, and communication. This is especially significant, given the fact that Muḥammad was

468

"unlettered," unable to read or write.

This first revelation did not begin with the injunction to listen, or look, or witness, but to read. Implied in this is the primary relationship between the human being, represented by Muḥammad, and the Rabb (Lord, Sustainer, Nourisher), a relationship of education, teaching, and communication through a divinely-revealed language. Islam is a religion that has at its very beginning this affirmation of the importance of reading, reflection, and understanding. Humanity is taught, and has been taught what it did not, could not otherwise have known, and this teaching has been transmitted by *the pen,* a way of conveying meaning through the symbolic means of language. It is language which establishes, fixes, and clarifies meanings which can be shared among human beings, and it is a sacred language, preserved as much as possible from subjectivity and distortion, which helps us to find our relationship with, our connection to the Divine.

It is good to read and hear the actual sound of this first revelation:

ᶜIqraᶜ bismi Rabbikal-ladhī khalaq,

Khalaqal-ᶜinsāna min ᶜalaq.

ᶜIqraᶜ wa Rabbukal-akram,

ᶜAlladhī ᶜallama bil-qalam

ᶜAllamal-ᶜinsāna mā lam yaᶜlam.

It is not difficult, even for a non-Arabic speaker, to recognize the musicality of this passage, but it is also interesting to focus on certain key words.

The first of these is *Rabb,* conventionally translated as Lord, but more properly understood as something or someone in charge in a nurturing way, for the verb *rabba* means to raise up a child. The second is *khalaq,* which signifies creation *from nothing.*

Khalaq is repeated in the third line in which it is said that this "Sustainer" created the human being from *ᶜalaq,* another important and fascinating term. *ᶜAlaq* has sometimes been mistranslated as "clot," or worse yet, "blood clot," a true embarrassment, for there is no scientific evidence to suggest that the human being is created from such a clot. Rather, the word signifies something indefinite which has a linkage, a linked or "clinging substance" would be a fair if wordy translation of ʿalaq.

Here we have an example of the suggestive and symbolic power of language offered to us almost immediately in the first words of the revelation. ʿAlaq, this linked substance, is full of meaning, including meanings that could not have been anticipated in the seventh century of the current era. DNA, the double helix of linked chromosomes, for instance, was only discovered in the middle of the twentieth century. ʿAlaq is a word that describes the whole creative geometry behind life. It is a word that leaves room for possibly even more discovery. It does not confine or limit meaning, but offers a lens for seeing into creation. It also describes and affirms a quality of *relatedness* between the Creator and the human being. (Helminski)

ʿIqraʿ may mean "read," or "recite," or "rehearse," or "proclaim aloud," the object understood as being Allāh's message. In worldly letters the Prophet was unversed, but with spiritual knowledge his mind and soul were filled, and now had come the time when he must stand forth to the world and declare his mission. The declaration or proclamation was to be in the name of Allāh the Creator. It was not for any personal benefit to the Prophet: to him there was to come bitter persecution, sorrow, and suffering. It was the call of Allāh for the benefit of erring humanity. Allāh is mentioned by his title of Lord and Cherisher (*rabb,* Sustainer), to establish a direct nexus between the source of the Message and the one addressed. The Message was not merely an abstract proposition of philosophy, but the direct concrete message of a personal Allāh to the creatures whom He loves and cherishes.

Who created the human being out of a connecting cell. The lowly origin of the animal in man is contrasted with the high destiny offered to him in his intellectual, moral, and spiritual nature by his *Most Generous* Creator.

No knowledge is withheld from man. On the contrary, through the faculties freely given to him, he acquires it in such measure as outstrips his immediate understanding, and leads him ever to strive for newer and newer meaning.

The One Who taught by the pen. Compare to *By the Pen and by that which they write* [68:1]. The Arabic words for "teach" and "knowledge" are from the same root. It is impossible to produce in a translation the complete orchestral harmony of the words for "read," "teach," "pen" (which implies reading, writing, books, study, research), "knowledge" (including science, self-knowledge, spiritual understanding), and "proclaim," an alternative meaning of the word for "to read." This proclaiming or reading implies not only the duty of blazoning forth Allāh's message, as going with the prophetic office, but also the duty of promulgation and wide dissemination of the Truth by all who read and understand it. The comprehensive meaning of *qarā* [the root of ᶜ*iqra*ᶜ] refers not only to a particular person and occasion but also gives a universal direction. And this kind of comprehensive meaning, as we have seen, runs throughout the Qurʾān for whose who will understand. Allāh teaches us new knowledge at every given moment. Individuals learn more and more day by day; nations and humanity at large learn fresh knowledge at every stage. This is even more noticeable and important in the spiritual world.

No, but humankind goes beyond all bounds. . . . All our knowledge and capacities come as gifts from Allāh. But man, in his inordinate vanity and insolence, mistakes Allāh's gifts for his own achievements. The gifts may be strength or beauty, wealth, position, or power, or the more subtle gifts of knowledge or talents in individuals—or science, or art, or government, or organization for mankind in general.

. . . when it considers itself self-sufficient. In truth, to their Sustainer all will return. Man is not self-sufficient, either as an individual or in his collective capacity. If he attributes Allāh's gifts to himself, he is reminded—backwards, of his lowly physical origin (from a drop of animal matter) and

forwards, of his responsibility and final return to Allāh. (A. Yusuf Ali, pp. 1761–1762)

Bow Down

Bow down in adoration and draw near!

[*Sūrah al-ᶜAlaq* 96:19]

The righteous man has no fear. He can disregard all the forces of evil that are brought against him. But he must learn humility: that is his defense. He will bow down in adoration to Allāh. He must have the will to bring himself closer to Allāh. For Allāh is always close to him, closer to him *than his life blood in the jugular vein* [50:16]. Man's humility and adoration remove him from being an insolent rebel on the one hand and, on the other, prepare his will to realize his nearness to Allāh. (A. Yusuf Ali, p. 1763)

The Night of Power

In the Name of God, the Infinitely Compassionate and Most Merciful
We have indeed revealed this during the Night of Power.[14]
And what will explain to you what the Night of Power is?
The Night of Power is better than a thousand months.
Within it the angels descend bearing divine inspiration
by God's permission upon every mission:
Peace! . . . This until the rise of dawn!

[*Sūrah al-Qadr* 97:1-5, complete]

The Night of Power is when revelation comes down to a benighted world—it may be to the wonderful cosmos of an individual—and transforms the conflict of wrongdoing into peace and harmony, through the agency of the angelic host, representing the spiritual powers of the Mercy of God.

The 23rd, 25th, or 27th night of Ramaḍān, as well as other nights, have been suggested as the Night of Power. It is best to take this in conjunction with verse 3, which says that *the Night of Power is better than a thousand months*. It transcends time: for it is Allāh's Power dispelling the darkness of ignorance, by His revelation, in every kind of affair. *A thousand* must be taken in an indefinite sense, as denoting a very long period of time. This does not refer to our ideas of time, but to "timeless time."

---

[14] The night during which the Prophet Muḥammad received the first revelation. Tradition reports that historically it was one of the last ten nights of the month of Ramaḍān, probably the 27th. The Night of Power is a night when inspiration arrives and closeness with one's Sustainer. One must be watchful for its coming.

One moment of enlightenment under Allāh's Light is better than thousands of months or years of animal life, and such a moment converts the night of darkness into a period of spiritual glory.

Within it the angels descend bearing divine inspiration: this could also be translated *Therein come down the angels and the Spirit by Allāh's permission on every errand.* "The Spirit" or *rūh* in this case is usually understood to be the angel Gabriel.

Peace! . . . This until the rise of dawn! When the night of spiritual darkness is dissipated by the glory of Allāh, a wonderful peace and a sense of security arise in the soul. And this lasts on until this life closes, and the glorious day of the new world dawns, when everything will be on a different plane, and the checkered nights and days of this world will be even less than a dream. (A. Yusuf Ali, pp. 1764-1765)

Accumulation

In the Name of God,
the Infinitely Compassionate and Most Merciful
The desire to accumulate distracts you
all the way to the graves,
but soon you will know.
Yes indeed, you will know.
If you were to know with the knowledge of certainty,
you would see Hell;
you would see with the eyes of certainty;
and on that Day you will be asked about true happiness.

[*Sūrah at-Takāthur* 102:1-8, complete]

Seeing with the Eyes of Certainty

The principle word here is *takāthur*, which can be translated as mutual rivalry, competition, greed for more and more. Its root meaning is related to *kathīr*, many, and it is the opposite, in a sense, of *tawhīd*, oneness. This greedy, acquisitive state is just the opposite of the state of living in the knowledge and wholeness of God's unity. *Takāthur* also contrasts with *kawthar*, true abundance, the name of another *sūrah*.

This state of distraction is contrasted with knowing. The time will come when we will know whether that which we pursued had any value. But what if we could know now? What if we could know with the knowledge of certainty? Then we might see ourselves more objectively. For some people, it would be the painful realization that their state of greedy busyness, worldly preoccupation is actually Hell. When that fated day comes we will have to answer for how we spent our lives.

The voice of the Qur'ān may sound threatening to some people, but this shocking reminder is actually a form of Mercy. It is God's Mercy reaching out to us, telling us it is not too late to awaken to true happiness and well-being. (Helminski)

You have been preoccupied by sensual pleasures, and perishing fantasies of the bounties of the life of this world by which you have been veiled, and have trapped your perfection within it, and have squandered the goodness you have of the light of receptivity and the purity of your essential nature and intellect, and the possibilities of intellectual delights and the enduring extraordinary meanings from the bounties of the other world.

Your boasting and flaunting over these perishing matters, of wealth, offspring, and ancestral honor has gone so far that you have become dissatisfied with what exists of these things and have gone to boasting of what has passed of the degenerated bones of past non-existent things. This is due to your extreme veiling, and the dominance of the pleasures of fantasy and the power of the evil forces of illusions over you. This will go on until you perish and waste your whole life in these matters never paying attention throughout your lives to the cause of your salvation.

Beware of the unhealthy and bad consequences of this behavior. For you shall come to know, when your bodies become ruined, and the cover that conceals the universes is lifted, and knowledge will avail you nothing since when death comes, all apparent causes as well as the means by which you could reach completion will have vanished. Then you will know the unhealthy consequences of your preoccupation with these senses and those quickly vanishing delusions that are of great harm due to the persistence of their traces and the torment that is caused by their forms, and the fiery hold of their traces. This you shall know.

If you could taste the true delights of the knowledge of certainty, and the attainments of lights that are far above these senses and perishing fantasies, your regrets and bitterness for wasting your dear lives over these matters would be beyond description. By God you would see the fire of the hell of your animal nature due to the veils of your senses. You will taste this fire with certainty not through learning but through direct experience and in your conscience. Then you shall be asked on that day which is the true bounty; the worldly things with their perishing delights or the otherworldly things that are everlasting in their state which you used to deny.

Alternatively, if you only knew the knowledge of certainty and have reached its station you would have seen the fire of the hell of the particular nature of those who are veiled by the vileness caused from their immersion in base desires and in illusionary delights, and in the excessive sensuality in which you have buried your heads and have coveted in an extreme way; and that would have made you desist completely from all these things.

And if you could attain to the rank of certain knowledge you would have tasted, and would have known its delight and its permanence and beauty, and its brilliance and nobility. And you would have known the perpetual condition that you are in and its degeneration and ugliness and its wickedness and illness. You would have been elevated to the rank of insight and witnessing so that you would see the truth as it is in its sacred light and its divine attributes. And you would have witnessed with the light of insight the truth of hell and the harmfulness of these pleasures with the pain they bring to our constitution and the torment of the flames and of deprivation.

Is your current state of the otherworldly bliss or is it this worldly bliss? If you knew the knowledge of certainty, O you who are veiled by these facades and superstitions, you would surely see hell from the intensity of longing and from the engulfing of the fire of love. Then you would be elevated through this longing to the rank of the eye of certainty and witnessing so that you would see the truth of the fire of love with

478

real insight. Then you would be asked after this tasting about the bliss that is the truth of certainty, what is it? That is, you will certainly find the taste of having arrived, and the trace of the truth of certainty so you would be able to tell of it. And God knows best. (Kashani, translated for the Book Foundation by Mahmoud Mostafa)

The Multiplication of Wealth

In the Name of Allāh, the Beneficent, the Most Merciful
Abundance distracts you until you come to the graves.

Man worships the Essence of bounty, of increase (and everything in this world increases), and thus he inadvertently looks for increase in every aspect of life even though it may mean a decrease in another way. For example, an increase of one's arrogance or expectation is in reality a decrease of one's awakening, of one's light.

The specific reference of this *āyah* was to a time when the number of the Prophet's followers was being counted by his enemies in Mecca, the Quraish. They would continually congratulate themselves.

A similar example is to be found in the story of the man who boasted arrogantly about his great wealth, wealth of which, in fact, he had little, and which, during those times, was measured by the number of palm-trees one owned. Whenever anyone asked about the number of trees in his plantation he would say, qualifyingly, "I and the Naqi'd family have 3,500," although of the figure he perhaps owned only six. We count many things in this life as being among our strengths, and often they are almost non-existent. Another way of looking at these *āyāts* is that the grave represents the body. If we look to our bodies as strengths, then we are not looking in the right direction. Thus, these two *āyāts* are saying, "Your wealth, family, tribes, and their number bring you pride, and that is the opposite of fear." The object of our life is to be in a state of awareness, of *dhikr*, in which we see that anything which distracts us puts us in a state of forgetfulness. In truth, however, anything other than Allāh is non-existent. If we try to see anything other than that which is, has been, and will be, then we are indulging in false thinking. Increase is one of our first troubles because it brings about its own affliction. If we have wealth, then others try to take it; if we have family, then we have to ensure constant provision, and so on. Abundance brings about distraction unless we are totally on the path. If it is *fi sabil Allāh* (in the way of Allāh), then it will be Allāh's business. The dead things we count as increase are of no use, whether they are belongings, relatives, or supporters.

> *Nay! You will soon come to know.*
> *Nay! If you but knew with the knowledge of certainty.*
> *Nay! If you but knew with the knowledge of certainty.*

We will come to know if only we seek the knowledge of certainty, *'ilm al-yaqīn*. By carefully watching events, we will know their consequences, so that at least we will have certainty at the time of their end. In this life, however, there is an injunction upon all men and women to seek knowledge. The Prophet Σ said, "Seek knowledge, even though it may be in China." From the moment we are born we want to know. Knowledge here means inner knowledge, and true inner knowledge is certainty.

> *You would certainly see the fire of Hell;*

If man seeks knowledge he will see hell, the Fire, here and now. Many people interpret this as indicating that the Fire will come later, and when asked about *āyāts* which imply that the Fire is here and now, they say that its root is here and that it has been willed by Allāh to be here, but that it will be manifest in the next life. Imām Riḍāʾ *'alayhisalām* says, however, that the Fire certainly is here, and that whoever denies it "is not among us, nor from us," and has, in fact, already been cast away. Man can see the meaning of the Fire here and now if he looks into his innermost

480

heart, if he wants to have that inner knowledge.

Then you will certainly see it with the eye of certainty.

First the Fire is known by *ʿilm al-yaqīn* (knowledge of certainty), and if anything is left of us after that, we will see it by the *ʿayn al-yaqīn* (the eye of certainty). After that we will come to know the truth of it in *ḥaqq al-yaqīn* (the truth of certainty). If nothing is left of us after that, and we are only pure awareness, then we become *ḥaqq al-ḥaqq* (the truth of truth). The state of the Fire is justice and absoluteness, clear and profound, in which obscurity or ambiguity will cease to be.

Then, on that day you will be questioned about the benefits and favors.

Then, on that final day, on the Day of Judgement, in that absolute state, we will be asked about the favors and comforts of life which we were given. We will suddenly see what we have squandered and how we abused and denied the bounty of Allāh and the potential we had been given for seeking knowledge and gaining it. What was *ḥalāl* (permitted) for us will be accounted for and we will be asked to account for the way in which we spent our time, whether it was spent sleeping, or waiting for the next meal, and so on. Then we will ask ourselves why we did not awaken to the certainty of this day, and we will see that we did not be-cause we were distracted by the multiplication and increase of our wealth in all its form. (Shaikh Fadhlalla Haeri, pp. 271-274)

Acquisitiveness, that is, the passion for seeking an increase in wealth, position, the number of adherents or followers or supporters, mass pro-duction and mass organization, may affect an individual as such, or it may affect whole societies or nations. Other people's example or rivalry in such things may aggravate the situation. Up to a certain point it may be good and necessary. But when it becomes inordinate and monopolizes attention, it leaves no time for higher things in life, and a clear warning is here sounded from a moral point of view. Man may be engrossed in these things until death approaches, and he looks back on a wasted life, as far as the higher things are concerned.

The desire to accumulate distracts you all the way to the graves, that is, until the time comes when you must lie down in the graves and leave the pomp and circumstance of an empty life. The true Reality will then appear before you. Why not try to strive for a little understanding of that Reality in this very life?

If you were to know with the knowledge of certainty. . . . Three kinds of *yaqīn* (certainty of knowledge) are described in the Qur'ān (see 69:38-53). The first is *certainty of mind or inference,* mentioned here. We hear from someone, or we infer from something we know: this refers to our own state of mind. If we instruct our minds in this way, we should value the deeper things of life better, and not waste all our time in ephemeral things. But if we do not use our reasoning faculties now, we shall yet see with our own eyes the penalty for our sins. It will be *certainty of sight.* We shall see Hell. The *absolute certainty of assured truth* is that described in 69:51; that is not liable to any human error or psychological defects.

And on that Day you will be asked about true happiness. We shall be questioned, i.e., we shall be held responsible for every kind of joy we indulge in—whether it was false pride or delight in things of no value, or things evil, or the enjoyment of things legitimate, the last to see whether we kept this within reasonable bounds. (A. Yusuf Ali, pp. 1780-1781)

Everyone Is in Loss, Except . . .

In the Name of God,
the Infinitely Compassionate and Most Merciful
Consider time:
Truly, human beings are in loss,
except those who have faith and do righteous deeds
and encourage each other in the teaching of Truth
and of patient perseverance.

[*Sūrah al-ʿAṣr* 103:1-3, complete]

Al-ʿAṣr may mean (1) time through the ages, or long periods, in which case it comes near to the abstract idea of time, *dahr;* (2) or the late afternoon, from which the ʿAṣr canonical prayer takes its name. In 2:238, it says *Guard strictly your prayers especially the middle prayer and stand before Allāh in a devout frame of mind.* Most authorities interpret the middle prayer, *ṣalāt-ul-wusṭa,* as the ʿAṣr prayer in the middle of the afternoon. This is apt to be the most neglected, and yet this is the most necessary, to remind us of God in the midst of our worldly affairs.

An appeal is made to Time as one of the creations of Allāh, of which everyone knows something but of which no one can fully explain the exact significance. Time searches out and destroys everything material. No one in secular literature has expressed the tyranny of "never-resting time" better than Shakespeare in his sonnets. For example, see sonnets 5 ("never-resting time"), 12 ("Nothing 'gainst Time's scythe can make defense") and 64 ("When I have seen by Time's fell hand defaced The rich proud cost of outworn buried age"). If we merely run a race against

Time, we shall lose. It is the spiritual part of us that conquers Time, as expressed in verse three of this *sūrah*.

Truly, human beings are in loss. . . . If life be considered under the metaphor of a business bargain, man, by merely attending to his material gains, will lose. When he makes up his day's account in the afternoon, it will show a loss. It will only show profit if he has faith, leads a good life, and contributes to social welfare by directing and encouraging other people on the path of truth and constancy.

. . . *except those who have faith and do righteous deeds and encourage each other in the teaching of Truth and of patient perseverance.* Faith is his armor, which wards off the wounds of the material world; and his righteous life is his positive contribution to spiritual ascent. If he lived only for himself, he would not fulfill his whole duty. Whatever good he has, especially in moral and spiritual life, he must spread among his brethren, so that they may see the Truth and stand by it in patient hope and unshaken constancy amidst all the storm and stress of outer life. For he and they will then have attained peace within. (A. Yusuf Ali, pp. 1783, 95)

This Surah (Al Asr) offers a condensed version of the ethos of the early Meccan revelations. There is no doctrine of original sin in Islam, no doctrine of an innate sinfulness that makes every human inherently unworthy of salvation without the saving grace of the deity. Instead, the Qur'an affirms that humankind is in a state of forgetfulness, confusion, and loss, and in need of reminder.

The Sura affirms that each human being is at a loss, except those who engage in four activities. The first activity is holding or keeping the faith *(iman)*. This word is often translated as "belief," but *iman* includes not only intellectual assent to certain propositions but also engagement in just actions. These actions include l) defending belief in the face of persecution or ridicule; 2) sharing wealth; 3) protecting those who are disinherited or in need; and 4) performing the ritual prayer, *salat*—the second activity explicitly mentioned in this Sura. The word *iman* also has connotations of being secure or protected. In other words, to keep the faith through an active witness that exposes one to persecution and danger, is, ironically, to gain refuge.

The last two items tie two primary virtues, the seeking of truth *(haqq)* and patience *(sabr)*, to the social nature of such activity, the mutual counseling and encouraging of friend to friend toward such ends. (Michael Sells)

Allah promises by time, that is by the expanding subsistence of time and what is contained therein and what occurs in it by its Originator and Cause, which is Eternity. People attribute the changes of conditions and states to time and they let it influence their intellect, as is said of them in the Quran, "Only time causes our demise." But what influences our intellect is Allah. The Prophet said, "Do not curse time for Allah is Eternal Time." He said this in order to give time its due respect since it is through time that Allah is manifest in His attributes and actions.

The one who is veiled from time is in loss. A person loses in it his very capital, which consists of the light of his essential nature and original guidance that comes from the timeless potentialities. This loss is due to choosing worldly life, and fleeting pleasures being veiled by them over time, thus losing what is everlasting in what is ephemeral.

Only those who have faith based on certain knowledge are spared this loss. Those are the ones who know that there is no influencer other than Allah. They are the ones who have emerged from the veil of time and their actions are good and everlasting and so they gain the light of completion in addition to the light of potentialities that is their capital. And they are ever mindful of the constant, and everlasting state of unity and justice. This is *Tawhid* that is essential, descriptive, and practical. This

485

is the secure truth and it is sufficient. And by being upright and grounded they are ever mindful of being patient with Him and for Him to the exclusion of all other than Him.

Arriving to Truth is relatively easy but to subsist in Him and to be patient with Him through uprightness in worship, that is indeed more rare than red sulphur and white crows. The fact is that humankind is in loss except for those who are complete in knowledge and actions and are completed by them.

And it is possible to understand Asr as the extraction or purification. So, Allah purifies a person through trials, striving, and spiritual exercise until his essence is made clear.

Indeed those who persist in the dregs of life, who continue to be veiled by their animal nature are in loss except for those who are characterized by knowledge and action, they are the ones who are persistent in the firm truth which is the certain faith that is necessary for lasting purity after the dregs are gone. They are the ones who are persistent in patience with trials and tests, this is why the Prophet (puh) said, "Trial is ordained for the prophets, then for the saints, then for those most like them." And he also said, "Trial is one of Allah's whips which He uses to drive His servants to Him."

(Haeri)

Hypocritical Worshippers

In the Name of God, the Infinitely Compassionate and Most Merciful.
Do you see the one who denies the Reckoning?
Such is one who shuns the orphan
and doesn't encourage the feeding of the poor.
So grief to the worshippers who do not pray with their hearts,
but only wish to be seen,
those who turn away from neighborly needs.

[*Sūrah al-Māʿūn* 107:1-7, complete]

Do you see the one who denies the Reckoning? Dīn may mean either (1) the Judgment to come, the responsibility in the moral and spiritual world, for all actions done by men, or (2) faith, religion, the principles of right and wrong in spiritual matters, which often conflict with selfish desires or predilections. It is men who deny faith or future responsibility, that treat the helpless with contempt and lead arrogant selfish lives.

Such is one who shuns the orphan and doesn't encourage the feeding of the poor. The charity or love which feeds the indigent at the expense of self is a noble form of virtue, which is beyond the reach of men who are so callous as even to discourage or forbid or look down upon the value of charity or kindness in others.

So grief to the worshippers who do not pray with their hearts. True worship does not consist in the mere form of prayer, without the heart and mind being earnestly applied to seek the realization of the presence of Allāh, and to understand and do His holy Will.

. . . but only wish to be seen. . . . Compare 4:142: *When they stand up*

487

to prayer, they stand without earnestness, to be seen of men, but little do they hold Allāh in remembrance.

Those who turn away from neighborly needs. Hypocrites make a great show of hollow acts of goodness, devotion, and charity. But they fail signally if you test them by little acts of neighborly help or charity, the thousand little courtesies and kindnesses of daily life, the supply of needs which cost little but mean much. (A. Yusuf Ali, p. 1796)

The small kindness relates a series of activities in a way that grounds much of Islamic moral theology. The first act is rejecting or calling a lie the *din,* a word that can mean either the religion or the day of reckoning. Just as the word often translated as "believe" is more passive than the Qur'anic conception of holding fast to the belief or keeping the faith, so the concept of calling the reckoning (or religion) a lie is more active than standard English translations such as "unbelief." Those who reject the reckoning—which, in early Meccan revelations, is the foundation of religion—are those who abuse the orphan, who are indifferent to those suffering in their midst, and who are neglectful in performing the prayer. This neglectfulness has been interpreted in two ways by Qur'anic commentators: either as neglecting the proper timing and posture in performing the physical movements or as performing them mechanically while thinking about other things, without following through on the implications of the prayer for other aspects of life and behavior. The second interpretation is supported by the fact that the verse on prayer is followed by two verses on self-display and neglecting the small kindness.

Display, particularly of one's own acts of worship or piety, betrays a lack of true generosity. Self-display ends as a form of self-delusion, as a person ignores what the Qur'an announces will be ultimate in the evaluation of each life at the moment of reckoning: a genuine act of kindness, however small it might seem. There is a moral circle of causality implied

488

in the Qur'anic passages on this issue. The refusal to acknowledge the moment of reckoning results in blindness to the small act of kindness. On the other hand, the true weight of that small act will be revealed on the day of reckoning to those who have carried it out and to those who have neglected it alike. (Michael Sells)

The Source of Abundance

In the Name of God,
the Infinitely Compassionate and Most Merciful.
We have bestowed on you the source of abundance.
So to your Sustainer turn in prayer and sacrifice.
For the one who despises you will be cut off.

[*Sūrah al-Kawthar* 108:1-3, complete]

The name of this *sūrah*, *Al-Kawthar*, is an intensive form of the noun *kathrah* (Zamakhsharī), which, in its turn, denotes "copiousness," "multitude," or "abundance"; it also occurs as an adjective with the same connotation. In the above context, which is the sole instance of its use in the Qur'ān, *al-kawthar* obviously relates to the abundant bestowal on the Prophet of all that is good in an abstract, spiritual sense, like revelation, knowledge, wisdom, the doing of good works, and dignity in this world and in the hereafter (Rāzī); with reference to the believers in general, it evidently signifies the *ability* to acquire knowledge, to do good works, to be kind towards all living beings, and thus to attain to inner peace and dignity. (Asad, p. 980)

We have bestowed on you the source of abundance. Al-Kawthar literally means *good in abundance*. It is the heavenly fountain of unbounded grace and knowledge, mercy and goodness, truth and wisdom, spiritual power and insight, which was granted to the holy Prophet, the man of God, and in some degree or other, to all men and women who are sincere devotees of God. That fountain quenches the highest spiritual thirst of man: it con-

490

fers overflowing benefits of all kinds. *And he to whom wisdom is granted receives indeed a benefit overflowing* [2:269]. Such a person wants for nothing: worldly pomp and wealth are a dust beneath his feet.

So to your Sustainer turn in prayer and sacrifice. He Who grants these blessings is Allāh, and to Allāh alone must we turn in adoration and thanksgiving, and in sacrifice. *Nahr* means sacrifice; in a restricted ritual sense, the sacrifice of camels, such as described in 22:36. But the ritual is a mere symbol. Behind it is a deep spiritual meaning; the meat slaughtered feeds the poor, and the slaughter is a symbol of the self-sacrifice in our hearts. *It is not their meat nor their blood that reaches Allāh; it is your piety that reaches Him* [22:37].

For the one who despises you will be cut off [*from all that is good*]. Hatred and spite are not constructive contributions to the work of this world, but its opposites. Abū Jahl and his pagan confederates vented their personal spite and venom against the holy Prophet by taunting him with the loss of his two infant sons by Khadījah, but where were these venomous detractors a few years afterwards, when the divine Light shone more brilliantly than ever? It was these that were cut off from all future hope, in this world and the next. (A. Yusuf Ali, p. 1798)

Although Muhammad had nine wives and several concubines, he did not have a surviving male heir. This short Sura is thought by Qur'anic commentators to have been revealed to Muhammad in consolation for the death of his son in infancy, his lack of a male heir, and the taunts he is reported to have endured because of it. It is not Muhammad who is the *abtar* (one cut, mutilated, deprived of posterity) but rather those who hate him.

According to the values of traditional tribal society in Arabia, a man's honor and status depended upon his patrilineal ancestors. It was vital for every man to have a son to carry on this lineage of honor. Men were named after their fathers and were called *ibn* or *bin* (son of). Frequently, after the birth of his first son, a father would be given anew name: (Abu (father of) followed by the given name of the son. In some cases, this Abu designation could be inherited from one's ancestors). Thus, Muhammad's uncle was called Abu Talib (the father of Talib). Muhammad's cousin 'Alt was then known as 'All bin Abi Talib ('Ali the son of Abu Talib).

The Qur'an transforms radical tribal adherence to male lineage by redefining the individual and the community in ways that weaken the absolute authority of patriarchal kinship. The practice of naming children in a patrilineal manner remained, but the Islamic notion of a community *(umma) of* believers offered a strong balance to clan affiliation. Thus it becomes possible in this Sura for an orphan without male heirs to hear a divine voice saying "To you we have given fully"—a statement that by tribal standards of lineage-based honor would have been inconceivable.

The etymology *of kawthar* and its usage during Muhammad's time indicate the clear meaning of "abundance." According to early biographers of Muhammad, the Prophet himself believed al-Kawthar was a place name for a river in paradise or a pond near the zenith of his heavenly ascent *(mi'raj)*. The glorious waters of al-Kawthar have become proverbial in Islam and resonate with a wider Mediterranean symbolism concerning the waters of life. (Michael Sells)

492

"You Who Deny the Truth"

In the Name of God,
the Infinitely Compassionate and Most Merciful.
Say: "O you who deny the Truth!
I do not worship that which you worship
Nor will you worship that which I worship.
And I will not worship that which you are used to worshipping
Nor will you worship that which I worship.
To you your way and to me mine."

[*Sūrah al-Kāfirūn* 109:1-6, complete]

Say: "O you who deny the Truth!" could also be translated *Say: "O you that reject Faith!"* Faith is a matter of personal conviction, and does not depend on worldly motives. Worship should depend on pure and sincere faith, but often does not: for motives of worldly gain, ancestral custom, social conventions or imitative instincts, or a lethargic instinct to shrink from inquiring into the real significance of solemn acts and the motives behind them, reduce a great deal of the world's worship to sin, selfishness, or futility. Symbolic idols may themselves be merely instruments for safeguarding the privileges of a selfish priestly class, or the ambitions, greed, or lust of private individuals. Hence the insistence of Islam and its Prophet on the pure worship of the One True God. The Prophet firmly resisted all appeals to worldly motives, and stood firm to his Message of eternal unity.

I do not worship that which you worship, nor will you worship that which I worship. These verses describe the conditions as they were at the time when this *sūrah* was revealed, and may be freely paraphrased: "I am a

493

worshipper of the One True God, the Lord of all, of you as well as of myself; but you on account of your vested interests have not the will to give up your false worship of idols and self."

The following verses describe the psychological reasons. *And I will not worship that which you are used to worshipping, nor will you worship that which I worship.* This can be paraphrased as: "I, being a prophet of Allāh, do not and cannot possibly desire to follow your false ancestral ways; and you, as custodians of the false worship, have not the will to give up your ways of worship, which are wrong." The "will" in the translation represents less the future tense than the will, the desire, the psychological possibility; it tries to reproduce the Arabic noun-agent.

To you your way and to me mine. "I, having been given the Truth, cannot come to your false ways: you, having your vested interests, will not give them up. For your ways the responsibility is yours: I have shown you the Truth. For my ways the responsibility is mine: you have no right to ask me to abandon the Truth. Your persecutions will be vain: the Truth must prevail in the end." This was the attitude of faith then, but it is true for all time. Hold fast to Truth, "in scorn of consequence." (A. Yusuf Ali, p. 1800)

Help at the End

In the Name of God, the Infinitely Compassionate and Most Merciful.
When the help of God comes and victory,
and you see people enter God's Way in throngs,
celebrate the praises of your Sustainer and pray for His forgiveness:
for He is ever turning one towards repentance.

[*Sūrah an-Naṣr* 110:1-3, complete]

The Prophet migrated from Mecca to Medina, a persecuted man. In Medina, all the forces of truth and righteousness rallied round him, and the efforts by the Meccans and their confederates to destroy him and his community recoiled on their own heads. Gradually all the outlying parts of Arabia ranged themselves round his standard, and the bloodless conquest of Mecca was the crown and prize of his patience and constant endeavor. After that, whole tribes and tracts of country gave their adhesion to him collectively, and before his ministry was finished, the soil was prepared for the conquest of the wide world for Islam. What was the lesson to be learnt from this little epitome of the world's history? Not man's self-glory, but humility; not power but service; not an appeal to man's selfishness or self-sufficiency, but a realization of Allāh's Grace and Mercy, and the abundant outpouring of Allāh's praises in word and conduct.

Celebrate the praises of your Sustainer and pray for His forgiveness: for He is ever turning one towards repentance. Every man should humble himself before Allāh, confess his human frailties, and seek Allāh's grace; attributing any success that he gets in his work, not to his own merits, but to the goodness and mercy of Allāh. But the Prophet of Allāh had also another duty and privilege—to pray for grace and forgiveness for his people in case any of them had exulted in their victory or done anything that they should not have done. (A. Yusuf Ali, p. 1802)

This short sura is thought to be from the later Medinan period of Muhammad's prophecy. After years of struggle, Muhammad found himself increasingly acknowledged and his Islamic community expanding. Some place the Sura after Muhammad's triumphal return to Mecca, whence he had been expelled to Medina at the time of the hijra. After three battles between his Meccan opponents and his supporters based in Medina, he returned to Mecca victorious and made the pilgrimage there. This would be the "opening" *(fath)* of the city to the party of Muhammad. Others place the Sura before the return to Mecca and interpret the opening in more general terms, as the opening up of the way to vindication after years of struggle.

The passage opens with a "when" clause that is never finished—a distinctive feature of Qur'anic discourse. After reminding the prophet of his success, the Qur'an exhorts him to ask forgiveness.

By the grim standards of tribal warfare, the people of Mecca, having lost the war, expected looting, massacre, and the enslavement of the survivors. To the consternation of his adversaries and supporters alike, Muhammad not only refused to carry out mass revenge against the Meccan persecutors, he brought them into his movement and allowed many to rise to the highest levels of leadership in the Islamic community.

The phrase *istaghfir Allah* has now become part of everyday language in Arabic and is a common response to any kind of compliment. The term *istaghfir* means literally "ask forgiveness." It can also be translated more figuratively as "God forgive" or "God forbid"—that is, "God prevent me from taking credit or becoming proud and forgive me for having done so." From the point of view of Islamic psychology, the exclamation "God forgive" is used here to petition divine help in avoiding egoism before the prayer (poisoning the intention and thus the act of prayer before the fact) and also to ask forgiveness for egoism that occurs after the prayer (as self-congratulation poisons the act after the fact). In reference to Muhammad, the words would be an injunction to him against taking credit or becoming prideful after the victory. (Michael Sells)

The Eternal Originator

In the Name of God, the Infinitely Compassionate and Most Merciful.
Say, "He is the One God;
God the Eternal Originator;
He does not bear children, nor was He born;
and He is beyond compare."

[*Sūrah al-Ikhlāṣ* 112:1-4, complete]

The nature of Allāh is here indicated to us in a few words, such as we can understand. The qualities of Allāh are described in numerous places elsewhere, e.g., in 59:22-24, 62:1, and 2:255. Here we are specially taught to avoid the pitfalls into which men and nations have fallen at various times in trying to understand Allāh. The first thing we have to note is that His nature is so sublime, so far beyond our limited conceptions, that the best way in which we can realize Him is to feel that He is a personality, "He," and not a mere abstract conception of philosophy. He is near us; He cares for us; we owe our existence to Him. Secondly, He is the One and Only God, the Only One to whom worship is due; all other things or beings we can think of are His creatures and in no way comparable to Him. Thirdly, He is Eternal, without beginning or end, Absolute, not limited by time or place or circumstance, the Reality. Fourthly, we must not think of Him as having a son or a father, for that would be to import animal qualities into our conception of Him. Fifthly, He is not like any other person or thing that we can know or can imagine: His qualities and nature are unique.

The opening line could also be translated: *Say: He is Allāh, the One and Only*. This is to negate the idea of polytheism, a system in which people believe in gods many and lords many. Such a system is opposed to our truest and most profound conceptions of life. For unity in design, unity in the fundamental facts of existence, proclaim the Unity of the Maker.

God the Eternal Originator could also be translated *Allāh, the Eternal, Absolute. Ṣamad* is difficult to translate by one word. I have used two, "eternal" and "absolute." The latter implies (1) that absolute existence can only be predicated of Him; all other existence is temporal or conditional; (2) that He is dependent on no person or thing, but all persons or things are dependent on Him, thus negating the idea of gods and goddesses who ate and drank, wrangled and plotted, depended on the gifts of worshippers, etc.

He does not bear children, nor was He born: this is to negate the Christian idea of the godhead, "the Father," "the only-begotten Son," etc.

And He is beyond compare. This sums up the whole argument and warns us specially against anthropomorphism, the tendency to conceive of God after our own pattern, an insidious tendency that creeps in at all times and among all peoples. (A. Yusuf Ali, p. 1806)

The Mischief within Creation

In the Name of God, the Infinitely Compassionate and Most Merciful
Say, "I seek refuge with the Lord of the Dawn
from the mischief of created things;
from the evil of Darkness as it overspreads;
from the harmfulness of those who blow on knots;[15]
and from the harm of the envious one as he envies."

[*Sūrah al-Falaq* 113:1-5, complete]

In God's created world there are all kinds of forces and counter-forces, especially those put in motion by beings who have been endowed with some sort of will. The forces of good may be compared to light, and those of evil to darkness. God can cleave the depths of darkness and produce light (6:96) and therefore we should cast off fear and take refuge in divine guidance and goodness.

Falaq is the dawn or daybreak, the cleaving of darkness and the manifestation of light. This may be understood in various senses: (1) literally, when the darkness of the night is at its worst, rays of light pierce through and produce the dawn; (2) when the darkness of ignorance is at its worst, the light of God pierces through the soul and gives it enlightenment (24:35); (3) non-existence is darkness, and life and activity may be typified by light. The author and source of all true light is God, and if we seek Him, we are free from ignorance, superstitions, fear, and every kind of evil.

---

[15] Those who cast spells; those who spread constriction, who exacerbate difficulties.

Our trust in God is the refuge from every kind of fear and superstition, every kind of danger and evil. Three special kinds of mischief are specified, against which our best guard is our trust in God, the Light of the heavens and the earth. They are: (1) physical dangers, typified by darkness; (2) psychical dangers within us, typified by secret arts; and (3) physical dangers from without us, resulting from a perverted will, which seek to destroy any good that we enjoy.

From the evil of Darkness as it overspreads: the darkness of the night, physical darkness, is a good type of physical danger and difficulty. Many people are afraid of physical darkness, and all are afraid of physical injuries, accidents, and calamities. We should not fear, but having taken reasonable precautions, trust in God.

From the harmfulness of those who blow on knots: this having been a favorite form of witchcraft practiced by perverted women. Such secret arts cause psychological terror. They may be what is called black magic, or secret plottings, or the display of false and seductive charms, or the spreading of false and secret rumors or slanders to frighten men or deter them from right action. There is fraud in such things, but men are swayed by it. They should cast off fear and do their duty.

And from the harm of the envious one as he envies. Malignant envy, translated into action, seeks to destroy the happiness of the material or spiritual good enjoyed by other people. The best guard against it is trust in God with purity of heart. (A. Yusuf Ali, p. 1808)

Inner Whisperings

In the Name of God, the Infinitely Compassionate and Most Merciful
Say, "I seek refuge with the Sustainer of humankind,
the Sovereign of humankind,
the God of humankind,
from the mischief of the slinking whisperer
who whispers in the hearts of human beings
among jinns and among humankind."

[*Sūrah an-Nās* 114:1-6, complete]

The previous *sūrah* pointed to the necessity of seeking God's protection against external factors which might affect an individual. Here the need of protection from internal factors, mankind being viewed as a whole, is pointed out. For this reason a threefold relation in which man stands to God is mentioned: (1) God is his Lord, Maker, and Cherisher. God sustains him and cares for him; He provides him with all the means for his growth and development, and for his protection against evil; (2) God is the king or ruler, more than any earthly king. God has authority to guide man's conduct, and lead him to ways which will make for his welfare, and He has given him laws; and (3) God is He to Whom mankind must return, to give an account of all their deeds in this life. *To Allāh we belong and to Him is our return* (2:156). God will be the Judge. He is the goal of the hereafter, and the only being entitled to man's worship at any time. From all these aspects man could and should seek God's protection against evil.

Evil insinuates itself in all sorts of insidious ways from within so as to

502

sap man's will, which was given to man by God. This power of evil may be Satan or his host of evil ones, or evil men or the evil inclinations within man's own will for there are *evil ones among men and jinns, inspiring each other with flowery discourses by way of deception* [6:112]. They secretly whisper evil and then withdraw, to make their net the more subtle and alluring.

Who whispers in the hearts of human beings among jinns and among humankind: this last clause amplifies the description of the sources from which the whisper of evil may emanate: they may be men you may see or invisible spirits of evil working within. So long as we put ourselves in God's protection and trust in God, evil cannot really touch us in our essential and inner life. (A. Yusuf Ali, p. 1810)

References Cited by Muhammad Asad

Abū Dāʾūd   Abū Dāʾūd Sulaymān al-Ashʿath (d. 275 H.), *Kitāb as-Sunan.*

Baghawī   Al-Ḥusayn ibn Masʿūd al-Farrāʾ al-Baghawī (d. 516 H.), *Maʿālim at-Tanzīl.*

Bayḍāwī   ʿAbd Allāh ibn ʿUmar al-Bayḍāwī (d. 685 or 691 H.), *Anwār at-Tanzīl wa-Asrār at-Taʿwīl.*

Bayhaqī   Abū Bakr Aḥmad ibn al-Ḥusayn al-Bayhaqī (d. 458 H.), *Kitāb as-Sunan al-Kubrā.*

Bukhārī   Muḥammad ibn Ismāʿīl al-Bukhārī (d. 256 H.), *Al-Jāmiʿ aṣ-Ṣaḥīḥ.*

Ḥākim   see *Mustadrak.*

Ibn Ḥanbal   Aḥmad ibn Muḥammad ibn Ḥanbal (d. 241 H.), *Al-Musnad.*

Ibn Hishām   ʿAbd al-Malik ibn Hishām (d. 243 H.), *Sīrat an-Nabī.*

Ibn Kathīr   Abu 'l-Fidāʾ Ismāʿīl ibn Kathīr (d. 774 H.), *Tafsīr al-Qurʿān*, Cairo 1343-47 H.

Ibn Mājah   Muḥammad ibn Yazīd ibn Mājah al-Qazwīnī (d. 273 or 275 H.), *Kitāb as-Sunan.*

Jawharī   Abū Naṣr Ismāʿīl ibn Ḥammād al-Jawharī (d. about 400 H.), *Tāj al-Lughah wa-Ṣiḥāḥ al-ʿArabiyyah*, Būlāq 1292 H.

Lane   William Edward Lane, *Arabic-English Lexicon*, London 1863-93.

Lisān al-ʿArab   Abu 'l-Faḍl Muḥammad ibn Mukarram al-Ifrīqī (d. 711 H.), *Lisān al-ʿArab.*

Manār   Muḥammad Rashīd Riḍāʾ, *Tafsīr al-Qurʿān* (known as *Tafsīr al-Manār*), Cairo 1367-72 H.

Mughnī   Jamāl ad-Dīn ʿAbd Allāh ibn Yūsuf al-Anṣārī (d. 761 H.), *Mughnī 'l-Labīb ʿan Kutub al-Aʿārīb.*

Muslim	Muslim ibn al-Ḥajjāj an-Nīsābūrī (d. 261 H.), *Kitāb aṣ-Ṣaḥīḥ*.
Nasā'ī	Aḥmad ibn Shuʿayb an-Nasā'ī (d. 303 H.), *Kitāb as-Sunan*.
Nihāyah	ʿAlī ibn Muḥammad ibn al-Athīr (d. 630 H.), *An-Nihāyah fī Gharīb al-Ḥadīth*.
Qāmūs	Abu 't-Ṭāhir Muḥammad ibn Yaʿqūb al-Fīrūzābādī (d. 817 H.), *Al-Qāmūs*.
Rāghib	Abu 'l-Qāsim Ḥusayn ar-Rāghib (d. 503 H.), *Al-Mufradāt fī Gharīb al-Qurʾān*.
Rāzī	Abu 'l-Faḍl Muḥammad Fakhr ad-Dīn ar-Rāzī (d. 606 H.), *At-Tafsīr al-Kabīr*.
State and Government	Muḥammad Asad, *The Principles of State and Government in Islam*, University of California Press, 1961.
Ṭabarī	Abū Jaʿfar Muḥammad ibn Jarīr aṭ-Ṭabarī (d. 310 H.), *Jāmiʿ al-Bayān ʿan Taʾwīl al-Qurʾān*.
Tāj al-ʿArūs	Murtaḍā az-Zabīdī (d. 1205 H.), *Tāj al-ʿArūs*.
Tirmidhī	Muḥammad ibn ʿIsā at-Tirmidhī (d. 275 or 279 H.), *Al-Jāmiʿ aṣ-Ṣaḥīḥ*.
Zamakhsharī	Maḥmūd ibn ʿUmar az-Zamakhsharī (d. 538 H.), *Al-Kashshāf ʿan Ḥaqāʾiq Ghawāmiḍ at-Tanzīl*. (For the same author's lexicographic works, see *Asās* and *Fāʾiq*.)

Bibliography

Ali, Abdullah Yusuf. *The Holy Qur^cān: Text, Translation, and Commentary*. Lahore, Pakistan: Sh. Muhammad Ashraf, first published in 1938.

Asad, Muhammad Asad. *The Message of the Qur^cān*. Gibraltar: Dar Al-Andalus, 1980, 1984.

Ayoub, Mahmoud M. *The Qur^can and Its Interpreters: Volume II, The House of ^cImrān*. Albany, New York: State University of New York Press, 1992.

Bennabi, Malik. *The Qur^canic Phenomenon: an Eassy of a Theory on the Qur^can*. Translated and annotated by Mohammed El-Tahir El-Mesawi. Kuala Lumpur: Islamic Book Trust, 2001.

Draz, M.A. *Introduction to the Qur^can*. London and New York: I.B. Tauris & Co., Ltd., 2000.

Haeri, Shaykh Fadhlalla. *Beams of Illumination from the Divine Revelation: Juz^{cc}Amma, the last section of the Qur^cān*. Blanco, Texas: Zahra Publications, 1985.

Helminski, Camille Adams. *The Light of Dawn: A Daybook of Verses from the Holy Qur^cān*. Boston: Shambhala Publications, 1998.

Helminski, Kabir. *The Book of Language*. Watsonville, California: The Book Foundation, 2004.

Rūmī, Jalālu'ddin. *Open Secret*. Translated by John Moyne and Coleman

Barks. Putney, Vermont: Threshold Books, 1984.

Rūmī, Jalālu'ddin. *Signs of the Unseen: The Discourses of Jalaluddin Rumi (Fihi Mā Fihi)*. Translated by William M. Thackston, Jr. Putney, Vermont: Threshold Books, 1994.

Sells, Michael. *Approaching the Qurᶜān: The Early Revelations*. Ashland, Oregon: White Cloud Press, 1999.

Shah-Kazemi, Reza. *The Metaphysics of Interfaith Dialogue*. (An essay yet to be published.)

At **The Book Foundation** our goal is to express the highest ideals of Islam and the Qur'an through publications, curricula, and other learning resources, suitable for schools, parents, and individuals, whether non-Muslims seeking to understand the Islamic perspective, or Muslims wanting to deepen their understanding of their own faith. Please visit our website: **thebook.org**

The Book of Revelations

A Sourcebook of Themes
from the Holy Qur'an,

Edited by Kabir Helminski
$33   £16.95   6 x 9"   508pp
1-904510-12-4

This book invites us to recognize and reflect upon the essential spiritual themes of the Qur'an. It offers 265 titled selections of ayats, presented in a fresh contemporary translation of high literary quality, with accompanying interpretations by Muhammad Asad, Yusuf Ali, and others. It is an essential sourcebook for Muslims and non-Muslims alike.

The Book of Character

An Anthology of Writings on Virtue
from Islamic and Other Sources
Edited by Camille Helminski
$33   £16.95   6 x 9"   484pp
1-904510-09-4

A collection of writings dealing with the qualities of our essential Human Nature: Faith and Trust; Repentance and Forgiveness; Compassion and Mercy; Patience and Forbearance; Modesty, Humility, and Discretion; Purity; Intention and Discernment; Generosity and Gratitude; Courage, Justice, and Right Action; Contentment and Inner Peace; Courtesy and Chivalry. From the Prophets Abraham and Moses, to the sages Confucius and Buddha, to the Prophet Muhammad, his wife, Khadija, and his companions Abu Bakr and 'Ali, through great saints like Rumi, and humanitarians like Florence Nightingale, Mother Theresa, and Martin Luther King, and even in the personal story of the bicyclist Lance Armstrong, we find stories and wisdom that will help us toward spiritual well-being.

The Book Foundation *has embarked on an important effort to develop books and teaching tools that are approachable and relevant to Muslims and non-Muslims.* ~**Shabbir Mansuri**, *Founding Director, Council on Islamic Education (CIE)*

The Book of Essential Islam
The Spiritual Training System of Islam
Ali Rafea,
with Aisha and Aliaa Rafea
$21   £10.95   6 x 9"   276 pp
1-904510-13-2

This book examines the main teachings and practices of Islam with lucidity and depth. It is a corrective to the distortions and misconceptions of Islam that abound. It can serve equally well to introduce non-Muslims to Islam, as well as to enhance Muslims understanding of their own faith. This book presents Islam as a spiritual training system that supports us in harmonizing ourselves with the Divine Order and thus with each other and our environment. It reveals the intent and inner significance of practices like ablution, ritual prayer, fasting, and pilgrimage.

The Fragrance of Faith
The Enlightened Heart of Islam
Jamal Rahman
$15.95 £9.95   6 x 9"   176pp
1-904510-08-6

The Fragrance of Faith reveals the inner Islam that has been passed down through the generations. Jamal is a link in this chain, passing along the message, just as he received it from his grandfather, a village wiseman in Bangladesh. We need reminders of this "enlightened heart of Islam" in our lives, our homes, and our schools. In Jamal Rahman's book Islam is alive and well. ~**Imam Feisal Abdul Rauf**, Author *Islam: A Sacred Law* and *What's Right With Islam*.

This heartfelt book is perfect for the classroom, whether in a Muslim context, or outside of it. It conveys a tradition of compassion and humor passed through one family that represents the best Islam has to offer. And Mr. Rahman is highly entertaining. ~**Michael Wolfe**, *The Hadj: An American's Pilgrimage to Mecca*, Producer of the PBS Documentary: *Muhammad: The Legacy of a Prophet*.

The Message of the Qur'an

by Muhammad Asad

- Newly designed and typeset
- Available in two formats: a single hardback volume,
  and a boxed set of six parts in paperback
  for ease of handling and reference
- Original artwork by the internationally renowned
  Muslim artist and scholar, Dr. Ahmed Moustafa
- A Romanised transliteration of the Arabic text
- A newly compiled general index

As the distinguished British Muslim, Gai Eaton, explains in a new Prologue to the work, there is no more useful guide to the Qur'an in the English language than Muhammad Asad's complete translation and commentary, and no other translator has come so close to conveying the meaning of the Qur'an to those who may not be able to read the Arabic text or the classical commentaries. Generous sponsorship has enabled the Foundation to offer this work at a very reasonable price for a publication of this exceptional quality.

Price: Hardback $55, £28, 39 Euros
  Boxed set of 6 deluxe paperback volumes: $60, £33, 45 Euros
ISBN: Hardback 1-904510-00-0 Boxed set 1-904510-01-9
  Hardback cover size: 8.5 x 11. Approximately: 1200 pages

To Order In the USA:
  The Book Foundation: 831 685 3995
  Bookstores: IPG 800 888 4741
In England: Orca Book Services 01202 665432

Or visit our website: TheBook.org

Printed in the United States
51549LVS00004B/7-54